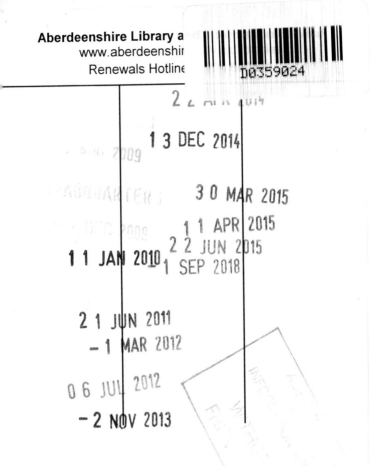
25 albums that rocked the world!

25 ALBUMS THAT ROCKED THE WORLD!

Copyright © 2008 Omnibus Press
(A Division of Music Sales Limited)

Cover designed by Chloe Alexander.
Picture research: Sarah Bacon.

ISBN: 978.1.84772.626.1
Order No: OP52635

Exclusive Distributors
Music Sales Limited,
14/15 Berners Street,
London, W1T 3LJ.

Music Sales Corporation,
257 Park Avenue South,
New York, NY 10010, USA.

Macmillan Distribution Services,
56 Parkwest Drive
Derrimut, Vic 3030,
Australia.

Every effort has been made to trace the copyright holders of the photographs in this book but
one or two were unreachable.
We would be grateful if the photographers concerned would contact us.

Printed by: Gutenberg Press Limited, Malta.

A catalogue record for this book is available from the British Library.

Visit Omnibus Press on the web at www.omnibuspress.com

CONTENTS

INTRODUCTION

URING THE NINETIES Omnibus Press published a series of books under the generic title *The Complete Guides To The Music Of...* They were shaped like CD jewel cases and designed to sit alongside the CDs on your record shelf, and were written by experienced rock critics whose brief was not just to be objective about the music and sort out the wheat from the chaff in any given artist's repertoire, but also to offer background information about the circumstances in which the albums were recorded.

As the commissioning editor of this series, it was my hope that the books would most benefit newcomers to the increasingly large catalogues of rock's greatest performers. I envisaged a teenager in a Virgin or HMV megastore being bewildered and discouraged by the amount of different CDs in, say, the Jimi Hendrix or David Bowie sections, and not knowing what to buy. Our *Complete Guide* books were designed to steer them in the right direction, especially when commenting on the merits of compilations and whether they offered value for money.

In the end, Omnibus published almost 50 books on artists ranging from Frank Sinatra to The Sex Pistols. The first batch of six - on Elvis Presley, The Beatles, The Doors, Bob Marley, Queen and Led Zeppelin - were chosen because I thought their catalogues were complete and the books would therefore not require any further updating. How wrong I was! Even though with all these acts the artist or a member of the group had passed on, I wasn't taking into consideration the ingenuity of record labels when it came to reissuing back catalogues. All these books were soon out of date, as were most of those that followed, so keeping the series up to date became a bit like painting the Forth Bridge - an endless task.

Talking of record labels, one major approached Omnibus with a view to packaging our miniature books with CDs by the acts in question. It sounded like a great marketing opportunity but I was obliged to point out to the label representative that the books were objective, that there were occasions when the author may have been a bit harsh about this or that album and suggested, perhaps, that the creative muse had somehow failed the artist on this particular record, and offered opinions on the music that the artist might not necessarily share and which might therefore cause some embarrassment in the boardroom. The major label took the point and discussions were aborted.

I believe the books worked best with those acts whose back catalogues are best described as "untidy". These were artists who, like Jimi Hendrix or Bob Marley, signed unpropitious record deals early in their careers long before they recorded their best-known work. Once the artists were famous these early recordings would come back to haunt them, often marketed under dubious titles like *The Fabulous Early Years* or *The Roots Of Genius*, clearly designed to hoodwink the unwary into parting with their money for substandard product. Anyone who read the *Complete Guide* books would know what to avoid in this regard. For those acts with "tidy" catalogues, like The Beatles or U2, the books served more as reference works than consumer guides, but I like to think they contained some useful information, fine writing and thoughtful analysis, even if everyone already knew that *Sgt. Pepper's Lonely Hearts Club Band* and *The Joshua Tree* are pretty good records.

Both those albums are in this book, along with 23 others that I think either defined their era, pushed the boundaries back a bit or, in one or two cases, simply sold in such huge quantities that they are impossible to ignore. For this reason I thought it worthwhile to combine into one single volume critiques of 25 of the greatest records of the last 50 years.

The first long playing record, with finely spaced grooves that turned at 33^1/$_3$ rpm, was introduced by Columbia Records in the USA in 1931, and the first compact disc for commercial release rolled off the assembly line in 1982 at a Philips factory in Germany. In the first decade of the 21st century, music largely exists as a non-tangible entity that can be accessed down a telephone line in a fraction of a second, and it is possible to carry 20,000 songs around on a gadget not much larger than a cigarette packet. Albums, as such, are giving way to individual tracks. Soon they will be no more, redundant because most new consumers won't want to buy them as tangible entities anyway.

But for now, here's 25 of the best ever made.

Chris Charlesworth, 2008.

ELVIS PRESLEY

The Sun Years

1954/5

By Peter Doggett

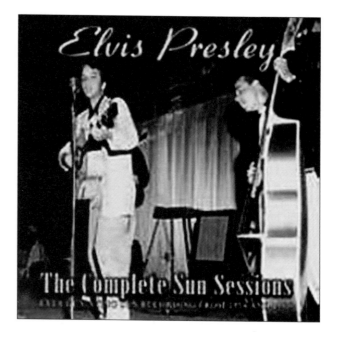

A T 706 UNION Avenue, Memphis, Tennessee, stands Sun Studios – the birthplace of the most important collection of rock'n'roll tracks ever recorded. Between 1954 and 1960, Sun's owner, Sam Phillips, produced pioneering rockabilly, blues, country and pop sides by artists such as Carl Perkins, Jerry Lee Lewis, Johnny Cash, Charlie Rich – and Elvis Presley.

Before Elvis was signed to Sun, in the summer of 1954, Phillips' label was renowned as a centre of excellence for the blues. Like scores of independents in the Southern states, Sun scuffled to survive from one release to the next. Phillips financed the label's early years by freelance production work, handling sessions with artists such as Howlin' Wolf and B.B. King for larger companies. He supervised the making of what's generally regarded as the first rock'n'roll record, Jackie Brenston's 'Rocket 88'. He proved to be an equally sympathetic producer of hillbilly country music. And in 1954, the future King of Rock'n'Roll fell into his lap.

Elvis Presley had been born on January 8, 1935, in a tiny shack in Tupelo, Mississippi. He was raised in Memphis, and working as a truck driver for the local firm of Crown Electric when he made his first amateur recordings – at the Memphis Recording Service, part of the small Sun empire. Presley had been performing blues, country, gospel and pop songs in public for a year or two by then, and had attracted the attention of some of the hottest gospel quartets in the State. But he needed the reassurance of hearing his voice on a record before he felt confident enough to make his music into a career.

Under the guise of cutting a record for his mother's birthday – already several months past – Elvis approached Marion Keisker, Sam Phillips' right-hand-woman, in the late summer of 1953. She captured him singing two songs, 'My Happiness' and 'That's When Your Heartaches Begin', to his own simple guitar accompaniment. The following January, he was back, cutting another pair of songs: 'Casual Love Affair' and 'I'll Never Stand In Your Way'. Impressed by the haunting melodicism of his voice, which was pitched intriguingly between a crooner's smooth slide and the low moan of the blues, Keisker kept Elvis's details on file, and reported his existence to her boss.

When Phillips needed a singer to cut a demo a few months later, he invited Presley into the studio. Their initial sessions were unproductive, but when Phillips teamed Elvis with two of the label's regular sessionmen, bassist Bill Black and guitarist Scotty Moore, sparks rapidly grew into an inferno. After cutting restrained renditions of two ballads, 'Harbor Lights' and 'I Love You Because', Presley, Moore and Black jammed around the changes of a blues song, Arthur "Big Boy" Crudup's 'That's All Right (Mama)', while Phillips was away from the studio board. When the producer returned, he asked them what on earth they were doing – and whether they could do it again. After a handful of takes, Elvis Presley's first single was on tape, and the world of popular music was changed for ever.

Elvis issued five singles on Sun, scoring regional hits and making brief inroads into the national country charts. He also taped around a dozen other songs during his sessions with Sam Phillips – a dozen that have survived, that is, as rumours persist of a treasure trove of missing Sun sides.

Each of his Sun singles was carefully programmed to couple a blues tune with a country song, thereby maximising the potential for sales and airplay. Before his name and face became known, no one was sure whether Elvis was black or white – which was precisely the sound that Phillips had been looking for. Elvis's voice was part Hank Williams, part Bobby Bland, part Dean Martin, part Johnnie Ray, and part the kind of divine accident that only happens once in a century. Whether or not Sam Phillips ever voiced his much-quoted aim of finding a white man who had a "Negro sound and feel", Presley fitted the bill. Equally at home in the black or white musical traditions, he effectively moulded them into one. And his appreciation for mainstream pop music, and the tight harmonies of the top gospel quartets, enabled him to branch out way beyond the strict ghetto boundaries of blues and country. Outside, the world was waiting.

THE SINGLES

That's All Right (Mama)/Blue Moon Of Kentucky
(1954)

Blues purists trace a path of exploitation, of white musicians ripping off blacks, from the release of this record – which mixed a taste of hillbilly country with a Delta blues tune and produced the concoction known as rock'n'roll. Play Crudup's original alongside Presley's cover, however, and their theory implodes. Fine though Crudup's record is, it lends nothing but its basic lyrical framework to Presley's interpretation. In the hands of Elvis, Scotty and Bill, as the trio were credited on the Sun singles, 'That's All Right (Mama)' was transformed from a laboured complaint into a celebratory jubilee. Set Crudup's lugubrious vocal alongside the effortless verve of Presley's singing, and all comparisons disappear.

Presley worked similar magic on the flipside, a bluegrass tune by the father of the genre, Bill Monroe. His original had the "high lonesome" sound of Forties bluegrass, with keening vocals and a tight, restrained rhythm. Elvis started out singing the song that way, then cut loose the chains and played it like an uptempo blues tune. By the time the record was finished, it was hard to tell which side was country and which was blues.

Good Rockin' Tonight/I Don't Care If The Sun Don't Shine
(1954)

The same formula was repeated on the second Sun single. 'Good Rockin' Tonight' came from a blues single by Roy Brown – an uptown, citified blues this time, rather than the rural model Presley souped up on his début. Stopping the world in its tracks with the arrogance of his opening vocal wail, Presley set off on a roller-coaster ride across musical boundaries, calling out for everyone to recognise his power. "Tonight she'll know I'm a mighty mighty man", Presley swaggered on the middle verse, and every second of his performance matched his boast.

'I Don't Care If The Sun Don't Shine' sounded like another hillbilly song waiting for a fresh tank of gas. But it actually belonged to Tin Pan Alley, having been recorded by such sophisticates as Patti Page and Elvis's idol, Dean Martin. Elvis, Scotty and Bill turned up the tempo and played it hard and furious, and the result was every bit as dynamic as 'Blue Moon Of Kentucky'.

Milkcow Blues Boogie/You're A Heartbreaker

(1955)

The lyrical imagery of 'Milkcow Blues Boogie' had appeared in dozens of blues (and hillbilly) songs in the decades before Elvis solidified the song for all time. It's not certain where he learned the lines – whether they came from a bluesman like Kokomo Arnold, or from the Western swing rendition of Bob Wills and his Texas Playboys. Nor is it certain whether the memorable opening seconds of his recording were contrived or improvised on the spot. Elvis, Scotty and Bill begin the song at a dirge-like tempo, before Elvis calls the band to a halt. "Hold it, fellas. That don't move me," he complains. "Let's get real, real gone for a change." And they do, the musicians struggling to keep pace as Elvis drives them forward with a vocal that hiccups and swoops up and down the octaves with barely contained delirium at its heart.

By complete contrast, 'You're A Heartbreaker' – actually a pop song, originally recorded by one Jimmy Heap – was presented as Presley's most sedate country performance to date. Elvis abandoned the vocal pyrotechnics of the A-side, and swung through the melody as confidently as another of his early role models, Lefty Frizzell.

I'm Left, You're Right, She's Gone/Baby Let's Play House
(1955)

Pitched midway between full-bore rockabilly and uptempo hillbilly, 'I'm Left, You're Right, She's Gone' was the first original song that Presley ever recorded. Written by Sun Records insider Stan Kesler, it started out as a slow blues, under the title 'My Baby's Gone' (as first heard on a legal release via *The Complete Sun Sessions* CD).

That track was completely overshadowed by its coupling, an R&B tune based on a country hit by Eddy Arnold, and fuelled by imagery that had passed down the blues tradition for generations. Elvis launched the track with an almost inhuman series of whoops and hollers, before slicing through the lyrics with a confidence that defined the concept of "machismo". Mean, threatening, half sung and half sneered, 'Baby Let's Play House' encapsulated everything that was dark and enticing about the young Elvis Presley.

Mystery Train/I Forgot To Remember To Forget
(1955)

Stan Kesler and self-styled rockabilly pioneer Charlie Feathers concocted the pun-filled honky-tonk ballad, 'I Forgot To Remember To Forget' – a stone country tune that Elvis sang with the flair of a Lefty Frizzell or a George Jones. Once again, though, it was the blues coupling that set the world on fire. Sam Phillips had produced Junior Parker's original version of 'Mystery Train', an eerie harbinger of doom based around the lyrical theme of a Thirties country song. For Presley's version, fellow blues fan Scotty Moore set the rhythm with a clipped, insistent guitar riff, while Elvis opened his throat and wailed, like an engineer powerless to control a ghost train heading full-tilt for a fallen bridge.

In commercial terms, this was probably the strongest of the five Sun singles; and it was certainly the most successful, topping the Billboard Country and Western charts towards the end of 1955. Its chart showing ensured that a major label like RCA couldn't help but be aware of Presley's potential — both as an artist and a profit-making machine.

THE EVER EXPANDING SUN COLLECTION

When RCA purchased Elvis's contract in November 1955, they secured a case full of Elvis session tapes, which was raided to make up the numbers on RCA's studio albums and singles between 1956 and 1959. Another Sun recording surfaced in 1965; after that, there were merely persistent rumours, until bootleg collections began appearing in the early Seventies, presenting a batch of alternate takes (including the near-legendary 'My Baby's Gone', the bluesier role model for 'I'm Left, You're Right, She's Gone').

For anyone who didn't have access to the original, mono singles, the Sun recordings were available only in ludicrous fake stereo from the early Sixties through to 1975, when RCA finally released their first Sun-centred Presley album. There have been several subsequent attempts at the same operation, but still hard-core Presley-philes maintain that there is a secret vault filled with previously unheard Sun masters. That there may be; but it's near certain RCA doesn't have access to it, or else those tracks would surely have been released by now.

The late Seventies and Eighties also saw the legal (or semi-legal, in some cases) release of other material long rumoured to have survived — live recordings of Elvis, Scotty Moore and Bill Black taped during the Sun era, plus the fabled 'Million Dollar Quartet' tape, recorded at Sun a year after Elvis left for RCA.

THE ELVIS PRESLEY SUN COLLECTION
(1975)

It took British Presley fans — notably the NME journalist Roy Carr — to force RCA into compiling a long-overdue album of what seemed, at the time, like the complete Sun recordings. With the exception of an alternate take of 'I Love You Because', issued on 1974's *A Legendary Performer* LP, everything on the original pressing of this album had been issued in the Fifties. But here it was on sale in one budget-priced package, and without the distorted, artificial remixing of previous reissues. It was also the first Presley LP to include lengthy, informative, factual sleeve notes.

A few months after this LP appeared, RCA "discovered" a previously unknown Sun out-take: a cover of the crooner's favourite, 'Harbor Lights'. This was added to the subsequent pressings of the Sun Collection, only for the process to be repeated. This time the addition to the canon was 'When It Rains, It Really Pours', a 1955 prototype for the recording included on 1965's Elvis For Everyone LP. That surfaced on A Legendary Performer Vol. 4 in 1983. Next to be uncovered was the undubbed recording of 'Tomorrow Night', which had first surfaced with additional instrumentation on that same 1965 LP. Stripped of its later ornamentation, it appeared on the 1985 collection, Reconsider Baby.

A few months earlier, the boxed album set A Golden Celebration had offered an entire suite of Sun out-takes. Among them was the legendary 'My Baby's Gone', so titled by bootleggers in the early Seventies, but actually an early, bluesy arrangement of 'I'm Left, You're Right, She's Gone'; a pure country fragment of 'Blue Moon Of Kentucky'; an equally brief 'I'll Never Let You Go'; alternate versions of 'Harbor Lights', 'That's All Right' and 'I Don't Care If The Sun Don't Shine'; and that magical 'When It Rains, It Really Pours'.

When RCA announced it now had access to more than a dozen alternate takes from the Sun years, it was obviously time for a complete revamp.

THE COMPLETE SUN SESSIONS
(1987)

To a chorus of praise from most sides, blurred only slightly by howls of disgust by perfectionists, The Complete Sun Sessions gave these seminal recordings their most prestigious setting to date. The lengthy notes by Presley biographer Peter Guralnick set the scene and cast aside some myths, while the two-LP set itself gathered up every Sun track released to date and added nine further out-takes.

These weren't quite as thrilling as they might have been, as they comprised three additional takes of 'I Love You Because' and six of 'I'm Left, You're Right, She's Gone'. Confirmation of their existence suggested to the detractors that RCA must be sitting on similar treasure troves for other songs in its archive – a theory for which the release of *The Complete Fifties Masters* in 1992 added more evidence.

Sadly, this was one release where the vinyl edition outstripped the CD. Two full LPs contained too much music for one 5" disc, so six tracks were dropped to prevent the need for a two-CD set: takes one and four of 'I Love You Because' and takes eight, 10, 11 and 12 of 'I'm Left, You're Right, She's Gone'. At least RCA had the honesty to drop the "Complete" from the title of the CD.

THE BEACH BOYS

Pet Sounds

May 1966

By Andrew Doe & John Tobler

HAVING BOUGHT TIME (and handed Capitol a purely incidental hit album) with *The Beach Boys' Party!*, Brian Wilson now turned his full attention to his new project. Inspired by The Beatles' *Rubber Soul* LP (released in December 1965), which he considered to be "full of all good stuff, no filler", he told wife Marilyn: "I'm gonna make the best rock album in the world"... and, in the view of many expert critics, he succeeded. In three Nineties UK polls, *Pet Sounds* emerged at or near the top of the pile each time – and these are critics' polls, the considered opinions of professional rock journalists, and not merely a reflection of the flavour of the month. An artistic validation 30 years too late, true, but very welcome all the same.

Wilson's compositional style for *Pet Sounds* bordered on the impressionistic; rather than writing a complete melody, he instead sketched out what he called "feels... specific rhythm patterns, fragments of ideas". The melody and lyric would come later, inspired directly by the mood of the "feels". As a writing method, it was luxurious, organic... and time consuming, to the extent that, when Capitol reminded Wilson that a "proper" LP was again overdue, just one song had been completed ('Sloop John B') and one basic track recorded ('In My Childhood' – which he decided he hated).

Gripped by a mild panic, and with the band away on tour, Wilson recalled a chance acquaintance, advertising jingle writer Tony Asher, whom he asked to help out with lyrics. Asher immediately agreed, but soon found out that collaborating with Wilson (whose chemical experimentation was escalating) was a distinct chore outside the strictly musical arena, and in later years offered the famous quote that Brian Wilson was "a genius musician, but an amateur human being".

The Beach Boys, largely absent on tour while their resident Svengali was creating, offered a more considered, if fragmented, critical opinion. Dennis and Carl Wilson loved the new music; Al Jardine decided "it sure doesn't sound like the old stuff"; and Mike Love was memorably forthright – "don't fuck with the formula"; (Bruce Johnston also loved the music, but as a wage slave like Jardine – rather than a voting member of the corporation – he had no real clout in such matters).

Love's disapproval also concerned certain lyrical themes, which Wilson, ever diplomatic, duly ensured were revised. In other matters, however, Wilson was totally intransigent, and this benign dictatorship resulted in *Pet Sounds* being, essentially, a Brian Wilson solo album with guest vocalists. The rest of the band barely contributed instrumentally, and there is strong documentary evidence that, after group vocal sessions, Wilson would return alone to the studio and re-record them his way; which is not to imply that vocals by his colleagues were in any way substandard, but rather was an example of his increasingly perfectionist nature – something that session musicians were already well aware of.

As was his habit, Wilson spent much longer in the studio than Capitol deemed fit, with the result that, apart from the previously released 'Sloop John B' and 'Caroline, No', all of *Pet Sounds*' complex backing tracks and vocals were mixed in a single nine-hour session (which probably explains the chatter heard on some tracks).

Pet Sounds has been called an early concept album; while all the main participants repeatedly deny this, it is not difficult to discern a uniting theme – of hopes and aspirations dashed, of a search for love doomed to failure – and even, some claim, by judicious reprogramming of the CD track order, to produce a coherent storyline tracing the rise and fall of a relationship… and certainly the pervading air of *Pet Sounds* is one of gentle melancholy. Perhaps that's why, even though it included three US Top 40 hits, *Pet Sounds* sold significantly fewer copies than any Beach Boys LP since *Surfin' Safari* and only just made the US Top 10, although it was a major commercial success in Britain, where it became their first Top 10 LP and their first to spend over six months in the chart.

Artistically, however, it was a different story: the music business understood that something very special indeed was happening in southern California, and Wilson suddenly found himself at the vanguard of the nascent pop revolution, regarded as an innovator, a man with something to say of whom much was expected. Fortunately, the next step was already well in hand: during the Pet Sounds sessions, Wilson had also taken a couple of stabs at another title – 'Good Vibrations'.

It had been the intention of Capitol Records to mark the 30th anniversary of the release of Pet Sounds with a revolutionary four CD box set comprising a remastered mono version (using HD/CD technology), session material as per the fifth CD of the Good Vibrations box set (including the first ever 'Good Vibrations' session), the instrumental and vocal tracks in isolation (and stereo!) and, at long last, the first true stereo mix of the complete album. This was lovingly and excellently constructed by Mark Linnett, using the original instrumental four-track and vocal eight-track session tapes. Synchronisation was possible because once he was satisfied with the instrumental backing, Wilson had mixed it down to mono on one of the eight tracks on the eight-track tape, leaving seven tracks for vocals. Linnett thus was able to work with what were effectively 11 tracks for each song once he had synchronised the start of the instrumental four track with the mixed-down mono instrumental track.

Well, that's how it has been explained. The results were stunning, opening up new windows on each song, and the deconstructed vocal and instrumental versions not only allowed intimate study of Brian Wilson's working methods (as did the session tapes, which were also in stereo), but also confirmed that the majority of the vocals on the album were (as had long been rumoured) by Brian Wilson.

Whether or not this rankled with the rest of the group is not known, but the fact is that the box had been approved by Wilson and scheduled for a May 1996 release but was postponed several times; once because the band wanted the booklet(s) revised, and on another occasion because they (allegedly) demanded the stereo mix be done again. The Pet Sounds Sessions box set was eventually released in late 1997, to huge critical acclaim. In 1999, and again in 2001, the album was reissued in a single CD format that comprised both the mono and stereo mixes, and yet again in 2003 in a DVD-A format, comprising the following versions: advanced resolution surround sound, advanced resolution stereo, advanced resolution mono, DTS

5.1 surround sound and DVD-video compatible Dolby digital 5.1.

The package also included video footage from the *Sessions* EPK, and a stereo remix of 'Summer Means New Love'. Not bad for an album conceived and originally released in mono.

(NB: Where Mike Love's composer credit is followed by *, these songs were decreed by a 1994 Los Angeles court decision to have been co-written by him, although he was never previously credited as such; the bonus tracks included on Capitol's 1990 CD reissue programme are noted by +.)

Wouldn't It Be Nice
(B. Wilson/Asher/Love*)

Recorded at LA's Gold Star Studios (where many of Phil Spector's masterpieces were created), this classic US Top 10 hit's lilting guitar intro and explosive drum shot usher in a bittersweet tale of longings as yet unfulfilled, hopes tempered by reality. An accordion-driven track of impressive complexity overlaid with Brian Wilson's keen lead and Love's wonderfully mellow middle-eight vocal, cushioned by sumptuous group harmonies, the lyrical hints at immorality in the first two verses are allayed by the matrimonial hopes of the bridge.

A 24-carat masterpiece, this was carelessly released in Britain as the flip side of the Top Three 'God Only Knows' single; a classic case of losing an obvious hit through bad judgement – in the US, 'God Only Knows' was the flip side of 'Wouldn't It Be Nice', but in Britain, 'God Only Knows' was the favoured track on pirate radio and thus became a smash hit. Included on the boxed set collectors CD in vocal split format, the vocals are even more stunning... and curiously, it's Wilson and not Love singing the middle-eight (a point remedied on the second reissue of the mono/stereo single CD).

You Still Believe In Me
(B. Wilson/Asher)

The odd bicycle bell and horn interjections in this stately, almost hymn-like number are relics of the song's original incarnation as 'In My Childhood', a number that Wilson abandoned, but which had been recorded in such a way that these extraneous sounds could not be erased when he decided to recycle the track... yet strangely, they still fit. His lead vocal is sweetness personified, and the chorus harmony blocks are truly angelic. The bell-like piano intro was achieved by plucking the strings of the instrument, which apparently required extensive practice!

That's Not Me
(B. Wilson/Asher)

The eccentric drum patterns underpinning this track heighten the sense of uncertainty evident in the lyric, while a melodic bass line weaves in and around Love's questioning vocal and Wilson's plaintive counter. As spellbinding, in the view of some commentators, as the two previous tracks.

Don't Talk (Put Your Head On My Shoulder)
(B. Wilson/Asher)

The last track recorded for the album, and a solo vocal performance from Wilson, this languid confection is one of his most romantic compositions and, according to some critics, exudes almost overwhelming emotion.

I'm Waiting For The Day
(B. Wilson/Love)

An attention-grabbing timpani intro leads into a track of great contrasts, juxtaposing reflective passages with aggressive verses to great effect. Similarly, Wilson's lead vocal swings from tender to strident as required. Originally copyrighted in 1964 and credited to Wilson alone, Love's compositional contribution was apparently to amend eight words.

Let's Go Away For A While

(B. Wilson)

A year after the release of *Pet Sounds*, Brian Wilson considered this wistfully atmospheric track to be "the most satisfying piece of music I've ever made", a statement with which many Beach Boys fans and commentators would concur. Although presented as an instrumental, and long thought to have been conceived as such – even though lyrics were written by Asher – it emerged in 1995 that a session for vocals was scheduled, but – at Capitol's insistence – was used instead to mix the album. The story goes that as part of a running joke then current, the song was semi-seriously called 'Let's Go Away For A While (And Then We'll Have World Peace)'.

Sloop John B.

(Trad. arr. B. Wilson)

Released as a single in March, 1966, and a Top Three hit on both sides of the Atlantic, this version of a traditional folk song (a 1960 UK hit for Lonnie Donegan as 'I Wanna Go Home') was recorded in late 1965 at Jardine's instigation, although the arrangement is 100 per cent Brian Wilson. The sore thumb of the album in lyrical terms, it was long assumed that the song was included at Capitol's insistence, as a recent hit; however, research has unearthed a mid-February track listing that Wilson handed to the company, on which the then-unreleased 'Sloop John B' is included. A totally compelling vocal performance, especially during the a cappella break. Love and Wilson share lead vocals.

God Only Knows

(B. Wilson/Asher)

Possibly Carl Wilson's crowning vocal achievement, this has been described by one noted Beach Boys historian as the most beautiful suicide song ever (presumably on the strength of the lines, "The world would show nothing to me, so what good would living do me?"). Be that as it may, Carl's honeyed lead is matched by a shimmering backing track and a gorgeous rotating tag featuring Brian Wilson and Johnston. A US Top 40 hit as the B-side to 'Wouldn't It Be Nice?' and a UK Top Three smash (see above), Brian reputedly had some misgivings about including the word "God" in the song title; Asher successfully talked him round.

A major highlight of the 1993 *Good Vibrations* boxed set was a nine-minute session track, illustrating the importance of the studio musicians in developing the song, and culminating with a version featuring not only Brian's original guide vocal but also an awesome and previously unheard vocal tag of immense complexity and beauty. Why this was consigned to the vaults remains a complete mystery. The *Sessions* box included a (wisely rejected) mix featuring a (lamentable) sax break during the middle-eight in place of the vocals we all know. Finally, *Endless Harmony* featured a very down-home rendition recorded live in the studio in 1967 for the unreleased *Lei'd In Hawaii* project.

I Know There's An Answer
(B. Wilson/Asher/Sachen/Love*)

Initially written and recorded as 'Hang On To Your Ego', this was the item that sent Love's blood pressure soaring, and caused Brian Wilson to get road manager Terry Sachen to marginally revise the lyrics. The track is driven nicely by bass harmonica and banjo, and to many fans, the voice on the verse after Love's first line sounds awfully like Jardine rather than Wilson.

Here Today
(B. Wilson/Asher)

A cascading bass line into the chorus and the mid-song chatter highlight this forceful song, taken from an ex-boyfriend's point of view. If the chords behind the verse sound familiar, they should – Brian Wilson recycled the progression in 'Good Vibrations'. Love is spot on as usual. The instrumental track was recorded at Sunset Sound.

I Just Wasn't Made For These Times
(B. Wilson/Asher)

A less-than-subtle cri de coeur from Brian Wilson, this near-solo performance boasts what may be the first ever use on a rock song of a theremin (a strange instrument, to say the least, later used extensively on 'Good Vibrations'), played by Paul Tanner. The three-part vocal chorus has attracted great attention as the second and third lines are less than clear; session tapes reveal them to be, "Ain't found the one thing I can put my heart and soul into" and, "My friends don't know (or want) me". The instrumental track was recorded at Gold Star.

Pet Sounds
(B. Wilson)

'Sloop John B' aside, this spiky instrumental was long thought to be the first track recorded for *Pet Sounds* (further research has since disproved the notion), and was originally called 'Run, James, Run' (the James in question reportedly being Bond, as in 007).

Caroline, No
(B. Wilson/Asher)

Ushered in by drummer Hal Blaine tapping on an empty soda siphon bottle, this bittersweet US Top 40 ballad was issued as a Brian Wilson solo single. As with 'Surfin'', father Murry Wilson insisted the master be sped up a tone to make Brian sound younger. The barking on the tag was supplied by the latter's dogs at the time, Banana (a beagle) and Louie (a Weimaraner).

Unreleased Backgrounds+
(B. Wilson)

... to 'Don't Talk': probably a wise omission from the LP in 1966.

Hang On To Your Ego+

(B. Wilson/Asher)

Brian Wilson handles the original lyric in a working vocal over a slightly incomplete track. Some find it difficult to understand precisely what Love found so objectionable. Brian Wilson's appeal to engineer Chuck Britz at the end is priceless, as is the latter's response. As with 'God Only Knows', the boxed set included enlightening session material on this title, as well as an alternate version.

Trombone Dixie+

(B. Wilson)

According to David Leaf's excellent *Pet Sounds* CD booklet notes, it says 'Trombone Dixie' on the tape box and features a trombone, so that'll have to do. Reprising (among others) a riff from 'The Little Girl I Once Knew', Brian Wilson would later recycle part of this perky instrumental into 'Had To Phone Ya' on *15 Big Ones*, the group's 1976 comeback LP.

BOB DYLAN

Blonde On Blonde

August 1966

By Patrick Humphries

WITH BACKING GROUP The Band on board, Bob Dylan set off to terrorise the civilised world. Established as a bona-fide pop star, Dylan played nearly 50 shows between May and July 1966, but diehard Dylan fans still couldn't take the idea of their idol fronting a pop group; it seemed to them that Bob was debasing himself before the false gods of money and fame.

Only Dylan could inspire such devotion and provoke such feelings of betrayal. If you went to a concert by Cliff Richard, you didn't go to boo. Crispian St Peters never aroused such hostility in his fans. This was only the second generation of rock'n'roll, the amplification in halls was primitive, achieving a sound balance was nigh-on impossible... but the over-riding feeling left by that incendiary 1966 concert tour was of betrayal.

Loyal fans who had stood by Bob and put up with all the disparaging comments ("Can't sing for toffee, what are his songs about..?") went along and heard their hero drowned out by a pop group. Pop groups were Freddie and The Dreamers, not Bob Dylan and The Band. Guitarist Robbie Robertson recalled: "You get off the plane and play – people booed you. We thought, 'Jesus, this is a strange way to make a living!'"

The head-on collision between Dylan and The Band has been one of rock's great mysteries. The reality is that a secretary in Dylan's manager's office took Bob out to see the boys somewhere in the swamps of New Jersey, sometime in 1965. In *Dont Look Back*, when asked why he had other musicians on his record, Dylan smiles and says they're his friends... "And I have to give my friends work, don't I?"

It's a theory Marianne Faithfull enthusiastically explored in her 1994 autobiography. She gives a compelling fly-on-the-wall account of Dylan at the height of his pop star adulation: "When he came back... with The Band... he was so happy... and it made you realise just what a drag it must have been being out there all by himself with an acoustic guitar, just moaning away. This was exacerbated by being in England, where all the musicians he was meeting were in groups... All that boys' club stuff that makes it so much easier."

Out on a limb, Dylan was also under pressure to deliver a

novel – he couldn't let John Lennon be the only literary pop star. He was touring, his manager had committed him to a TV special, his contract with CBS was due to expire. And there was the question of that new album... The pressure was on. Begun in New York at the end of 1965, *Blonde On Blonde* was wrapped up in Nashville by February 1966.

Nashville didn't have a skyline in 1966. Nashville was where country & western was diluted to taste, in studios light on atmosphere but heavy on time-is-money. The Nashville Sound was lush, wraparound strings, drowning out any real emotion on production-line pop songs, which were only made "country" by virtue of a weeping steel guitar. It wasn't quite what Bob Dylan had in mind...

Blonde On Blonde is a dark and brooding collection. As rock'n'roll's first double album, it beat Frank Zappa's *Freak Out* by a clear two months. Recorded with the cream of the Nashville session aces and a little help from "mathematical guitar genius" Robbie Robertson, the album's 14 songs were quixotic examples of where Dylan's Medusa-like head was at during those punishing first months of 1966.

From the scowling, unfocused Bob on the cover, through to the 10-minute homage to his bride Sara on 'Sad-Eyed Lady Of The Lowlands', *Blonde On Blonde* just teems and overflows. The bulk of the songs were busked in the studio; Dylan only had shadows of what he wanted. His outlines were given flesh by the musicians, initially wary of the wiry-haired pop star, and a sort of camaraderie emerged in the Nashville bunker.

In the past, it had been relatively easy for Dylan to scat his way through an album, when there was only him, his guitar, harmonica and occasionally piano to satisfy. With *Blonde On Blonde*, Dylan had to try and convey the sounds inside his mind not only to other musicians, but to session men with precious little sympatico. Remarkable then that for Dylan, *Blonde On Blonde* came the "closest I ever got to the sound I hear in my mind... It's that thin, that wild mercury sound. It's metallic and bright gold..."

Touring, though, was taking its toll. Dylan sounded as hazy on vinyl as he looked on the album cover. Hindsight again lends a different perspective on the album; knowing that it was to be his last original work for 18 months – a lifetime in rock'n'roll back then – there seem all manner of omens and portents within Blonde On Blonde.

Some of Dylan's best work is to be found among the autumnal hues of Blonde On Blonde, but the relentless pressures of an increasingly successful career meant that, for the first time since his début, he was too busy to be original. He was now to be found borrowing from those he had previously left far behind. 'Fourth Time Around' is an engaging rewrite of The Beatles' 'Norwegian Wood', which had appeared on Rubber Soul six months before, while 'Temporary Like Achilles' and 'Obviously 5 Believers' sounded like Bob Dylan trying to ape the Bob Dylan of a year before.

There is no real "country" on the first album by a rock star to be recorded in Nashville. 'I Want You', 'Rainy Day Women # 12 & 35', 'Leopard-Skin Pill-Box Hat' were lightweight pop, although the refrain, "Everybody must get stoned" (from 'Rainy Day Women...') found easy favour at the time.

'Stuck Inside Of Mobile With The Memphis Blues Again' was another of those great Dylan songs about places. Few American songwriters have conveyed the space and variety of their nation as well as Dylan, the poet of the place-name. He manages to convey the full awfulness of being marooned in Mobile, Alabama, burning with the blues from Memphis, Tennessee. It doesn't mean a lot, but with a talent as blazing as Dylan's, his vagueness is frequently far more satisfying than the precision of others.

'Just Like A Woman' is a song with English overtones and images (fog, royalty, pearls), and one that sits uneasily on today's ears, with its litany of selfish, sexist slurs. Of its time though, its smoky melancholy slots neatly into the weary and resigned world Dylan created in Blonde On Blonde.

'Most Likely You Go Your Way (And I'll Go Mine)' and 'Absolutely Sweet Marie' rock along best without much scrutiny (surely, if you live outside the law, you are, perforce, dishonest?). There is the usual, utility cast of Dylan characters – Persian drunks, guilty undertakers, neon madmen and the Queen of Spades. Bowled along by the composer's relentlessness, much of Dylan's stuff at this time was swallowed without scrutiny.

At his best, though, he could carry you along on the strength of his performance and the conviction of his lyrics. The magnificently wasted 'One Of Us Must Know (Sooner Or Later)', is a bitter farewell played out against desolate landscapes beneath glowering, leaden skies. However, the whole side devoted to 'Sad-Eyed Lady Of The Lowlands' suggested Dylan was out-reaching his grasp. 'Desolation Row' was longer and still managed to squeeze three more songs alongside it, on Side 2 of *Highway 61 Revisited*.

Of all Dylan's atmospheric songs of the period, 'Sad-Eyed Lady...' weaves its own world around Dylan, sounding as world-weary as Humphrey Bogart in the neon-lit Rick's Bar in *Casablanca*, as Ilsa quits him, again. There is a lot of puff here (what, please, is a "geranium kiss"? Describe a "cowboy mouth") but there is also a rolling hymn of devotion with some extraordinarily intense commitments and pledges contained therein.

The masterpiece of the set is 'Visions Of Johanna'. A New York song cut in Nashville – that estrangement lends atmosphere to the work. The first verse is perhaps Dylan's finest evocation of time and place. Wide-ranging and ubiquitous, 'Visions Of Johanna' switches from a clammy attic room to a courtroom where Infinity is judged; from empty parking lots on West 4th Street to a no-show Madonna, prowling an empty cage.

A mournful harmonica plays, a drug-induced nightmare follows halfway through the fourth verse: women with faces like jelly and missing knees, a donkey standing draped with "jewels and binoculars" (an image The Rolling Stones would borrow three years later for the cover of their 1970 live album, *Get Yer Ya-Ya's Out*).

'Visions Of Johanna' has Dylan sounding wise as leader, old as Time. Few have attempted cover versions of this impossibly convoluted song. At his iconoclastic best, Dylan explains Mona Lisa's inscrutable, enigmatic smile as a bad case of the "highway blues", but there aren't many laughs to be had here. This is mystery and imagination, with an organ playing skeleton keys in the wispy background and, near the end, Dylan's conscience explodes and he is gone, while all that remains are his 'Visions Of Johanna', ambiguous and dazzling images that he has entertained over a lifetime.

The summer of 1966 saw The Beatles unleash *Revolver*, their most mature album to date. The Beach Boys' *Pet Sounds* sounded like the only American album to tackle the Fabs head-on. Dylan's manager, Albert Grossman, had scheduled 60 more concerts for the remainder of the year, significantly including a date at Shea Stadium. The Beatles had played the New York baseball stadium the previous year, establishing a record for the largest-ever attendance at a pop concert. Grossman was now determined to put Dylan on a commercial par with The Beatles.

Dylan had established a base at the artists' community of Woodstock, north of New York. It was while riding his motorcycle around the muddy, tree-lined paths of Woodstock that the back wheel on Dylan's machine locked, and he was hurled over the handlebars.

The few people who had been close to Dylan in the weeks before the crash remarked on the singer's ghost-like pallor. You could hear how weary he sounded on record and in interview. There was a tragic inevitability to the crash, the legend of James Dean loomed large. Youth needed another martyr.

Dylan's legendary status was enhanced by the crash, marking as it did a period of withdrawal, when the only stories to emerge from Dylan's Woodstock retreat were rumours. As pop convulsed during the summer of 1967, Bob Dylan sat far away in upstate New York, looking out at the trees and staring at the sky.

THE BEATLES

Sgt. Pepper's Lonely Hearts Club Band

June 1967

By Peter Doggett

"THE BIGGEST INFLUENCE on *Sgt. Pepper* was *Pet Sounds* by The Beach Boys," said Paul McCartney in 1980. "That album just flipped me. When I heard it, I thought, 'Oh dear, this is the album of all time. What the hell are we going to do?' My ideas took off from that standard. I had this idea that it was going to be an album of another band that wasn't us — we'd just imagine all the time that it wasn't us playing. It was just a nice little device to give us some distance on the album. The cover was going to be us dressed as this other band in crazy gear; but it was all stuff that we'd always wanted to wear. And we were going to have photos on the wall of all our heroes."

That's the standard view of *Sgt. Pepper*, from the man who almost single-handedly created the album, and its legend. In this reading, *Pepper* is the best pop record of all time — the album that customarily wins critics' polls, the masterpiece that first persuaded "serious" musical critics that pop was worth their consideration.

There's a rival view of the whole affair, however, and it was put forward most cogently by McCartney's supposed partner, John Lennon. "Paul said 'come and see the show' on that album," he moaned a few years after its release. "I didn't. I had to knock off a few songs so I knocked off 'A Day In The Life', or my section of it, and 'Mr Kite'. I was very paranoid in those days. I could hardly move."

More than any other Beatles album bar *Abbey Road*, *Sgt. Pepper* was a Paul McCartney creation. It was he who dreamed up the concept, the title, the idea behind Peter Blake's remarkable cover, the orchestrations, and the device of pretending that the entire LP was the work of another band entirely — which in turn became one of the major themes of the *Yellow Submarine* movie, then in its pre-production stages.

Meanwhile, John Lennon was deep in a creative trough. For the first time, Lennon and McCartney appeared — to Lennon, at least — to be in competition rather than on the same side. Since the Beatles had played their final live shows in August, McCartney had been composing — first the musical themes for the film *The Family Way*, then the songs that would appear on the next Beatles album. Lennon had also been involved in film work, but as an actor, in Dick Lester's *How I Won The War*. Required for the part to shed his Beatle locks, he adopted the granny specs that soon became his trademark, stared into the mirror, and wondered what the future might bring for an unemployed Beatle. Back in England at the end of filming, Lennon regarded McCartney's enthusiasm to get into the studio as a threat. Aware that he was likely to be outnumbered in the songwriting stakes, he raised the emotional barriers and took against the *Pepper* album from the start.

In the end, Lennon came up with the requisite number of songs for the album, but he never warmed to the concept. On *Revolver*, and again on the majestic 'Strawberry Fields Forever', cut early in the sessions, he'd experienced the relief and satisfaction of writing from the heart. For *Pepper*, he was back where he'd been in 1964, writing songs to order. Hence the sarcastic, dismissive comments he reserved for this album throughout the rest of his life.

Whatever else *Sgt. Pepper* may or may not have been, it was certainly an event. It unified British pop culture in a way no other occasion could match. Maybe in hindsight it wasn't The Beatles' strongest album, but it had an impact unlike any record before or since. It literally revolutionised the direction of pop, helping to divide it between those who were prepared to follow the group along the path of experimentation (thus creating "rock") and those who mourned the loss of the less significant Beatles of yore (the champions of "pop"). After Pepper, nothing was ever the same again – within or without The Beatles.

All songs written by John Lennon and
Paul McCartney unless otherwise indicated.

Sgt. Pepper's Lonely Hearts Club Band

Complete with the appropriate sound effects, the album's uptempo title track introduced the record, the concept and the Club Band. It performed the function of an overture in an opera, preparing the audience for what was to follow, and introducing the themes that supposedly unified the piece.

With A Little Help From My Friends

The Beatles' official biographer, Hunter Davies, watched Lennon, McCartney and their associates completing work on Paul McCartney's original idea, aware from the start that this would be a vehicle for Ringo Starr – or "Billy Shears", as he was billed in the opening seconds of the song. Though the song's theme was tailored towards Ringo's warm public image (right down to the line, "What would you think if I sang out of tune?" a real possibility), at least one observer saw a hidden meaning. Speaking in 1970, US Vice-President Spiro Agnew told an audience that he had recently been informed that the song was a tribute to the power of illegal drugs – news to its composers, perhaps.

Not often did other performers outclass The Beatles with cover versions of their songs, but Joe Cocker's gut-wrenching version of 'Friends' in 1968 left Ringo floundering.

Lucy In The Sky With Diamonds

The minor furore over the meaning of 'Friends' had nothing on the frenzied response to this piece of whimsy from the pen of John Lennon. "I was consciously writing poetry," he admitted, shifting blame for the line about "newspaper taxis" to his nominal co-writer. But the *Alice In Wonderland* style imagery, supposedly inspired by a drawing John's son Julian had brought home from nursery school, was widely believed to be a description of an acid trip. As soon as someone noticed the initials of the song's title (LSD), that seemed to clinch the story – except that Lennon continued to deny it until his dying day. Having owned up to so much else down the years, there was no reason for him to lie – especially over a song which he always felt was "so badly recorded".

Getting Better

Based on a favourite saying of Beatles' stand-in drummer Jimmy Nicol (who briefly deputised for Ringo on tour in 1964), 'Getting Better' was a McCartney song augmented by Lennon, who contributed the self-accusing verse that began,

"I used to be cruel to my woman". Ever since Lennon's death, McCartney has bemoaned his inability to find a co-writer who, like John, would answer a line like, "It's getting better all the time" with, "Couldn't get much worse". Even in the midst of what was intended to be a concept album, McCartney could turn out a song that was clever, melodic, memorable and universal in its application.

Fixing A Hole

For the first time in England, The Beatles left Abbey Road studios for the session that provided the basic track for this fine McCartney song, often overlooked by critics and fans alike. EMI's studio was fully booked for the night, so the group moved to Regent Sound on the West End's Tottenham Court Road.

While John Lennon's writing veered between fantasy and obvious self-revelation, McCartney's skirted from the romantic to the delightfully oblique. This song definitely fell into the latter category, with lyrics that unveiled as many mysteries as they solved. Instrumentally, too, 'Fixing A Hole' was a minor classic, from McCartney's opening trills on the harpsichord to the lyrical guitar solo.

She's Leaving Home

"Paul had the basic theme for this song," said John Lennon, "but all those lines like, 'We sacrificed most of our life... We gave her everything money could buy', those were the things Mimi used to say to me. It was easy to write."

Paul's rather precious piece of fictional writing wasn't helped by Mike Leander's ornate score for the song, one of the few occasions when The Beatles were left sounding pretentious. It took the realism of Lennon's answer-lines to cut through the sweetness of the piece.

Being For The Benefit Of Mr. Kite

A masterpiece of ingenuity rather than inspiration, 'Mr. Kite' was written when John transcribed the wording from a vintage circus poster into verse form, and recorded with the help of scores of small segments of fairground organ tape, tossed into the air and then stuck back together to produce the eerie noise that dominates the instrumental sections. Lennon dismissed it as a throwaway – which, when you remember how it was made, is pretty apt.

Within You, Without You
(George Harrison)

Though it was John Lennon who resented Paul McCartney's domination of the *Pepper* sessions, George Harrison probably had more cause to be aggrieved. He was restricted to just one number on the LP, his other contribution ('Only A Northern Song') being rejected.

Like 'Love You To', 'Within You, Without You' blatantly displayed Harrison's infatuation with Indian culture. Recorded with the assistance of several Indian musicians, plus Beatles aide Neil Aspinall on tamboura, the song required no help from any other member of the group. "It was written at Klaus Voorman's house in Hampstead, one night after dinner," George explained a decade later. "I was playing a pedal harmonium when it came, the tune first, then the first sentence." Some thought it a masterpiece, some a prime example of mock-philosophical babble. Either way, it was pure Harrison.

When I'm Sixty Four

Paul began writing this song when he was a teenager, needing only to add the middle sections for this revival of a 10-year-old melody. Within the concept of the album, it fitted the image of the Edwardian Pepper band, whereas it would have seemed mawkish on any of the group's earlier LPs. The addition of clarinets to the mix heightened the pre-First World War feel.

Lovely Rita

The anthem for traffic wardens ("meter maids") everywhere, 'Lovely Rita' was a glorious throwaway, full of musical jokes and brimming with self-confidence. Nothing on the record expressed that as fully as the piano solo, ironically played by keyboard maestro George Martin.

Good Morning, Good Morning

Using a TV commercial for Kellogg's cereal as his starting point, John Lennon concocted a wonderfully dry satire on contemporary urban life. Several points to watch out for here: the reference to the popular BBC TV sitcom, *Meet The Wife*; the ultra-compressed brass sound provided by members of Sounds Incorporated; a stinging McCartney guitar solo; and the cavalcade of animals, in ascending order of ferocity, which segues into a reprise of the title track.

Sgt. Pepper's Lonely Hearts Club Band (Reprise)

For the first but definitely not last time, Paul McCartney topped and tailed a set of songs by reprising the opening melody, in true Hollywood musical fashion.

A Day In The Life

Delete 'A Day In The Life' from *Sgt. Pepper* and you'd have an elegant, playful album of pop songs. With it, the LP assumes some kind of greatness. Some might vote for 'Hey Jude' or 'Strawberry Fields Forever' as the finest Beatles recording, but 'A Day In The Life' would run anything close – and it's certainly the best collaborative effort between Lennon and McCartney.

Lennon wrote the basic song, its verses a snapshot from his own life and the world around him – the death of a friend in a car crash, a newspaper cutting about the state of the roads in Blackburn, Lancashire. The tag line, "I'd love to turn you on", brought a broadcasting ban by the BBC in Britain: more importantly, it led twice into an overwhelming orchestral assault, with 40 musicians headed helter-skelter up the scales towards a crescendo of silence. First time around, the barrage leads into McCartney's stoned middle-eight, another day in another life; second time, there's a pause, and then a piano chord that resounds for almost a minute. Then bathos: a whistle only dogs could hear, followed by the locked-groove gibberish that brought the side to a close and is sampled briefly at the end of the CD. Stunning, magnificent, awesome: there's nothing in rock to match it.

JIMI HENDRIX
(The Jimi Hendrix Experience)

Electric Ladyland
October 1968

By Peter Doggett

THE JIMI HENDRIX EXPERIENCE ELECTRIC LADY LAND

FOR PURE EXPERIMENTAL genius, melodic flair, conceptual vision and instrumental brilliance, The Jimi Hendrix Experience's *Electric Ladyland* is a prime contender for the status of rock's greatest album. During its 75-minute passage, it flirts with electronic composition, soft-soul, Delta blues, psychedelic rock, modern jazz and proto-funk, without ever threatening to be confined by any of those labels. It climaxes with a display of musical virtuosity that has never been surpassed in rock music. Small wonder that Hendrix found the task of matching this album insuperable: despite the splendour of much of his post-1968 work, he could never again capture the effortless magic of *Electric Ladyland*.

The album was a landmark in personal terms as much as artistic. During the early sessions, Chas Chandler effectively resigned as Hendrix's producer; his formal disengagement as co-manager followed the next year. Meanwhile, internal dissension within the Experience led bassist Noel Redding to be absent for many of the *Ladyland* sessions. Sometimes Hendrix covered Redding's parts himself; sometimes he augmented the three-man studio line-up to incorporate keyboards, brass or woodwinds.

Most importantly, Hendrix was able to expand the visionary painting-in-sound techniques he'd employed on tracks such as 'Third Stone From The Sun' (from *Are You Experienced*) and 'EXP' (from *Axis: Bold As Love*), to the point that he was able to build an entire side of the original double-LP – from 'Rainy Day, Dream Away' to 'Moon, Turn The Tides' – into an exotic suite, a seamless composition of fragments and improvisation that couldn't quite be categorised as jazz or as rock. Fracturing those genre boundaries merely made it more difficult for Hendrix to reconstitute them in the future.

ELECTRIC LADYLAND (VERSION 1)
October 1968

Tracks: CD1: ...And The Gods Made Love/Have You Ever Been (To Electric Ladyland)/Crosstown Traffic/Voodoo Chile/Still Raining, Still Dreaming/House Burning Down/All Along The

Watchtower/Voodoo Child (Slight Return)
CD2: Little Miss Strange/Long Hot Summer Night/Come On (Part 1)/Gypsy Eyes/The Burning Of The Midnight Lamp/ Rainy Day, Dream Away/1983... (A Merman I Should Turn To Be)/Moon, Turn The Tides... Gently, Gently Away

The original CD release retained the naked "glory" of the original UK album cover, with its parade of slightly distorted female flesh. Hendrix hated that design, and he would have loathed this CD release even more. Not only was the mastering very poor, bathed in hiss and excess noise, but Polydor destroyed the original album concept by combining sides one and four of the double LP on the first disc, and two and three on the second. This magnificent piece of logic meant that 'Rainy Day, Dream Away' appeared after its intended sequel, 'Still Raining, Still Dreaming'.

ELECTRIC LADYLAND (VERSION 2)
June 1991

Tracks: ...And The Gods Made Love/Have You Ever Been (To Electric Ladyland)/Crosstown Traffic/Voodoo Chile/Little Miss Strange/Long Hot Summer Night/Come On (Part 1)/ Gypsy Eyes/The Burning Of The Midnight Lamp/Rainy Day, Dream Away/1983 ...(A Merman I Should Turn To Be)/Moon, Turn The Tide... Gently, Gently Away/Still Raining, Still Dreaming/House Burning Down/All Along The Watchtower/ Voodoo Child (Slight Return)

During the initial phase of remastering for the *Sessions* box set, *Electric Ladyland* was sensibly reduced to a single CD (without shedding any of its contents) and the running order was restored to Hendrix's original instructions. But the sound quality was only marginally more satisfactory than the first release.

ELECTRIC LADYLAND (VERSION 3)
1993

Tracks: as per Version 2

Excellently re-mastered, Electric Ladyland now sounds as breathtaking on CD as it did on vinyl in 1968. Michael Fairchild's notes in the lengthy booklet are superb, and so is the sound quality − from the tumultuous sonic landslide of 'Voodoo Child (Slight Return)' to the delicacy of 'Moon, Turn The Tides' − which, bizarrely, is listed on the back cover as lasting for just one minute, not 10.

All songs written by Jimi Hendrix unless otherwise indicated.

...And The Gods Made Love

Conceived under the more prosaic title 'At Last The Beginning', this solo guitar concoction presaged the multi-dubbed delights to come, as Hendrix conjured magnificent pictures from musical genius and technical brilliance. Taped on June 29, 1968, during a single lengthy session.

Have You Ever Been (To Electric Ladyland)

Unlike the slightly later solo rendition captured on the posthumous *Loose Ends* collection, this soft-soul classic added studio trickery to the obvious influence of Curtis Mayfield's guitar. With Noel Redding absent from proceedings, Hendrix handled the bass as well, and topped off a delightfully airy confection with some precise falsetto vocals.

Crosstown Traffic

Having just exhibited his command of the most subtle forms of soul music, Hendrix unveiled an aggressive, swaggering funk track − the basic track cut live in the studio by the Experience line-up back in December 1967 and then overdubbed in April and May 1968. Twenty-two years later, the Estate sanctioned the creation of a video to accompany the song's belated release as a single: both visually and aurally, it felt stunningly contemporary alongside the funk/rock crossovers of Lenny Kravitz and Living Colour.

Proof that someone at the sessions had a sense of humour was the involvement of Traffic guitarist, Dave Mason – whose sole contribution to the track was to sing the name of his band in every chorus.

Voodoo Chile

Throughout 1967, Muddy Waters' Chicago R&B song, 'Catfish Blues', was a regular inclusion in the Experience's live set. By early 1968, it had mutated into an original Hendrix song, built around an identical riff, and with lyrics that paid their dues to some of the most unsettling images from the Delta blues tradition.

During a lengthy session on May 1, 1968, Hendrix, Experience drummer Mitch Mitchell, Jack Casady (bassist from Jefferson Airplane) and Steve Winwood (from Traffic) worked their way through a series of lengthy free-form jams around the 'Voodoo Chile' changes. This was the longest, and most successful, with Hendrix's surprisingly orthodox blues playing acting as counterpoint to Winwood's sustained organ chords.

Down the years, there's been much confusion over the exact spelling of this song, and its counterpart at the end of this album. I've settled on 'Voodoo Chile' and 'Voodoo Child (Slight Return)', as being Hendrix's preferences. What matters most, though, is that the two songs – offering vastly different takes on the blues – are the twin pillars of *Electric Ladyland*.

Little Miss Strange

(Noel Redding)

For the second album running, Noel Redding was allowed to contribute – and sing – one number. Sadly, 'Little Miss Strange' did little more than repeat the ingredients of 'She's So Fine' from *Axis*, and *Electric Ladyland* would be a stronger album without it. Like much of this set, it was taped during April and May 1968.

Long Hot Summer

Hendrix doubled up on bass and guitar, while Al Kooper's keyboards took a minor role on this piece of urban soul, which was mixed idiosyncratically, to say the least. Mitch Mitchell's drums were marooned on the far left of the stereo picture, while the other instruments never quite cohered into any kind of whole – as if the tape had picked up musicians from different rooms who happened by chance to be performing the same number.

Come On (Part 1)
(Earl King)

The final song to be recorded for the album was this cover of a blues by New Orleans guitarist Earl King, cut on August 27, 1968. The Experience ploughed through the standard chord changes and lyrical imagery, take after take, and several near-identical versions have appeared on bootlegs in recent years. Pleasant but undemanding, its last-minute addition to the album was strange, in view of the fact that Hendrix left out-takes from these sessions like 'South Saturn Delta' and 'My Friend' unreleased.

Gypsy Eyes

From its train-in-tunnel drum phasing to its staccato guitar licks, 'Gypsy Eyes' was a masterpiece of creating substance out of little more than a riff and a message of love. Hendrix's guitar patterns on this track, and the interplay he built up with his own bass runs, can be heard resounding down the history of subsequent rock/funk crossovers, notably Prince's early-to-mid Eighties work.

The Burning Of The Midnight Lamp

Already issued as a single long before the release of *Electric Ladyland*, 'Midnight Lamp' still fitted the album with its dense production (reminiscent of Phil Spector), unusual voicings

(Hendrix on harpsichord and mellotron) and evocative imagery. "They said that was the worst record we'd done," Jimi said in 1968, "but to me that was the best one we ever made."

Rainy Day, Dream Away

On June 10, 1968, Hendrix, Buddy Miles, organist Michael Finnigan, sax player Freddie Smith and percussionist Larry Faucette jammed through a set of jazzy changes with a cool, late-night feel, and an equally laid-back lyric. Suitably overdubbed and edited, their lengthy 'Rainy Day Jam' was divided between this track and 'Still Raining, Still Dreaming'. Initially, it introduced the brilliant suite of music that segued into...

1983... (A Merman I Should Turn To Be)

Delicate guitar passages established a mood that mixed psychedelic rock and jazz, before Hendrix began to paint in words the portrait of a world torn by war and despair, from which the only escape is the sea. Playing all the instruments apart from flute (supplied by Chris Wood, the third Traffic member to guest on this album), Hendrix created an orchestral tapestry of sound, which flowed elegantly into a gentle chaos of tape effects, backwards guitar and chiming percussion, and then to...

Moon, Turn The Tides... Gently, Gently Away

Multi-dubbed guitar motifs restored the psychedelic jazz feel, vamping melodically for several minutes until the mood became almost frenzied and shifted into an electronically treated drum solo. At last, the familiar themes of '1983' re-emerged, to guide the suite to its conclusion, and complete 20 minutes of stunningly complex and beautiful instrumental tonalities. These two tracks were taped in a single remarkable session, on April 23, 1968.

Still Raining, Still Dreaming

Still jamming, too, first through another verse of 'Rainy Day, Dream Away', and then into a coda that gradually wound down the mellow jazz groove of the original track.

House Burning Down

Another collaboration between Hendrix and Mitchell (Noel Redding played on just five *Electric Ladyland* songs), 'House Burning Down' twisted through several key changes in its tight, swirling intro, and then shifted again as the strident chorus moved into the reportorial verses. Like so many of Hendrix's songs from this period, there was an atmosphere of impending doom in the air, inspired by the outburst of black-on-black violence that had shaken some of America's ghettos earlier in 1968. "Try to learn instead of burn," Jimi advised hopefully, before (as ever) finding salvation somewhere other than the land – this time via a friendly visitor from another galaxy.

All Along The Watchtower

(Bob Dylan)

'I Dreamed I Saw St. Augustine' was Hendrix's first choice of material when he listened to Bob Dylan's 1968 album, *John Wesley Harding*, for the first time. In 1970, he recorded another song from the set, 'Drifter's Escape'; but his arrangement of 'All Along The Watchtower' was so convincing that Dylan himself has been using it ever since.

In its original acoustic form, Dylan threw the emphasis of the song on its apocalyptic imagery. Hendrix used the sound of the studio to evoke the storms and the sense of dread, creating an echoed aural landscape that remains the most successful Dylan cover ever recorded. Dave Mason of Traffic contributed bass and acoustic guitar to the basic session on January 21, 1968; Hendrix completed his overdubs four months later, and the song subsequently became a worldwide hit single.

Voodoo Child (Slight Return)

Two days after recording the epic 'Voodoo Chile', Hendrix was back at New York's Record Plant, with Mitchell and Redding, ready for this 'Slight Return'. What evolved, over eight takes, was the single most impressive piece of guitar-playing this writer has ever heard, on a track that compresses every ounce of Hendrix's ambition, musical technique, production skill and uncanny sense of impending disaster into five minutes. From its opening wah-wah chatter to the wails of feedback that bring the song to its close, it's an extravaganza of noise and naked emotion. Its verbal imagery is ablaze with destruction and imminent death; and the music is equal to every last nuance. By its very nature, feedback evokes loss of control: during this performance, Hendrix handles it like a wizard controlling a hurricane.

JOHNNY CASH

Johnny Cash
At San Quentin

June 1969

By Peter Hogan

I N JANUARY 1969, Johnny Cash and June Carter had visited Vietnam to play concerts for the US troops stationed at Long Binh Air Force Base in Saigon. They slept in a trailer there during a night of heavy bombardment by the Viet Cong, and discovered the next morning that their trailer had been moved several feet by the shock waves. Cash later spoke of hearing the shells falling: "After you hear that sound, you never want there to be a war again, ever." During their stay in Vietnam they often played ten shows a day for the troops. Cash came down with a fever, and was prescribed Dexedrine tablets – which quickly sparked drug-related problems that were a hangover from earlier addictions. He went on to play more concerts throughout the Far East, but when the show reached Tokyo he was unable to sing or even stand. Once again, he fought to get his habit under control.

Since the Folsom Prison album had been so successful, the decision was made to attempt to repeat the winning formula – though this may have been sparked by the fact that Britain's Granada TV wanted to film Cash playing a prison concert. This time, the venue chosen was the San Quentin State Prison in California's Marin County, overlooking the San Francisco Bay. Larger and older than Folsom, the maximum security prison held 6,000 hardened inmates and had 1,500 staff. Cash had first played there in 1959, when Merle Haggard was one of the inmates in the audience.

Both concert (and film) were recorded in San Quentin's mess hall on February 24, 1969, in front of approximately 1,000 inmates (and an unknown number of machine gun -toting guards). Bob Johnston was the album's producer, and the personnel of the Johnny Cash Show were the same as for Folsom Prison, with the exception of Bob Wootton as guitarist Luther Perkins' replacement. The atmosphere at the show was tense, due to escalating violence between rival prison gangs in the preceding weeks. "Best behaviour advised" read the prison poster announcing the concert. In Rolling Stone, Ralph Gleason called Cash's performance "right on the edge", since the singer skilfully whipped up the prisoners' enthusiasm without actually causing a riot. This time, Cash performed without the aid of drugs, and the results are even better than the Folsom Prison album – the sound quality is much better, and although Cash's voice sounds a little strained at times, he also sounds more self-assured. The band are also on great form, and far more energetic than at Folsom.

The resulting album spent 22 weeks at number one on the country charts, and four weeks at number one on the pop charts, and both the album and the 'A Boy Named Sue' single became certified million sellers. That year, LIFE magazine had claimed that Johnny Cash and Muhammad Ali were currently the two best-known people in the world. When the year ended, nine of Cash's albums were in the charts, and Columbia proudly announced that during that year in the USA, Johnny Cash had outsold The Beatles.

Three years later, Cash testified before a Senate Subcommittee on penitentiary reform. He also continued to play prison gigs until 1977 – when he played Folsom again – after which he stopped for good. Prisons had by this point become simply too dangerous, and Cash probably felt that he'd done enough for this particular cause. In 2000, an extended CD of the San Quentin concert was issued, containing nine previously unreleased tracks; the censor's bleeping was also removed.

All songs written by Johnny Cash unless otherwise indicated.

Big River

Cash got the inspiration for this song from reading an article about himself in TV Radio Mirror magazine, the first line of which read: "Johnny Cash has the Big River blues in his life." Cash wrote the song – once again about a love gone wrong and gone missing – in the back seat of a car in White Plains, New York, and later commented, "I finished the song before I ever finished the article."

Cash had wanted to record it as a slow 12-bar blues, but producer Sam Phillips chose to go for a rockabilly treatment instead, with Jack Clement playing an open-tuned Gibson with a bottleneck. Cash later admitted that Phillips had been right: "I thought it was fabulous. The groove he'd heard in his head was so much more powerful than mine."

In fact, the guitar playing totally makes the record. Bob Dylan later described the lyrics as: "words turned into bone". Released as the B-side of Sun single 283, this went to number one on the country charts in its own right.

Added for the extended CD.

I Still Miss Someone

(Johnny Cash/Roy Cash Jr)

Written with his brother Roy, this is possibly Cash's most covered composition, with versions to date by (among others) Joan Baez, Julie Andrews, Fairport Convention, Stevie Nicks, Emmylou Harris, Crystal Gayle, Linda Ronstadt and Percy Sledge. It's a wonderful song about carrying a torch for a lost love, and even the mildly irritating backing vocals of this version can't ruin it. The best thing on the album, it was released as the B-side of 'Don't Take Your Guns To Town' in December 1958.

Added for the extended CD.

Wreck Of The Old

(Arranged by J. Cash/B. Johnston/N. Blake)

A traditional folk song, loosely based on the true story of a 1903 train crash. Vernon Dalhart's 1924 recording of the song had been the first million-selling country record. Cash's version is respectful rather than inspired.

I Walk The Line

Cash would claim that the music for this song had been inspired by the accidental twisting of a rehearsal tape of one of his Air Force jam sessions during its playback, which resulted in the sound of backwards chords. "The drone and those weird chord changes stayed with me," he later said.

He finally completed the song in November 1955 while on the road with a Sun package tour. Backstage at a gig in Gladewater, Texas, Cash was strumming the chords he'd based upon the rehearsal tape, and told Carl Perkins that he was trying to write a song about "being true" – to oneself, to one's marital partner and to God – and that his working titles for it were 'I'm Still Being True' or 'I'm Walking The Line'. Perkins suggested that he abbreviate the latter to 'I Walk The Line', and Cash was sufficiently inspired by their conversation to finish writing the song. It supposedly only took him 20 minutes to complete, and he later commented that it was one of those songs just waiting to be written.

In a sense, Carl Perkins was simply repaying a favour – a few months earlier, Cash had told Perkins an anecdote from his service days, which Perkins used as the basis for his song 'Blue Suede Shoes'.

With this song, Cash was publicly pledging his fidelity to his wife, Vivienne, who had serious concerns that her husband might succumb to the temptations of young female fans while he was living the life of a touring musician. According to an article in Country Music International magazine, the phrase "walking the line" dates back to the era of railroad construction, when makeshift brothels sprang up alongside the rail tracks; "walking the line" thus meant to carry on walking past these temptations.

Sam Phillips thought the first version of the song that Cash recorded was too slow, and told him to play it again faster for a second version. Cash was upset that the faster version was the one Phillips chose to release in May 1956, but the producer evidently knew what he was doing, since the record (Sun single 241) went gold, selling over two million copies, hitting number one in the country charts and even breaking into the pop charts (at number 17). The song – which also won a BMI Award – has a truly epic quality, and the fact that Cash could write something this good this early in his career is ample proof of his talent.

The lyric's opening line inspired ex-Velvet Underground artist, John Cale's, song 'Close Watch'. The song would also provide the title for the 2005 Johnny Cash biopic, which starred Joaquin Phoenix as Cash and Reese Witherspoon as June Carter. See also The Complete Sun Recordings.

All of the above four songs are good, uptempo versions,

with some great guitar from Carl Perkins. Cash's voice occasionally sounds strained, but that's the only complaint.

Darlin' Companion
(John Sebastian)

One of the lesser-known items from The Lovin' Spoonful's songbook, performed as a country duet with June Carter. Not as good as the original, but not a disgrace either.

I Don't Know Where I'm Bound
(J. Cuttie)

Written by a prisoner in San Quentin, who had given Cash the sheet music for it the night before; since Cash couldn't read music, he set the lyrics to a tune of his own. It's an impressive folk ballad, verging on gospel.

Added for the extended CD.

Starkville City Jail

Written just before the concert, about Cash's arrest in Starkville, Mississippi in 1966 for picking flowers at 2 a.m. (while drunk and pilled-up, needless to say). Cash spent the night in jail and was fined $36 – and broke a toe after kicking the cell wall in frustration. The song itself is an impressive folk ballad.

San Quentin

Written two days before the concert, at the suggestion of Granada TV film director, Michael Darlow. It's a slow and powerful ballad written from the viewpoint of a prisoner questioning the point of the prison system, weakened slightly by unnecessary backing vocals. The song nearly caused a riot, as prisoners leapt up onto tables, yelling their approval of the lyrics. At its close, the song is reprised by popular demand.

Wanted Man
(Bob Dylan)

Dylan had co-written this song – a good country rocker about life on the run – with Cash shortly before, while staying at his house near Nashville. Cash publicly (and correctly) acclaimed Dylan as "the greatest writer of our time".

A Boy Named Sue
(Shel Silverstein)

The epic tale of a man who becomes a tough fighter because he's been saddled with an unfortunate first name. Humour writer and cartoonist Shel Silverstein gave Cash the "lyrics" to this at a party five days before the concert. It had no tune, but Cash and guitarist Bob Wootton improvised one on the spot, as Cash balanced the lyric sheet on a music stand in front of him. The song was released as a single in July 1969 and went to number one in the country charts and number two in the pop charts, making it Cash's all-time biggest hit. The word "bitch" in the phrase "son of a bitch" was censored with a bleep (removed for the extended CD version).

The inspiration for the song was a real person, Judge Sue K. Hicks from Madisonville, whom Silverstein had met at a juridical conference. The song also prompted two "answer" songs, Lois Williams' 'A Gal Called Sam' and Jane Morgan's 'A Girl Named Johnny Cash'.

(There'll Be) Peace In The Valley
(T. Dorsey)

Classic gospel tune that had been recorded by Sun Records' "Million Dollar Quartet" (Cash, Elvis Presley, Jerry Lee Lewis and Carl Perkins) and also by Presley solo. Cash's gentle and moving version has the benefit of autoharp and backing vocals from the Carter girls, but Presley's version still takes some beating.

Folsom Prison Blues

While in the Air Force, Cash had seen Crane Wilbur's 1951 film, *Inside The Walls Of Folsom Prison*, which starred Steve Cochran as a crusading prisoner. The movie – about a campaign to improve prison conditions – definitely made a big impression on him (he immediately asked for it to be shown again on the base), and he later claimed to have written this song the same night he saw the movie.

It's a moderately fast-paced rocker about a life gone wrong: the protagonist commits murder, ends up in prison and longs for life on the outside. The song's most famous line, about killing a man "just to see him die", Cash came up with after thinking hard about what would be "the worst reason a person could have for killing another person". A tale of violence and repentance, it can be viewed as concerning human limitation in its broadest sense; as Cash later pointed out, "Most of us are living in one little kind of prison or another."

Unfortunately, whether consciously or not, both lyrically and musically Cash based his song upon 'Crescent City Blues', a song from Gordon Jenkins' 1953 concept album, *Seven Dreams*. Cash subsequently stated that at the time he wrote the song, he "really had no idea I would be a professional recording artist. I wasn't trying to rip anybody off".

At the time of its initial release, Gordon Jenkins apparently wasn't aware of the song's existence, but when Cash re-recorded the song 13 years later for his Folsom Prison live album, Jenkins got to hear it and subsequently sued. Cash settled out of court in the early Seventies, and Jenkins was given a writing credit on the song from then on. Sam Phillips had originally wanted to send the song to Tennessee Ernie Ford to cover, but Cash insisted on releasing his own version instead.

Released as Sun single 232 in December 1955, this good, uptempo version, with great guitar and enthusiastic audience response, lacks the verve of the later live recording, but features some very nice guitar. The song is also at the root of the popular misconception that Johnny Cash actually served time in prison, and his resulting outlaw image.

Added for the extended CD.

Ring Of Fire
(J. Carter/M. Kilgore)

Written by June Carter about the pain of her affair with Cash, co-writer Kilgore would later be best man at their wedding. Apparently based upon a poem titled 'Love's Ring Of Fire', the song's original title was 'Love's Fiery Ring'. First recorded in 1962 by June's sister Anita; given the subject matter, it's somewhat ironic that Cash wanted to record the song himself as soon as he heard it.

The tune was supposedly inspired by music June had heard while travelling in Mexico, which fitted perfectly with the wonderful mariachi trumpet arrangement Cash uses on his version (the idea for which supposedly came to him in a dream). Since Cash wisely didn't trust producer Don Law to capture the sound he wanted, he drafted in his old Sun colleague, Jack Clement, to arrange the trumpet parts.

The song was recorded in March 1963 and released the following month, becoming a deserved hit that reached number one in the country charts (and stayed there for seven weeks) and number 17 in the pop charts. A few weeks after the original recording session, Cash recorded a Spanish-language version, 'Anillo De Fuego'. The song has since been covered by numerous artists, including Carlene Carter, Social Distortion and Wall Of Voodoo.

A so-so version, with one truly bizarre aspect: the Carters' attempt to vocally duplicate the trumpet part. See also *Ring Of Fire*.

Added for the extended CD.

He Turned Water Into Wine

A far better version than the one on *The Holy Land*. This is more like full-on gospel, with a bit of guts to it.

Added for the extended CD.

Daddy Sang Bass
(Carl Perkins)

Again, a far more spirited version than the studio recording on *The Holy Land*.

Added for the extended CD.

The Old Account Was Settled Long Ago
(L.R. Dalton)

The spirit was obviously moving them, since this is also far superior to the version on *Hymns By Johnny Cash*.

Added for the extended CD.

Closing Medley: Folsom Prison Blues/I Walk The Line/Ring Of Fire/The Rebel - Johnny Yuma
(J. Cash/J Carter/M. Kilgore/R. Markowitz/A. Fenady)

June Carter and Carl Perkins take lead vocals on two snippets of 'Folsom Prison Blues', the Carter Family deliver a snatch of 'I Walk The Line' and the Statler Brothers offer the chorus of 'Ring Of Fire', before Cash himself closes the concert out with a fragment of 'Johnny Yuma' and a final reprise of 'Folsom'.

Added for the extended CD.

SIMON & GARFUNKEL

Bridge Over
Troubled Water

February 1970

By Chris Charlesworth

AUL SIMON & Art Garfunkel were an odd couple, mismatched physically and emotionally, but their voices could produce the most gorgeous synthesis. Garfunkel was tall and gangling, with a shock of receding curly blond hair that seemed impervious to the attentions of a comb, and a personality that seemed both overtly romantic yet skittishly whimsical. Simon was short and stocky with flat, straight hair, of serious demeanour and ostensibly unyielding in his concentration and intensity. Garfunkel was light and airy; Simon dark and brooding.

By the time this album was released they were unquestionably the most successful duo in pop. They went out in style with this blockbuster, a multi-million seller that at the time set sales records and, if they weren't already, turned the duo into household names. As their career progressed, S&G took longer and longer to complete their work in the studio and, with the exception of two hastily contrived tracks, the lengthy gestation period of this album marks another important landmark in Simon's eternal search for perfection.

It also marked the end of the partnership. Paul and Artie weren't getting along any more: Simon wanted absolute control over the way his songs sounded, and Garfunkel wanted to be a film star. Work on the album was held up while Garfunkel filmed his scenes in *Catch 22*, which annoyed his partner. Simon was also annoyed, not to say insulted, when the hierarchy at CBS pleaded with him not to go it alone, suggesting that without Garfunkel he was unlikely to succeed. The record company's attitude, of course, was further intensified by the extraordinary sales figures the album notched up.

In many ways, *Bridge Over Troubled Water* became an icon of its era, its dull, blue-grey cover and washed-out picture of Simon & Garfunkel suggesting the doom and gloom that must surely follow the end of the 20th century's most colourful decade. So many homes had a copy of this album that its songs became as well known as classics by The Beatles, but two and a half decades later, it's difficult to justify exactly why it became the massive seller that it did. There were two huge hit singles, of course, in the title track and 'The Boxer', but at least four of the songs, all of them uptempo efforts, were inferior by the standards that Simon had set himself on earlier albums, and because of this there's a slightly patchy feel to *Bridge Over Troubled Water* that wasn't present on S&G's previous album, *Bookends*, or even its predecessor, *Parsley, Sage, Rosemary And Thyme* for that matter.

Perhaps it was because they split up that Simon & Garfunkel's final album attracted buyers in droves, all of them greedy for a final slice of the most successful duo of the Sixties now that the decade was over. Perhaps it was because the two singles were so good, as good as anything that S&G ever recorded, that buyers assumed the whole album must be chockfull of wonderful tracks. Or perhaps it was because the record industry as a whole was approaching a boom period and Columbia (CBS in the UK), under the guidance of the dynamic Clive Davis, was leading the way.

Bridge topped both the US and UK charts in February 1970. In the US it remained in the charts for 24 weeks but, in the UK, it stayed there for an extraordinary 303 weeks.

All songs written by Paul Simon unless otherwise indicated.

Bridge Over Troubled Water

This elegant, majestic, piano-led ballad, the effective climax to Simon & Garfunkel's partnership, has now become a popular standard, the most covered song that Simon ever wrote. Epic in its sweeping grandeur, 'Bridge' glides through three verses at a stately pace, evoking images of the power of healing followed by a transcendent conclusion to life's burdensome journey. The resonant piano is played by session man Larry Knechtel.

Art Garfunkel's reading of the song has a hymn-like quality, which suggests the gospel influence that Simon would bring out on later live versions after S&G split up. But Garfunkel's mellifluous tenor is a far cry from the heaving gospel interpretations that Simon performed with The Dixie Hummingbirds and which, he often stated, was his preferred reading of the song. Garfunkel, of course, felt differently and wasn't afraid to say so.

There have been over 50 cover versions of 'Bridge Over

Troubled Water' by such disparate artists as Elvis Presley, The Jackson 5, Perry Como, Lena Martell and Willie Nelson, not to mention a slew of male voice choirs. As a single, S&G's version topped the charts in both the US and UK in February and March of 1970.

El Condor Pasa

Although not nearly so well known as the stately title track, in retrospect 'El Condor Pasa' can be seen as the most important track on the whole album. More than any other song in the Simon & Garfunkel catalogue, it pointed to the direction that Simon's music would take for the next 20 years, insofar as it indicated his growing interest in music from regions other than North America (and Europe).

In its own way, 'El Condor Pasa' is also a stately anthem, flowing at the serene, somewhat deliberate pace established by the fretted instruments of the South American group, Los Incas, whom Simon had apparently first encountered and befriended in Paris many years before. The melody is borrowed from a Peruvian folk song to which Simon adds his own lyrics, subtitled 'If I Could', which offer a common sense, albeit somewhat prosaic, philosophy about life's choices.

Cecilia

A light-hearted, uptempo romp dominated by the percussive track over which Simon sings, probably fairly spontaneously, about a faithless ladyfriend who invites another man into her bed while the singer is in the bathroom! The track was conceived in Los Angeles, at a house S & G rented in Beverly Hills, while the duo experimented with the reverb on Garfunkel's tape machine. Joined by Simon's brother Eddie on guitar, they created the backing track there and then. Other instruments – and the vocals – were added later in the studio.

By Simon's standards, 'Cecilia' sounds like a throwaway, an experimental dance track with a carefree, singalong vocal, but it comes as a refreshing change after the solemn pace of the title track and the rather po-faced lyrics of 'El Condor Pasa'.

In 1996, it was covered without distinction by Suggs, the singer from Madness, who took it to number four in the UK singles charts.

Keep The Customer Satisfied

Maintaining the brisk pace, this is an update on 'Homeward Bound' but, instead of longing to return to his love life, our troubador is now quite simply fed up of the road, dead tired and longing for some peace and quiet. Some might argue that singing about the displeasures of rock stardom, and the boredom of being on the road, smacks of sour grapes when you've banked a million dollars and, off the road, enjoy a lifestyle akin to an emperor. But there can be no doubt that Simon, at least, was tired of Simon & Garfunkel, though not necessarily of his career in music. Not one of the most distinguished offerings on *Bridge*.

So Long, Frank Lloyd Wright

Sung by Garfunkel alone, this lush ballad operates on two levels, firstly as a tribute to the celebrated American architect, and secondly as a nostalgic look back to the S&G partnership as it comes to an end. It also acts as a tribute from Simon to his buddy, who might have become an architect had Simon's songs not got in the way.

With a melody that comes close to the grandeur of the title track, the lyrics suggest the parting round the corner; this is one of two instances on the album where Simon drops his guard slightly and admits to having second thoughts about ditching a partner who could sing as beautifully as Garfunkel. In the long fade-out, Simon and producer Roy Halee can be heard faintly chanting: "So long, already, Artie". Keep raising the volume and a logical conclusion can be heard just before the track fades to silence.

The Boxer

Staking its claim to stand alongside the very best songs Paul Simon has ever written, 'The Boxer' is a subtle commentary on man's inhumanity to man and, more crucially, a scathing castigation of American society's preoccupation with winners and lack of sympathy for losers. It's also a fine tune, propelled by a fast, intricate guitar figure that underpins the melody, lingering and returning over ebbs and flows from major to minor chords until the song breaks out into its swaggering, full-throated climax. It's quite possible, too, that 'The Boxer' was the first song to incorporate the word "whore" in its lyrics and, by extension, to reach US airwaves.

The possible identity of the "boxer" has been the subject of some speculation. Some have suggested it is about Bob Dylan, who covered the song on his *Self Portrait* album in 1970, while another school of thought thinks it is about Simon himself, though the details of the boxer's life are clearly not autobiographical. However, a song doesn't have to be literally true or about a specific individual. The hero of the song is the archetypal underdog, standing up bloody but unbowed to all that society (or even rock critics) can throw at him.

Unlike so many of the songs from the Simon & Garfunkel era, 'The Boxer' refuses to date, and Simon has repeatedly returned to the song in concert over the years, often changing the arrangement and, on many occasions, adding a central verse not heard in this original version, which suggests that time cannot erode the value of anything that is genuinely virtuous. Such sentiments – and the line, "After changes upon changes we are more or less the same" – inevitably win heartfelt applause from long-time fans.

As a single, 'The Boxer' reached number seven in the US charts and number six in the UK.

Baby Driver

It's to be hoped that Simon's point of view was tongue-in-cheek on this rocker, with apparently smug, self-satisfied lyrics about his well-to-do family, comfortable lifestyle and, in the final verses, determination to experiment sexually.

As seems to be the pattern on this album, the uptempo songs carry considerably less weight than the slower ones, into which far more thought and care has been invested. Like 'Keep The Customer Satisfied' and 'Why Don't You Write Me', which follows, 'Baby Driver' is quite dispensable, and it is the inclusion of these inferior tracks that always begs the question as to why the album as a whole sold as remarkably as it did.

Only Living Boy In New York

Unusually, Simon takes the lead vocals on a slow, dramatic ballad, which, in different circumstances might have been more suited to Garfunkel's style and voice. As the lyrics imply, however, Simon wrote this touching song while his partner was away in Mexico filming *Catch 22* – looking for a future without his old friend – and, like 'So Long, Frank Lloyd Wright', there's more than a suggestion of regret in Simon's words. Tom, of course, refers to Tom Graph, Jerry's partner in the Tom & Jerry days of long ago.

The song is carried by another beautiful melody, well up to the standard of the title track and the other outstanding ballads on this record.

Everything But The Girl's eloquent cover of this song scraped into the UK Top 50 in 1993.

Why Don't You Write Me

Simon's first stab at reggae is unconvincing. He would later admit as much and, to make amends, travel down to Jamaica to record the infinitely superior 'Mother And Child Reunion' on the next album he made. With slight lyrics that castigate a poor correspondent, the rhythm track is amateurish and clumsy, a poor imitation of the real thing, and a further example of the yawning gap between the quality songs on *Bridge* and the largely uptempo throwaway stuff.

Bye Bye Love
(Felice & Boudleaux Bryant)

Until the emergence of S&G, The Everly Brothers were the most successful duo in American popular music and an obvious influence on S&G, and it seems fitting that their successors should offer some sort of tribute as they retired from the contest. 'Bye Bye Love' was Don and Phil Everly's début hit in 1957, a sorry tale of lost love set to the kind of rhythm that suggests it doesn't really matter, because we're only young and we'll fall in love with somebody else next week anyway.

Simon & Garfunkel's version, recorded live during the previous year, stays faithful to The Everly Brothers' arrangement, and is executed with appropriate finesse and gusto.

Song For The Asking

This charming closing ballad is a plaintive declaration of love, touching in its simplicity, brief but heartfelt. Take me as I am, imperfections too, Simon is saying in this particularly honest declaration of modesty.

Significantly, the closing song on the final Simon & Garfunkel album features Simon solo, although ballads like this, and the three that precede it here, would be few and far between in his solo career. Without Garfunkel to sing them, Simon seemed less far inclined towards the smooth, harmonious ballads that grace this album. A pity.

ERIC CLAPTON
(Derek & The Dominos)

Layla And Other
Assorted Love Songs

December 1970

By Marc Roberty

I N MARCH 1970, after sessions for the guitarist's self-titled debut solo album were completed, Eric Clapton returned home to plan the album that is now widely regarded as the finest work of his career.

He had greatly enjoyed working on record and on tour with the American musicians surrounding Delaney and Bonnie Bramlett, and was keen to form a band and hit the road. Luckily for him, he was able to secure the services of keyboard player Bobby Whitlock, bassist Carl Radle and drummer Jim Gordon, all of whom had now left Delaney & Bonnie And Friends and were seeking berths elsewhere.

Rehearsals began at Clapton's home near Ewhurst in the Surrey Hills; almost simultaneously the team also cut their teeth at the sessions for George Harrison's stunning *All Things Must Pass* album. This was an ironic twist of fate, as Clapton's muse for his next album was actually Harrison's wife, Pattie Boyd, with whom he had fallen hopelessly in love. This as-yet unrequited affair would inspire the music he was soon to record but there was a downside, too: it hurled him headfirst into an addiction to heroin and alcohol that would take years to finally conquer.

The songs Clapton wrote and the cover versions he chose to record on *Layla And Other Assorted Love Songs* were all subliminal messages to Pattie, perhaps none more so than 'Have You Ever Loved A Woman?', with its stark references to adultery with the "woman who bears another man's name". Hindsight simplifies this analysis, but there can be little doubt that *Layla* is perhaps the greatest and most emotional love letter ever recorded by a rock musician.

The sessions took place at Miami's Criteria Studios under the production talents of Tom Dowd. Shortly after the start of recording, Duane Allman, at that time the finest slide player in America, was asked to join and, on top of everything else, the double album remains a fine testament to two guitarists at their peak, having a ball playing together.

Masterful, emotive, gargantuan, epic, heartfelt... all these epithets apply to this album. If Clapton had never played another note, *Layla And Other Assorted Love Songs* would have assured him an honourable mention in any rock history.

I Looked Away
(Clapton, Whitlock)

Wearing his heart on his sleeve, Clapton opens with a beautiful love ballad, as sad as it is innocent. With vocals shared between Clapton and keyboard player Bobby Whitlock, and a deceptively simple solo, 'I Looked Away' sets the romantic tone for all that will follow. It is backed with a solid rhythm section, the crucial factor that prevents the album's message from dragging or becoming self-absorbed.

Bell Bottom Blues
(Clapton)

Another hauntingly romantic song, rarely played live, and now a cult favourite among Clapton fanatics. Clapton throws in some delicate, chime-like harmonics before settling into a solo racked with pathos. His singing admirably complements his playing.

Keep On Growing
(Clapton, Whitlock)

Clapton chops his way into a song highlighted by lush, textured layers of intertwined guitars reminiscent of the Delaney & Bonnie sound.

Nobody Knows You When You're Down And Out
(Jimmie Cox)

Back to Clapton's main love – the blues. Duane Allman plays delicate slide fills beside Clapton's plaintive vocals. Whitlock provides some suitably bluesy Hammond sounds before Clapton offers up a throaty solo on his trusty Strat.

I Am Yours
(Clapton, Nizami)

A beautiful, Eastern-flavoured tabla drum-driven song with lyrics taken directly from Ganjavi Nizami's love poem *The Story Of Layla And Majnun*. Eric related heavily to the book, which inspired the album's title track.

Anyday
(Clapton, Whitlock)

A strong, self-assured number that again features rich, textured layers of guitars over which Clapton and Whitlock sing in unison about lost love.

Key To The Highway
(Charles Segar, Willie Broonzy)

Live and without overdubs, 'Key To The Highway' is a fine example of Clapton and Allman having fun with a blues jam. Their interplay is dynamic and unselfish, each giving the other plenty of space in which to stretch out. Clapton's vocals are authentic in feel, but take second place to his fluid and intense solos. A fair amount of the album came out of jams such as this, with Tom Dowd rolling the tapes pretty much constantly, which explains why the song fades in.

Tell The Truth
(Clapton, Whitlock)

'Tell The Truth' was originally recorded with Phil Spector during the sessions for George Harrison's *All Things Must Pass* but discarded by Clapton, who was dissatisfied with Spector's production. Re-recorded in Miami with Tom Dowd at the controls, this version was played at a much slower pace than the frantic original, with Clapton and Allman both playing slide guitar to great effect and the rhythm section of Carl Radle and Jim Gordon keeping the backing solid, as they did throughout the album.

Why Does Love Got To Be So Sad?
(Clapton, Whitlock)

A fast, guitar-led number with a title succinctly summing up Clapton's feelings. His playing is incendiary — as though he were exorcising some demon from his soul.

Have You Ever Loved A Woman?
(Billy Myles)

The autobiographical quotient on this emotional blues song seemed almost too apt for a man who'd fallen for the wife of his best friend. Perhaps the ultimate Clapton vehicle for sheer intensity, the emotion he displays in his playing is even rawer here than in 'Layla' itself. Putting every bit of himself into the song, he almost throttles the neck of his Strat, squeezing everything possible from wood and steel. Stunning, and the true highlight of the album.

Little Wing
(Jimi Hendrix)

Eric had been in awe of Jimi Hendrix's playing ever since they met shortly after the latter arrived in London in 1966. Hendrix jammed with Cream the following year and both players enjoyed a mutual respect. 'Little Wing' first appeared on Hendrix's second 1967 album, *Axis: Bold As Love*, and is one of his most lyrical ballads.

Clapton actually recorded the song in Miami just two weeks before Jimi died in London and, heartbroken when he heard the news, decided to retain his own haunting version on the album as a tribute to his friend.

It's Too Late
(Chuck Willis)

Back to the blues with a typical theme of lost love. Allman slides and Clapton sings.

Layla

(Eric Clapton, Jim Gordon)

Although not the foundation on which the Clapton legend was built, 'Layla' is certainly the pillar that has kept it strong for two decades. It is unquestionably his best-known song, a tearful plea to a girl, Layla – or Pattie as the case might have been – to take heed of his unrequited love. Certainly, it burns with fierce intensity, helped by Allman's screeching slide work, before mellowing out into Whitlock's piano lament, which is interwoven with Clapton and Allman's weeping guitars. Although it's a truly beautiful piece, it has become an albatross around Clapton's neck, as he is now expected to play it at every concert, and it suffers through over-familiarity as a result.

'Layla' became a hit single in the summer of 1972, almost two years after the album was released, and again in 1982.

Eric Clapton: "I had no idea what 'Layla' was going to be. It was just a ditty. When you get near to the end of it, that's when your enthusiasm starts building, and you know you've got something really powerful. You can be so-so as you're making the track, singing the vocals, but if, as you start to add stuff and mix it, it becomes gross, then you really are in charge of something powerful. What I'm saying is, when I started to do that, it didn't feel like anything special to me. If you try to write something that's already got all of that, it's impossible. You just try to write something that's pleasing, and then try to get it to that.

"I'm incredibly proud of 'Layla'. To have ownership of something that powerful is something I'll never be able to get used to. It still knocks me out when I play it. You know what? That riff is a direct lift from an Albert King song. It's a song off the *Born Under A Bad Sign* album ('As The Years Go Passing By'). It goes, 'There is nothing I can do/If you leave me here to cry'. It's a slow blues. We took that line and speeded it up.

"But the funny thing was that once I'd got 'Layla' out of my system, I didn't want to do any more with the Dominos. I didn't want to play another note. I went back home and stayed there and locked all the doors."

Thorn Tree In The Garden
(Whitlock)

After the storm, the album signs off with a gentle acoustic love song from Bobby Whitlock.

LAYLA - 20TH ANNIVERSARY EDITION
December 1990

A beautifully remastered version of *Layla And Other Assorted Love Songs* was released in a special three-CD box set to celebrate its 20th anniversary. The double album now fitted nicely onto a single disc, with two further discs of unreleased out-takes and jams from the original sessions. The package also included copies of the original studio session sheets.

DISC 1 – **Layla**
Track listing as above.

DISC 2 – **The Jams**
Jams 1 – 5

Of interest to die-hards only. These jams demonstrate clearly how well Derek & the Dominos gelled together and, of course, feature extended solos by Clapton and Allman that are particularly enlightening since they reveal how the sessions developed. Sadly, most buyers will probably content themselves with Disc One.

DISC 3
Alternate masters, jams and out-takes.

Have You Ever Loved A Woman?
(Alternate Master 1)

A good alternative version with a great guitar solo, but overall this lacks the intensity of the previously released version.

Have You Ever Loved A Woman?
(Alternate Master 2)

Yet another version, featuring some inspired playing during Clapton's solo but, again, failing to surpass the original.

Tell The Truth
(Jam 1)

Previously available only on the double album *History Of Eric Clapton*. An interesting jam without Allman but plenty of licks from Clapton.

Tell The Truth
(Jam 2)

This second jam is looser and lengthier than the first but still lacks inspiration, although there is enough interesting playing from Clapton to make it worthwhile listening. Just as you think the jam ends, Jim Gordon suddenly picks up the tempo and increases the pace, followed by the others, with Clapton playing different styles and throwing in the odd Chuck Berry lick here and there. If nothing else, the jam demonstrates how tight the band were at this stage.

Mean Old World
(Rehearsal)

Great blues number in its rehearsal stage that never made it onto the final album. Loose, but interesting.

Mean Old World
(Band Version – Master Take)

The finished version featuring Clapton and Allman on guitars and Jim Gordon on bass drum.

Mean Old World
(Duet Version – Master Take)

Previously available on a Duane Allman compilation, this version differs greatly from the band version. It's clear that Allman and Clapton had much in common musically, and it must have been a tough decision for Allman to return to his own band after these sessions.

It Hurts Me Too
(Jam)

Unspectacular version of the Elmore James song.

Tender Love
(Incomplete master)

Average rehearsal for a never-completed number. Mildly interesting at best.

It's Too Late
(Alternate Master)

Good alternate version.

THE WHO

Who's Next

August 1971

By Chris Charlesworth & Ed Hanel

W HO'S NEXT IS widely regarded as the finest studio LP The Who ever recorded and one of the best rock records ever. Certainly, it's far and away their most consistent in terms of quality songs – there isn't a duffer among them – and it introduces an important new element, the synthesiser, into the group's overall sound. More importantly, The Who were now at their creative peak, both as individual musicians and as a band: on stage they regularly performed with breathtaking panache, their confidence was at an all-time high, and their status as one of the world's greatest rock bands was secured for eternity.

Who's Next started life as another of Pete Townshend's concepts, this one a movie/musical called *Lifehouse*, which contained enough songs for a double LP. The project became bogged down in its futuristic, philosophical complexities, however, and was eventually reduced to a single LP and no movie. The concept of *Lifehouse* is long and bewildering, and the random nature of the songs on *Who's Next* gives little clue as to its storyline, such as it was. In view of what *Who's Next* became, there is little point in trying to explain it here, but among its many ideals was Townshend's design for The Who to somehow become one with their audience, to break down totally the barrier that exists between audience and performer. (For those interested in pursuing the subject, Townshend offered a detailed description in a book co-written with Jeff Young, entitled *Lifehouse*, which is the unedited transcript for a radio play first broadcast on BBC Radio 3 in December 1999. As part of the publicity for the project, Townshend made a credible argument that he had envisioned something like the web when he was originally struggling with the *Lifehouse* concept.)

What makes *Who's Next* different from any of its predecessors is the clarity of sound achieved by associate producer Glyn Johns, who took over from Kit Lambert midway through the project. Lambert was the perfect foil for Townshend to bounce ideas off, and his creative influence on The Who cannot be over-emphasised. Yet he was no technician, and as hi-fi equipment and recording studios became more and more sophisticated during the Seventies, far greater attention was being paid to the way records actually sounded.

The second great leap forward on *Who's Next* was Townshend's introduction of the Arp, an early synthesiser, into The Who's sound, most notably on 'Baba O'Riley' and 'Won't Get Fooled Again', the songs that open and close this album. Unlike so many of his less-imaginative peers Townshend didn't use his synthesiser simply as a solo keyboard that could make funny noises, but as a rotating musical loop that underpinned the melody and added a sharp bite to the rhythm track. In this respect, he and Stevie Wonder were the first musicians of their generation to make proper creative use of this new and subsequently much-abused electronic toy. Townshend's synthesiser style on *Who's Next*, in fact, is the first appearance on a rock record of the repetitive electronic sequencing that became predominant in pop and dance music in the Nineties.

There were other leaps forward here, too. Townshend's songwriting showed a sustained level of brilliance he would never again achieve (although he came close on *Quadrophenia*), John Entwistle's bass lines were more melodic but as fluid as ever, and Keith Moon managed to rein in his wilder antics while maintaining his usual key expressive role. But perhaps the greatest musical triumph belonged to Roger Daltrey: the *Tommy* experience, on record and on stage, had improved his confidence as a vocalist immeasurably and it shows, whether on the melodies of the beautiful 'Behind Blue Eyes' and 'The Song Is Over', or, at the other extreme, the defiant scream that climaxes 'Won't Get Fooled Again'.

Many of the songs that appeared on *Who's Next*, together with other *Lifehouse* material that later appeared on singles and on The Who out-takes compilation *Odds & Sods*, were originally recorded in New York with Kit Lambert as producer, but the band weren't satisfied with the results and returned to London to re-record them at Olympic Studios in Barnes with Glyn Johns.

Who's Next became the only Who album to make number one in the UK charts. It peaked at number four in the US, but songs from the album are played continually on US "classic rock" radio stations to this day.

Two upgraded CD versions have been released. The first followed the format of including a number of bonus tracks on a single disc, while the second, the Deluxe Edition, dropped four of the bonus tracks but included additional tracks from the New York Record Plant sessions, some of which feature Leslie West on guitar and Al Kooper on organ and had previously been heavily bootlegged. The real treat is a second disc that features one of the 1971 shows at London's Young Vic Theatre, where Townshend was trying to bring *Lifehouse* into being. For some reason, younger fans apparently found the roughness a little disconcerting, based on the comments found on Amazon.com. Considering the brief period between the times Townshend wrote the songs and when they were performed, the Young Vic show is staggering, every bit as worthwhile as the group's classic *Live At Leeds* album, and it catches The Who at a special time when their live performances made them the greatest rock band in the world.

All songs written by Pete Townshend unless otherwise indicated.

THE ORIGINAL RELEASE
This version consisted of nine tracks.

Baba O'Riley

Thirty seconds of spiralling solo synthesiser, excessively long for any intro, opens the album and one of its most memorable tracks. 'Baba', of course, is Meher Baba, Townshend's spiritual pal, and O'Riley, is Terry Riley, the electronic composer whose work 'A Rainbow In Curved Air' inspired Townshend's use of looping synthesiser riffs. Piano, voice, drums, bass and eventually guitar join in, but it's the cut and thrust between Daltrey's leonine roar and Townshend's tuneful pleading that gives the song its tension and best moments, though the free-form climax, a souped-up Irish jig featuring Dave Arbus on violin and Keith Moon playing as fast as he's ever played, is quite mesmerising.

"Teenage Wasteland", the starting point for Townshend's imaginary generation in their search to find nirvana, became a timeless Who entity in Daltrey's hands, and the downright disgust at the way things had turned out (post-Woodstock) was never better expressed in rock.

Pete Townshend: "This was a number I wrote while I was doing these experiments with tapes on the synthesiser. Among my plans was to take a person out of the audience and feed information – height, weight, autobiographical details – about the person into the synthesiser. The synthesiser would then select notes from the pattern of that person. It would be like translating a person into music. On this particular track I programmed details about the life of Meher Baba and that provided the backing for the number."

The synthesiser track that dominates 'Baba O'Riley' is part of a longer synthesiser piece that Townshend released privately on his Meher Baba tribute LP, I Am, in 1972. Further sections featured on his Psychoderelict solo album in 1993.

Bargain

Most songs addressed to "you" are sentimental love songs but Townshend's "you's" are almost always addressed to Meher Baba. Although used in songs that are often full-tilt rockers, like the 'See Me Feel Me' climax to Tommy, they are actually not-so-cunningly disguised prayers soliciting forgiveness for the writer's earthly foibles and unworthiness, seeking advice on spiritual advancement or simply offering thanks for his avatar's bountiful virtue. 'Bargain', which stands alongside any of the best tracks on Who's Next, is about the search for personal identity amid a sea of conformity, with lyrics such as, "I know I'm worth nothing without you", giving the Baba slant away, especially when sung by Townshend in a keening centre-piece counterpoint to Daltrey's harsher lines.

'Bargain' shows off The Who's ensemble playing at its very best. Block chords abound, there's a terrific guitar solo, bass lines pop and crackle, and Moon's drumming gives the song a rhythmic foundation that lifts The Who clean out of your speaker cabinets. A knock-out live version of 'Bargain' from San Francisco in December 1971 can be found elsewhere in The Who's catalogue.

Love Ain't For Keeping

Seriously upfront acoustic guitars feature strongly throughout one of the slighter (and shortest) songs on *Who's Next*, but the bouncy tempo, relatively simple compared with the album's other songs, and understated synthesiser hold this together well, as Daltrey sings about the difficulty of sustaining relationships in the modern world. This track is sequenced to run almost directly into...

My Wife
(John Entwistle)

John's song of marital discontent is arguably the best he ever wrote for The Who and it provided them with a terrific stage rocker, complete with the kind of block chords that Townshend loved to play while spinning his arm windmill-style. Although this version is no slouch, Entwistle was dissatisfied with the sound and re-recorded it himself for his third solo album. On live versions, Townshend would stretch out the end, duelling with Entwistle to mesmerising effect. 'My Wife' is possibly the most "Who-like" song Entwistle ever wrote, certainly the closest to Townshend's style of writing, and the lyrics are quite hilarious.

The Song Is Over

Among the most gorgeous ballads Townshend has ever written, 'The Song Is Over' again highlights the contrasting vocals of he and Daltrey, as well as some inspired synthesiser work, lovely piano playing by session man Nicky Hopkins, and Johns' sumptuous production. Because of its complexity, it was never played live. Doubtless intended as the climax to *Lifehouse*, it features as a coda the motif from 'Pure And Easy', another key *Lifehouse* song that was inexplicably left off this album. The closing passages are enhanced by an almost subliminal top-of-the-scale synthesiser harmonic line that traces the melody with a marvellous, undulating counterpoint.

It is only by listening to this song, in conjunction with others such as 'Pure And Easy', 'Baba O'Riley', 'Naked Eye',

'Time Is Passing' (which was included on Townshend's first solo album, 1972's *Who Came First*) and 'Behind Blue Eyes' that the real potential of *Lifehouse*, at least from a purely musical point of view, can be truly appreciated. A rock opera, or at least a song cycle, based around material as strong as this would surely have been the rock masterpiece to end all rock masterpieces. When it failed to materialise in the way he envisaged, Townshend's disillusionment led to his first nervous breakdown and almost broke up The Who.

Getting In Tune

Using the time-honoured tradition of tuning up before a show as an allegory for creating harmony between disparate societies, 'Getting In Tune' is another fearless rocker, perhaps not quite so breathtaking as others from the album, but certainly no slouch. Like 'The Song Is Over', this is a showcase for Daltrey at his absolute best.

Going Mobile

With its rolling, appropriately "mobile" rhythm and absence of harsh chords, 'Going Mobile' lacks the grandeur of many of the other tracks on *Who's Next*, but it's a witty and worthy contender nevertheless, a "travelogue" sung by Townshend about the joys of driving around, gypsy-style, in his newly acquired holiday home. Lines about "hippy gypsies" seem particularly apt in the current era of New Age travellers.

Apart from its tricky little acoustic rhythm signature, it's also notable for the guitar solo, in which Townshend wired his electric through a device similar to a wah-wah called an envelope follower, with the result that it sounds like he's playing underwater.

Behind Blue Eyes

Opening with one of the prettiest melodies Townshend has ever written, 'Behind Blue Eyes' rightly became a Who classic almost immediately. Crystal-clear acoustic guitar, Daltrey at his melodic best and a fluid bass line take the first verse, velvet three-part harmonies join in for the second, then, finally, in lurches Moon to give 'Blue Eyes' its third and final dimension.

The faster central passage, a plea to the creator for confidence and succour, contains the most moving lyrics on the whole album, before 'Blue Eyes' reverts back to its gentle opening lines at the close. The choir-like closing vocal harmony, drenched in reverb, is deliberately – and brilliantly – sequenced to contrast sharply with the shrill electronic synthesiser riff that heralds 'Won't Get Fooled Again'.

Won't Get Fooled Again.

If there is a key song on *Who's Next*, it is this lengthy call to arms that eventually became the traditional show closer at most Who concerts. Based on a clattering synthesiser riff that locks the group into a tight, rhythmic performance, 'Won't Get Fooled Again' is classic mid-period Who, Townshend's block chords firmly in place, Entwistle swooping up and down his bass, Daltrey singing his heart out and Moon an almighty presence, albeit slightly more disciplined than usual in view of the song's inflexible structure.

With lyrics that address the futility of revolution when the conqueror is likely to become as corrupt as the conquered, the song inspired many a clenched fist, especially when Daltrey came careering in at the end of the lengthy instrumental passage, declaiming the "bosses" and inciting the kind of scenes that in 1789 left the Bastille in ruins. His scream before the final verse is one of the most volatile vocal eruptions ever recorded.

Pete Townshend: "It's really a bit of a weird song. The first verse sounds like a revolution song and the second like somebody getting tired of it. It's an angry anti-establishment song. It's anti people who are negative. A song against the revolution because the revolution is only a revolution, and a revolution is not going to change anything at all in the long run, and a lot of people are going to get hurt."

Edited down for a single from its original eight minutes

and thirty seconds, 'Won't Get Fooled Again' reached number nine in the UK charts and 10 in the US.

REMIXED AND REMASTERED CD VERSION

This version kept the single disc format, adding the following bonus tracks.

Pure And Easy

This is the original version of 'Pure And Easy' recorded at the Record Plant, New York, on March 17-18, 1971. A later version was recorded at Olympic Studios, London, but not released until the *Odds & Sods* LP in 1974 (although, confusingly, John Entwistle recollected the recording stemmed from the preparatory sessions made at Mick Jagger's mansion, Stargroves, on the Rolling Stones Mobile).

A key song from *Lifehouse*, 'Pure And Easy' is a beautiful Townshend composition that should have appeared on *Who's Next* but was left off, probably because The Who weren't 100 per cent satisfied with the versions they'd recorded during the *Lifehouse/Who's Next* sessions. It is hard to find anything wrong with the version included here.

'Pure And Easy' is Townshend's rewrite on the myth of the "Lost Chord", a deeply felt song about the ultimate musical note, the loss of which symbolises mankind's decaying relationship with the universe. It is a song of yearning, almost a tearful lament, albeit fashioned over Who-style torrents. The guitar solo builds to a tremendous climax, rather like Jimmy Page's memorable solo in 'Stairway To Heaven'.

Townshend thought very highly of 'Pure And Easy' when he wrote it – so much so that its chorus forms a coda to 'The Song Is Over' on *Who's Next*, and he included it in demo form on his first solo album, *Who Came First*.

In the accompanying notes he wrote for *Odds & Sods*, the album on which this song first appeared in 1974, Townshend wrote: "This you might know from my solo album. This is the group's version. Not all of the group's versions of my songs are as faithful to the original demo as this one, but as usual the 'Oo make their terrible mark. Another track from the aborted Lifehouse story. It's strange, really, that this never appeared on *Who's Next*, because in the context of stuff like 'Song Is Over', 'Getting In Tune' and 'Baba O'Riley' it explains more about the general concept behind the Lifehouse idea than any amount of rap. Not released because we wanted a single album at the time."

It's remarkable to think that at this stage in his evolution as a songwriter, Townshend was able to discard material as strong as this.

The Who performed 'Pure And Easy' on stage briefly during 1971, on stage at the Young Vic and occasionally thereafter.

Baby Don't You Do It
(Brian Holland/Lamont Dozier/Edward Holland Jr.)

A stage favourite of The Who's from the 1964-66 era, this revived Motown classic by Marvin Gaye was perhaps an unusual choice for Lifehouse. Played at the Young Vic and in the band's concert act for the remainder of 1971, this version was recorded at the Record Plant, New York on March 16, 1971. Leslie West guested on lead guitar.

Naked Eye

This version was recorded live at the Young Vic on April 26, 1971. It was first released as part of the 1994 30 Years Of Maximum R&B box set, while a version recorded at Townshend's Eel Pie Sound home studio in 1970 appeared on the Odds & Sods LP in 1974.

A superb live song, 'Naked Eye' was developed on stage as part of the improvisation during extended versions of 'My Generation' (as heard on Live At Leeds) and, once fully formed, played at virtually every Who concert in the early Seventies. It took on enormous power as Townshend and Daltrey shared verses that contained some of the former's most powerful lyrical imagery ever.

Between oblique references to drugs and guns is a deep sense of frustration and failure, of not knowing where next to run to, yet at the same time realising that to stand still is suicidal, matters uppermost in Townshend's mind as he sought to justify his continued role in The Who and The Who's continued existence. Meanwhile, the band strains at the leash, while a strange, nagging riff holds the song together. This is the riff that made its first appearance at concerts during 1969 when the band were jamming at the climax to their shows, and only later did Townshend add lyrics to harness it into 'Naked Eye'.

Like 'Pure And Easy', 'Naked Eye' is an essential Who song, far more important than many found elsewhere in their catalogue.

Water

Also recorded live at the same Young Vic show as above.

An overlong, rather heavy-handed rocker, 'Water' is another *Lifehouse* reject, this one mixing a rather lascivious hook line ("water" rhymes with "daughter" throughout) into a song in which "water" becomes an allegory for quenching spiritual thirst. Considering the role it played on stage, it seemed destined for inclusion on whatever album that would follow *Tommy*. Eventually Townshend came up with several far better songs, and despite several stage comments at various shows and concerts during 1970/71 introducing it as a possible Who single, 'Water' was consigned to the scrap heap, only to resurface as the UK B-side of '5.15' in October 1973.

Too Much Of Anything

Another *Lifehouse* out-take, produced by The Who and associate producer Glyn Johns at Olympic Studios, London, on April 12, 1971. It was first released in 1974, with Daltrey's re-recorded vocal, on *Odds & Sods*.

'Too Much Of Anything' is a rather pedestrian rock ballad, with Nicky Hopkins on piano, that deals with greed and its consequences. It meanders along indifferently without the punch of other *Lifehouse* tracks. The Who occasionally played it on stage in 1971 but soon dropped it.

I Don't Even Know Myself

This is a 1970 Eel Pie recording that was part of a planned EP project. Instead, it appeared as the B-side of the 'Won't Get Fooled Again' single. A *Lifehouse* reject that wasn't quite up to the standard of the other songs Townshend was writing in 1970, 'Don't Know Myself' blends a fierce verse and chorus with a strange, country and western style middle eight, which features Moon tapping a wooden block. Often played live around the early Seventies, but dropped when *Who's Next* provided the band with better stage material.

Behind Blue Eyes

This original version of 'Behind Blue Eyes' was recorded at the Record Plant on March 17-18, 1971, and features Al Kooper on organ.

DELUXE EDITION DISC I

This double CD version begins with the original nine tracks and finishes off the first disc with the following bonus tracks from the March, 1971 New York Record Plant sessions.

Baby Don't You Do It
(Holland/Dozier/Holland)

This is the same track as on the remixed and remastered CD.

Getting In Tune

An alternative version from the Record Plant sessions, recorded March 18, 1971. Previously unreleased.

Pure And Easy

This is the same track as on the remixed and remastered CD.

Love Ain't For Keeping

Originally produced by Kit Lambert, this version of 'Love Ain't For Keeping' was recorded on March 17, 1971. It features a live vocal from Townshend, and Leslie West on second guitar. Previously released on the revamped *Odds & Sods* CD in 1998.

The *Who's Next* version was recorded with Glyn Johns at Olympic Studios in London two months later.

Behind Blue Eyes

This is the same track as on the remixed and remastered CD.

Won't Get Fooled Again

An early version from the Record Plant sessions, recorded March 16, 1971, featuring a different synthesiser pattern from the released version, with the famous lyric, "Meet the new boss, same as the old boss," occurring before the final synthesiser break and drum pattern, and lacking Daltrey's distinctive scream.

Pete Townshend: "No tape was used. What we did was play an organ through a VCS3 live with the session. So we had to keep in time with the square wave, but the shape was moveable. It was an experiment initiated by Roger and was fairly successful."

DELUXE EDITION DISC 2

Townshend had anticipated using live material from a number of small concerts before a specially invited audience to develop his *Lifehouse* project. The Young Vic Theatre, a South London venue with a reputation for the avant-garde, appreciated the rental and was set aside with the Rolling Stones Mobile for Townshend's efforts. By all accounts, the results were physically and mentally harrowing for Townshend, and the tapes were quietly put away as he failed to bring the concept into a format his fellow band members and audience could understand. The tracks on the Deluxe Edition's second disc were all recorded live on April 26, 1971.

Love Ain't For Keeping

As intimate an introduction a Who concert could ever produce, this is as close as a fan can get to having the band drop by for an afternoon and play a session for the neighbours. Considering that these are working versions of what were then unreleased songs, The Who clearly show that they are masters of their musical craft, even if mystified at what Townshend was trying to create

Pure And Easy

A very good version with Townshend's guitar work not quite as developed as that recorded on *Odds & Sods*, giving it the definitive title. The transition to 'The Song Is Over' is well developed in the latter part of this version, so it is now somewhat of a surprise to hear Townshend lead the band into…

Young Man Blues

(Allison)

The band begins aggressively enough, if not with quite the flair as on *Live At Leeds*, but Townshend's guitar goes dead at 1:40; and we can only imagine the off-stage demonstration in anger management that Townshend is not exercising. Entwistle and Moon carry on regardless with almost half a minute of interplay, brewing up a storm without the slightest need for a lead guitarist or vocalist. Townshend kicks back in and vents his frustration in a great guitar run, until he peels off into a very beautiful blues-orientated solo.

Time Is Passing

This version highlights the great mix on the Deluxe Edition's second disc, best heard in the contrast here between Townshend and Daltrey's vocals. This song was first widely heard on the former's solo album *Who Came First*. Originally recorded during the Olympic *Who's Next* sessions, a remastered studio version from a damaged master tape was released on the upgraded edition of *Odds & Sods* in 1998.

Behind Blue Eyes

Introduced as "probably a single", Townshend first takes on a fan who dared to stand up and dance during the previous song. He explains that he normally wouldn't care, but it is distracting as The Who are playing "a whole new show". That, of course, doesn't stop him from leading into the second of two well-used songs from Who history that appear in the six songs played so far.

I Don't Even Know Myself

Excellent version, as was to be expected with a song The Who had played live for some time.

Too Much Of Anything

Daltrey doesn't start off in a key that is comfortable for his range. Not so obvious at first, but as the song progresses he strains to get through. A great try, though, and fascinating to hear what worked as well as what didn't work for the band in developing *Who's Next*. The first official version of this song appeared on *Odds & Sods* in a version completed at Olympic on April 12, 1971, with Nicky Hopkins on piano.

Getting In Tune

Although this version sounds faster than the album version, it lasts for over six and a half minutes. Entwistle's bass line doesn't sound fully developed yet, and there is that rare experience of Moon playing without bass or guitar at 4:10. Still not a drum solo, as his band mates sing rounds of the title line over and over.

Bargain

Pete apologises that the new songs are "a wee bit lame, but they'll come together". For anyone interested in hearing The Who in this period, the apology is totally unnecessary. This version is played a little slower than fans have come to expect (and Moon initially has some problems with the time signatures), but it is primarily noteworthy for the lack of synthesiser that dominates the album version.

Water

No longer claiming it to be the next single, the band managed to work this version out to an eight-minute plus opus. While it is debatable that the song merits such an addressing, it is definitely good to have it in the collection considering the role it played in Who shows throughout 1970 and 1971.

My Generation

"Not trying to cause a bloody big sensation," as Daltrey sings. This straightforward treatment of the 1965 Who classic ends at about three minutes to segue into the next song.

Road Runner

(Elias McDaniel, aka Bo Diddley)

Originally written and recorded by blues master Elias McDaniel in 1959, the song has subsequently been covered by many artists, including Jr. Walker & The All-Stars' hit instrumental version in 1966. During the British R&B boom of the early to mid-Sixties many groups covered the song, including The Rolling Stones, The Animals, The Pretty Things, The Zombies and The Who. (In fact, it was this very song that The Who played during Keith Moon's drum-damaging audition at The Oldfield Hotel, Greenford, in April 1964.) During tours in the Seventies The Who often lurched into this medium-paced rocker during lengthy jams within the 'My Generation' framework.

Pete Townshend: "It was an afterthought to play this, probably not a good idea. It was a chaotic evening and I think that during this song some young boys started to fiddle around with some older women who were present, one of whom was Roger's ex, Cleo. We lost concentration as there were no bouncers."

Naked Eye

Probably noticeable to many fans on hearing this version is that the song (and certainly the middle break) had its genesis in parts of Pete's guitar work from the Leeds version of 'My Generation'.

A long-standing concert favourite from mid-1970, a studio version was recorded at Eel Pie Sound (completed at Olympic on June 7, 1971), and released on *Odds & Sods*.

Won't Get Fooled Again

The Who's second epic single (after 'I Can See For Miles') is pretty well worked out at this stage. There are some interesting guitar runs played over the synthesiser that will disappear, and the album version has a little added drive and aggression. This is worthwhile for hearing the verse-chorus sequence and hearing Daltrey's next step in developing, what is for many, the definitive rock'n'roll scream at the conclusion of the album version. All in all, put in the context of what Townshend was trying to do and what the band was trying to understand, this show is an exciting look into a work in progress. For Who fans wanting a CD of *Who's Next*, the Deluxe Edition is a must for the Young Vic show alone.

LED ZEPPELIN

November 1971

By Dave Lewis

N EARLY 1971, when Led Zeppelin returned to Headley Grange – a run-down mansion in Hampshire where some of 1970's *Led Zeppelin III* had been taped – they took along The Rolling Stones' mobile studio to record the whole process.

"We needed the sort of facilities where we could have a cup of tea and wander around the garden, and then go in and do what we had to do," said Jimmy Page. By moving into Headley Grange for the whole period of recording, many of the tracks were made up almost on the spot and committed to tape virtually there and then.

"A recording studio is an immediate imposition as compared to sitting around a fire strumming," said Robert Plant at the time. "With Headley Grange, we can put something down and hear the results immediately."

Initial sessions for the fourth album began at the new Island studios in December 1970, but the real work was done in the country. Once inside the great hall of Headley Grange, ideas flowed freely. It was here that Page stumbled on the monster snare and bass drum sound by spaciously miking Bonzo's newly acquired kit.

With the basic tracks recorded, many of them live, the band added overdubs at Island and, on the recommendation of engineer Andy Johns, took the completed master tapes to Los Angeles' Sunset Sound Studios for mixing. This mix proved to be a great disappointment, causing a delay in the release of the album. The band had hoped to have it out in time for their late-summer tour of the US, but further mixing back in London put the release back to November.

After the mixed reception that greeted the eclecticism of *Led Zeppelin III*, the group deliberately played down the new release. There had been talk of releasing a double set and at one stage, Page even came up with the idea of issuing the album as four EPs.

When it came to a title, instead of the expected *Led Zeppelin IV*, the band decided to set a precedent by selecting four symbols, each representing a member who chose his own symbol to form the title. John Bonham's came from a book of runes and took the form of three linked circles. Said to represent the man-wife-child trilogy, Plant was heard to remark that it resembled the emblem of Ballantine beer! John Paul Jones' came from the same book and was meant to represent confidence and competence. Plant's feather in a circle design was his own, based on the sign of the ancient Mu civilisation. Page's mysterious symbol, which has often been mistaken for a word that could be pronounced "Zoso", was also his own work. The group could hardly have known at the time what a deep and lasting impression these symbols would have on their career.

To further throw fans and the music industry, the gatefold sleeve design was entirely wordless, except for a barely decipherable Oxfam poster hanging amid the urban decay depicted on the front. (This cover print was actually bought from a junk shop in Reading by Plant.) A tarot card illustration of the Hermit formed the inner gatefold illustration, and the lyrics to 'Stairway To Heaven' were printed on the inner sleeve. Atlantic Records' reaction to this total lack of information on the sleeve was predictably negative.

As a result of all this mystery, no one has ever been quite sure what to actually call the album, and it has been variously referred to over the years as *Led Zeppelin IV*, *Untitled*, *Four Symbols*, *Zoso* and *The Runes*. And since no one from the Zeppelin camp has ever actually confirmed a title, the mystery is unlikely ever to be solved – which is exactly what the increasingly mysterious Led Zeppelin wanted.

In the run-up to the album's release, a series of teaser adverts depicting each symbol was placed in the music press. It didn't take fans too long to associate these mystical images with the album, and, title or no title, the fourth Zeppelin LP was an instant massive seller. It entered the UK chart at number one and stayed in the chart for 62 weeks. In America it remained on the chart longer than any other Zeppelin album, though it failed to knock Carole King's mega-selling *Tapestry* off the top spot. Ultimately, the fourth Zeppelin album would be the most durable seller in their catalogue and the most impressive critical and commercial success of their career.

In December 1990, this album, along with Def Leppard's *Hysteria*, was certified by *Billboard* magazine as being the biggest-selling rock album in American chart history. By that year's end it had registered some 10 million sales in the US alone. Not bad for an album whose wordless sleeve artwork was declared commercial suicide when it was first handed to the record company.

Black Dog
(Page, Plant, Jones)

If *Zeppelin III* had thrown up doubts in some corners as to Led Zeppelin's continued ability to flex the power displayed on their first two albums, here was the perfect antidote. From the moment Page warms up the Gibson, this is one of the most instantly recognisable Zep tracks.

'Black Dog' takes its title from a mutt that hung around at the Grange. The impossible part of the riff was Jones' input, while the a cappella vocal arrangement, Page would admit years later, was influenced by Fleetwood Mac's 'Oh Well'. The solo was constructed from four overdubbed Les Paul fills. The song is held in great esteem by Plant in particular, who would later add snippets of the song into two of his solo tracks, 'Tall Cool One' and 'Your Ma Said She Cried In Her Sleep Last Night'.

Rock And Roll
(Page, Plant, Jones, Bonham)

Another instantly identifiable Zeppelin anthem, and one that would be often used to open their concerts in the future. This track came out of a jam with Rolling Stones' roadie Ian Stewart on piano. Bonzo played the intro of 'Good Golly Miss Molly'/'Keep A Knockin'', and Page added a riff. Fifteen minutes later the nucleus of 'Rock And Roll' was down on tape – displaying the full benefit of recording on location with the tapes left running.

The Battle Of Evermore
(Page, Plant)

The tune for this was written by Page late one night at the Grange while he experimented on Jones' mandolin. Plant came up with a set of lyrics inspired by a book he was reading on the Scottish wars. Fairport Convention singer Sandy Denny was called in to sing the answer lines to Plant's vocal. Another impressive arrangement, a solo Plant guide vocal out-take remains in the vaults.

This song appeared in the 1992 grunge cult film *Singles*, performed by The Love Mongers, who featured Annie and Nancy Wilson of Heart.

Stairway To Heaven
(Page, Plant)

The big one. 'Stairway' started out as a fairly complete chord progression that Page brought in when the band commenced recording at Island studios in December 1970. At Headley Grange the song developed around the log fire, with Plant composing a set of lyrics full of hippy mysticism that told the tale of a search for spiritual perfection. The song's arrangement, with Jones contributing bass recorder on the intro and Bonzo entering as the track built to a crescendo, came together very quickly. This left Page to add the solo back at Island, for which he returned to the Telecaster. For the live version he would invest in a custom-made Gibson SG double-neck guitar.

'Stairway To Heaven' was undoubtedly the stand-out track on the fourth album, and was well received when performed on UK and US dates prior to the album's release. When the band went back to the States in the summer of 1972, Atlantic was naturally keen to issue the track as a single, but manager Peter Grant refused and was to do the same again the next year. The upshot of that decision was that record buyers began to invest in the fourth album as if it were a single.

'Stairway To Heaven' went on to become the most requested song on American radio, and achieve truly classic status worldwide. Far from being a mere rock song, it has become something of a people's favourite, cover-version fodder for symphony orchestras and night-club singers alike. So well known has the dreamy opening riff become that guitarists trying out guitars in British music shops must pay a fine of £5 if they play 'Stairway' in the shop!

In 1993, an entire album of cover versions of 'Stairway To Heaven' by various Australian performers, instigated by the Australian *Money Or The Gun* TV show, was released, and a spoof rendering by the inimitable Rolf Harris found its way into the UK Top Ten amid much jocularity.

Alongside songs like 'A Whiter Shade Of Pale' and 'You've Lost That Lovin' Feeling', 'Stairway' has a pastoral opening cadence that is classical in feel and which has ensured its immortality. This air of respectability may be the reason why Robert Plant has turned away from the song, declaring it a great song written at the right time for all the right reasons, but now sanctimonious in the extreme. Free from the burden of having to interpret the lyrics, Jimmy Page remains justly proud of the composition, happy to celebrate its legacy as an instrumental live showpiece.

On the 20th anniversary of the original release of this song, it was announced via US radio sources that the song had logged up an estimated 2,874,000 radio plays – back to back, that would run for 44 years solid. Its reverence in America remains unparalleled. In the UK there was a strong lobby from both Warners and Radio One to see the track issued as a single for the Christmas market in 1990. Ultimately – and unsurprisingly – the idea was vetoed. Rare original 7" promos pressed at the time, accompanied by a humorous in-house memo (Atlantic LZ3), are among the most sought-after Led Zeppelin UK rarities.

When sitting around that log fire all those years ago, the band certainly could never have envisaged the impact 'Stairway To Heaven' would have on their career, that the song would become the single most-requested track on American FM radio for most of the Seventies, or that it would inspire a whole album of cover versions.

The appearance of the superb delivery of the song drawn from their Earl's Court shows in May 1975 on the 2003 Led Zeppelin DVD finally restored some much overdue dignity to a track that, though much maligned, remains the band's most famous composition.

Misty Mountain Hop
(Page, Plant, Jones)

A happy, uptempo outing, written and recorded at the Grange, with Jones on electric piano and providing the central riff motif the song revolves around. This is another vintage Zeppelin song of which Plant has not grown tired. He has been more than happy to roll out its nostalgic hippy ideals during the Eighties, both on his solo tours and at reunions with Page and Jones.

Four Sticks
(Page, Plant)

A difficult track to record, this required many more takes than usual, and is so called because Bonzo employed the use of four drum sticks to create the relentless rhythm track. This was one of the tracks the band recut with members of the Bombay Symphony Orchestra in 1972. It also features Jones on Moog synthesiser. Another song that has enjoyed deserved renewed attention, it was one of the most-played Zep numbers on Page & Plant's 1995/96 world tour and remains a staple part of Plant's solo live set.

Going To California
(Page, Plant)

Another acoustic beauty with some memorable Plant lyrics, heavily influenced by Joni Mitchell. This started out as a song about Californian earthquakes and, when Page, Andy Johns and Peter Grant travelled to LA to mix the album, lo and behold the mountains did begin to tremble and shake. The track was then known as 'Guide To California'. It also tells of an unrequited search for the ultimate lady. "It's infinitely hard," Plant would often ad lib in the live rendition. Some

20 years later, at the Knebworth 1990 festival, he gave an indication during the show that his own search was ongoing, stating, "Do you know what – it's still hard…"

When The Levee Breaks
(Page, Plant, Jones, Bonham, Minnie)

On June 18, 1929, in New York, Memphis Minnie and Kansas Joe McCoy recorded a blues tune called 'When The Levee Breaks'. Forty years later in leafy Hampshire, Led Zeppelin reconstructed the song to form the spiralling finale of their fourth album. It had already been tried unsuccessfully at Island at the beginning of the sessions but, in Headley Grange it took on a whole new direction.

'Levee' goes down in the annals of Zeppelin history for Bonzo's crushing drum sound, performed, according to Page, on a brand new kit that had only just been delivered from the factory. Andy Johns has revealed that the unique drum sound came about after Bonzo complained that he wasn't getting the sound he wanted. Johns promptly repositioned the kit in the Headley Grange hallway and hung two M1160 mikes from the staircase. Back in the Stones mobile, he compressed the drum sound through two channels and added echo through Page's Binson echo unit. The result was the most sampled and envied drum track in rock history. Beyond the millennium it can be heard spinning on DJ turntables the world over as a perennial mixing backing track.

Alongside that drum sound, Page contributes a rampant bottleneck guitar, while Plant blows a mean mouth harp that cleverly winds it all up in a barrage of backwards echo.

THE ROLLING STONES

Exile On Main St.

May 1972

By Mark Paytress

STUDY A HANDFUL of rock magazines and you'll soon discover that every third musician is described as a "legend", and every band has turned in "one of the greatest rock albums of all time". The nature of the game is, after all, not puzzling but hyperbole. But if critical opinion is anything to go by, *Exile* – which, as some might remember, was greeted with a mixed press on its release – has emerged as one of the most complete rock double albums ever released.

The excuse for the less-than-revered Rolling Stones' 1967 album, *Their Satanic Majesties Request*, is, rightly or wrongly, usually cited as the undue pressure of court cases and an excess of drugs clouding the creative juices. A better explanation is probably an excess of contemporary musical fashion. In fact, the Stones work better when under pressure to deliver and, while far from starving artists working alone in an unwelcome world, their isolation in Keith Richards' villa in the South of France during the summer of 1971, combined with unsettled financial affairs and a frontman whose main concern appeared to be nursing his pregnant wife, were all factors that conspired to make *Exile* what it is. In the circumstances, the newly married Jagger, out to prove that he hadn't completely made his peace with conventional mores, turned in some of the best performances of his career.

What makes *Exile* so special? The album contained no era-defining songs like 'You Can't Always Get What You Want' or 'Sympathy For The Devil', nor any introspective epics like 'Moonlight Mile' or showy assertions of their satanic majesty, like 'Midnight Rambler'. No individual song is remembered as the highpoint, nor did the album in any way encapsulate the prevailing mood. With glam and progressive rock and singer-songwriters in the ascendant, it's perhaps little wonder that it was greeted with a hum and a ho first time around.

What *Exile* captured was a band wholly conversant with their own limitations. By defining their own terms, and by not falling foul of contemporary fads and fashions, the Stones touched base with what inspired them in the first place. The act of collective music-making, in the leisured ambience of a kitchen/basement, enabled them to fulfil what they weren't able to achieve back in 1962. And now able to draw on all the sources they'd accessed during their 10-year career, their vast musical education enabled them to fully control those influences, rather than let themselves simply become the sum of them.

There's nothing ostentatious or even immediately gripping about the results. But rarely has a group reacquainted itself with both the original, and a contemporary, vision of itself, and emerged with a hybrid that seemed quintessential and yet wonderfully out-of-sorts with both. Welcome to Main Street.

The album topped the LP charts in both the UK and US.

All songs written by Mick Jagger and
Keith Richards unless otherwise indicated.

Rocks Off

Fats Domino has never been acknowledged as a primary influence on The Rolling Stones. Yet an impressionable young Jagger was struck by a quote of his concerning diction and the contemporary popular voice. Fats believed that it wasn't necessary to sing the lyrics clearly: not only was the content secondary to the sound, but the sheer inability to decipher the words contributed to rock'n'roll's mystique. It was advice that Jagger never forgot. The production on the Stones' early records, in particular, was often derided for its sheer incomprehensibility, but rather than incompetence on the part of producer Andrew Oldham, it was as much a wilful exercise in obfuscation. And never was it put to better use than on this record.

Ostensibly a bar-room rocker, 'Rocks Off' was probably closer to The Velvet Underground's 'White Light/White Heat', both in its unadulterated onslaught of sound and in its speed-driven, brain-addled reportage. Jagger being Jagger, the sexual overtones were explicit, though who understood – on first hearing, at least – the underlying fear of impending impotence?

Rip This Joint

That the Stones took this set of songs out on the road to vast American stadiums was little short of criminal: 'Rip This Joint' was built for clubland, the audience showered by spit from Bobby Keyes' blistering sax, the floor caving in with the crush of bodies whipped into a frenzy by two minutes of classic rock'n'roll. With Ian "Stu" Stewart bashing out the piano keys and Bill Plummer testing the limits of his thick-stringed double bass, this – not Arthur Janov's – was the primal therapy John Lennon really desired.

Shake Your Hips

(James Moore)

Jagger's Slim Harpo impression was real enough to conjure up images of one of those weird Southern boys propping up a bar in Memphis. Thankfully, no eye contact was required here.

Like the band's take on Willie Dixon's 'I Just Want To Make Love To You', their version of 'Shake Your Hips' (alias 'Hip Shake') was handled well, without falling into parody or sophisticated, whited-out blues blandness. How the Stones completely lost the knack of doing this in the years that followed is something they probably don't even understand themselves.

Apparently, this track was taped as early as October 1970, at Olympic Studios, although it was later reworked at Keith's chateau Villa Nellcôte, pleasingly located in Villefranche Sur Mer, midway between Nice and Monte Carlo on the French Riviera.

Casino Boogie

Not one of the album highlights, 'Casino Boogie' (it sounds like its title suggests it might) is saved by Bobby Keyes' artful sax break and the fact that lines like, "Dietrich movies, close-up boogies" are incomprehensible without the aid of the sheet music.

Tumbling Dice

This song started life as 'Good Time Woman', with a completely different set of lyrics ("Red light woman sure like to party", etc.). Not for the first time on the album, Mick Taylor handled the bass duties, while Jagger's down-on-women line was tempered by the amusing aside that he was "all sixes and sevens and nines". Clydie King and Vanetta Fields provided the most effective backing vocals on a Stones' single to date, and it was one of the most unassuming, too. But there was little else on the album that would have done the job better: *Exile* was nothing if not a set of brilliantly executed half-singles.

Sweet Virginia

The nearest the Stones ever got to a round-the-campfire singalong, though Baden-Powell probably wouldn't have appreciated the refrain, "Got to scrape the shit right off your shoes", which suggested that the song may have been an obscure slant on the old standard 'Walking Blues'. But the blues (and the reds and the greens, for that matter) referred to in the song were in tablet form. If one Stones' song was written by Keith and Gram Parsons up in the Blue Ridge Mountains, 'Sweet Virginia' must have been it.

Torn And Frayed

The "restless" guitar player, with his coat "worn, it's torn and frayed", and his friends wondering "who's gonna help him to kick it", suggest a rare pen-portrait of Richards from the inside. But the "ballrooms and smelly bordellos"? The band "a bag of nerves on first nights"? Surely not. What could have been a throwaway was elevated by some splendid steel guitar, courtesy of Al Perkins, atmospheric organ from horn player Jim Price, and Jagger providing just the right featherlight touch the song required.

Sweet Black Angel

Even the Black and White Minstrels might have hesitated over a line like, "Ten liddle nigga, sittin' on deh wall", but Jagger's wildly exaggerated delivery of a tender message of support to black American radical Angela Davis ("She's a sweet black angel/not a gun totin' teacher/not a Red lovin' school mom") barely raised an eyelid. There is something distinctly odd about Jagger's most outrageous act of mimicry yet (not to mention the exotic, jungle-evoking backing) as he delivers the "free de sweet black slave" punchline, but the sentiments sideswept the almost painful parody.

Loving Cup

First recorded in spring 1969 and premiered at the Stones' July '69 Hyde Park concert, 'Loving Cup' had a long gestation period. With Nicky Hopkins and a punchy brass section in tow, the Stones furthered their own white gospel ambitions in tub-thumping fashion, a good way short of the plunge into caricature. That, in a few words, is what *Exile* is all about: a pivotal moment where they retained perfect control of their influences and their own destiny. They wouldn't always make it look so easy in the years ahead.

Happy

Almost entirely of Richards' making – he wrote the song, played guitar and bass, and even provided the template for his future lead vocal sorties – 'Happy' was basically cut as a warm-up, hence the impromptu backing group of just Jimmy Miller on drums and Bobby Keyes on sax. Jagger helped guide the melody at a later date, but essentially it's Richards' show.

Turd On The Run

With instrumental backing very much the outraged offspring of the obscure B-side 'Stoned' almost a decade earlier, 'Turd On The Run' belied its jokey title, providing just the mood of uptightness that Jagger revels in. He blew a pretty vitriolic harp, too.

Ventilator Blues
(Jagger/Richards/Mick Taylor)

So close to somnambulance and yet so far. It was a measure of the band's greatness during this period that they could walk the line marked turgid and transform a grizzly riff into something invested with all the "soul" they'd once sought to locate in second-rate covers of Otis Redding songs. 'Ventilator Blues' was white boy spit'n'sawdust blues at its best, and the first example of a Mick Taylor co-credit.

I Just Want To See His Face

Had *Exile* not been spread over four sides, the band probably would have played safe and songs like this Dr. John-influenced voodoo incantation would probably not have made the grade. Thankfully, it was, for it's in the album's margins that its true greatness lies.

Let It Loose

If the Stones' early excursions into gospel were tentative and sometimes painfully self-conscious, all doubts had been cast aside by 1971. Up to half-a-dozen backing singers joined Jagger in a rare display of genuine emotion (well, that's what it sounded like: don't study the lyrics too closely), while the horn arrangements were all but Memphis in name.

All Down The Line

'All Down The Line' preceded the main body of *Exile* sessions by a good 18 months, having first been recorded in acoustic form at Elektra Studios, Los Angeles, in October 1969. At one stage, this top-rate rocker, which features a rip-roaring Taylor slide solo, was tipped as the band's first post-Decca 45, but 'Brown Sugar' proved to be insurmountable opposition. It eventually surfaced on 7" in America, paired with 'Happy', as the follow-up to 'Tumbling Dice'.

Stop Breaking Down
(Traditional, arranged Jagger/Richards/Wyman/Taylor/Watts)

Learnt from the Robert Johnson version, originally recorded in 1937, this was exactly the kind of song Brian Jones wanted the Stones to make during the *Beggars Banquet* sessions. They didn't, but two years later, Mick Taylor was on hand to turn in some measured slide guitar. The basic track was recorded at Olympic between 17-31 October, 1970, with Jagger adding his ever-improving harp-playing at a later date.

Shine A Light

Another song originally laid down at the October 1970 Olympic sessions, 'Shine A Light' begins deceptively with a flashback of electronically generated psychedelic sound, before Jagger sermonises to the sound of Billy Preston's hotline-to-heaven organ-playing.

There was more than a hint of camp in his voice (the dropping of the "r"s, for instance), but the overall effect was more successful than 'Salt Of The Earth' (from *Beggars Banquet*) ever was. And the band weren't afraid to experiment, as the highly echoed guitar, and an "underwater effect" on the backing vocals, amply illustrate.

Soul Survivor

Typically evasive in his meaning, Jagger's 'Soul Survivor' ("gonna be the death of me") provides a fitting end to the Stones' finest hour (give or take seven minutes). A savage reassertion, not of the soul and gospel influences that soaked much of *Exile*, but of their immediately recognisable hard-rock style, the song captures the band at their best: getting the most out of a riff, verses that shy clear of melodic flamboyance, and a deceptively rousing non-chorus.

It's a pity the song never entered the band's regular concert repertoire. It wasn't conventionally crowd-pleasing (it's difficult to imagine a stadium audience clapping along as one to the song's jagged riff), though lack of exposure has frozen it in time. It's one of the last truly awesome expressions of the Stones' greatness — when they managed to make the instantly familiar sound like it had just been invented.

DAVID BOWIE

The Rise And Fall Of Ziggy Stardust And The Spiders From Mars

June 1972

By David Buckley

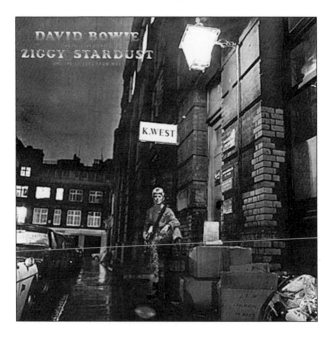

HE ALBUM THAT changed the perception of what rock as a medium could be was recorded almost immediately after *Hunky Dory* in 1971. In many ways Ziggy Stardust, again co-produced by Ken Scott, and recorded at Trident Studios in central London, now seems like the "son of" *Hunky Dory*. Musically, it may be slightly conservative by comparison with the astonishingly eccentric doo-wop meets sci-fi movie music of 1972's other crucial album, Roxy Music's eponymous debut, also released in the summer of that year. But together, the two records torched flower power for good, replacing it with a confused agenda of postmodern irony and theatricality that became the roots of British art rock.

By the time of *Ziggy*, Bowie had hit top form as a songwriter, and the album is a genuine classic. All of Bowie's self-penned songs are truly astonishing. Co-producer Scott gives the album a more hard-hitting rock sound without departing too far from the acoustic timbres of the previous album, and the sound is sparkling, clear and detailed, if lacking in the sonic weirdness of the later *Aladdin Sane*.

Although it is regularly touted as one of pop's great concept albums, telling the tale of the rise and fall of the fictional rocker, Ziggy Stardust, there is, in fact, no consistent plot development or narrative structure beyond an opener, which temporally places the events five years from the apocalypse, and an ending that neatly wraps things up with a suicide. An elaborate Ziggy stage show was planned by Bowie in late 1973, with a more developed narrative sketched in, but it never came to fruition.

What Bowie actually did was to collect a portfolio of songs that dealt with stardom and how it is manufactured within the entertainment business. Read like this, the album makes far more sense. 'Star', for example, then becomes a shameless exercise in destroying the myth of art for art's sake and reveals the grasping self-promotion that is at the centre of most popular music. 'Starman' loses the comic book sci-fi trappings and becomes a statement about the Messianic quality of our rock idols.

Ziggy Stardust is also heavily laden with images of rock's past, with Hendrix and Bolan making guest appearances.

This sense of history, taken together with the album's self-referential nature – a rock star making an album about a rock star – makes *Ziggy Stardust*, as writer Jon Savage pointed out, pop's first postmodern record. Fact/fiction, past/present are deliberately being played around with in a way new to pop.

And Bowie played the part with tireless aplomb. Soon neither he nor his audience were really sure whether this Kabuki-styled androgyne was the "real" Bowie or not. Bowie showed that everyone's personality could indeed be a "sack of things", and the idea that pop could not only comment on, but enable, these changes became central to how pop would develop from that day on.

In the UK, *Ziggy Stardust* reached number five in the LP charts and remained in the listing for just over two years, in the process giving a leg up to three earlier Bowie albums, *Hunky Dory*, *The Man Who Sold The World* and *Space Oddity*, all of which reached the charts for the first time in the months following its release. In the US, Ziggy failed to chart.

All songs written by David Bowie unless otherwise indicated.

Five Years

The inspiration behind this song has been the cause of discussion among Bowieologists for several years. Various theories have been put forward, including a take on a Roger McGough poem, a rewrite of a Wordsworth sonnet, and a dream Bowie had in which his dead father returned to warn him of the perils of flying. That heartbeat of a drum figure introduces what is arguably the strongest cut on the album, as the narrative locates the action five years from the end of the world.

The music moves with Bowie the narrator at a walking pace, and Bowie is once again treading the boards in an imagined real life: "It was cold and it rained so I felt like an actor". There's still a shrill, almost hysterical feel to many of the performances on the album, and 'Five Years' is a masterpiece of the overwrought. Swirling violins, impassioned cries, and this song, so full of danger and drama, is over. In 1985, Bowie was scheduled to perform the song at Live Aid, but it was dropped at the last minute when he discovered that there would be no room in the schedule to show a short film made by CBC TV of starving children in Addis Ababa, a film that would spur millions to donate on the day.

Soul Love

Only the most tortuous piece of hypothesising could actually fit this particular song into any sort of complete narrative concept. It's still a very fine song, full of remonstrations about the link between secular and non-secular love, and the infectious rhythm, neat pop guitar solo and singalong-a-Bowie coda make it.

Moonage Daydream

This is one of Bowie's best-ever songs, beautifully paced, beautifully played. The religion of the opening two tracks again resurfaces: "The church of man-love/ Is such a holy place to be", and Bowie is still playing the sci-fi card for all it's worth ("Put your ray-gun to my head").

It's also noticeable, as journalist Chris Brazier pointed out in a 1976 prize-winning essay, how much Bowie, in an attempt to comment on rock history, utilised slangy, hip Americanisms. 'Moonage Daydream' is a good example of this, filled as it is with lines such as "Mama-papa", "freak out", "lay it [the real thing] on me", and "rock-and-rolling-bitch". *Ziggy Stardust*, despite being regarded as the embodiment of the English obsession with style, is also, at least lyrically, peculiarly Americanised. The closing guitar freakout is Mick Ronson's greatest moment on a Bowie record.

Starman

Bowie's second UK Top 10 hit (and the single that really broke him big-time) finally came with this cartoonesque slab of highly contagious pop with its unforgettable chorus. Bowie's fascination with all things galactic tapped into an area of public fascination with sci-fi hitherto unexplored within popular music, although undoubtedly part of the national psyche, as the success of TV programmes such as *Dr Who* proved. Here, the arrival of the Ziggy figure, who, in another bout of Americanisms, thinks he'll "blow your minds", is equated with the second coming of Christ, and Bowie neatly draws attention to the Messianic qualities of superstardom.

Anyone around in the Seventies will never forget Bowie's appearance on *Top Of The Pops*, crimson of hair, pallid of complexion and pally of demeanour, a lovingly limp wrist dangling over Mick Ronson's shoulder. The instantly decodable melody, courtesy in part of a cheeky and nifty rewrite of 'Somewhere Over The Rainbow', is glam rock's finest show-tune.

It Ain't Easy
(Davies)

This cover of a little-known Ron Davies song just doesn't fit in, and its inclusion on the album is doubly puzzling given the stockpile of excellence Bowie had at the time.

Lady Stardust

Another effective piano part dominates this undemanding piece of pop. 'Lady Stardust' takes Marc Bolan and his myth as subject matter, and thus continues the idea of the album as a sort of self-referential universe dominated by fictionalised accounts of rock's real-life history.

Star

Backing vocals like air-raid sirens, a hammering piano and the best lyric on the album make this a pivotal song in the Bowie canon. Here, Bowie's lyric embodies his obsession with notoriety ("So inviting – so enticing to play the part"), and the hard-headed commercialism ("I could do with the money") behind pop's façade of integrity and authenticity.

Hang On To Yourself

Again the acoustic, rather than lead, guitar hogs the limelight in this out-and-out rocker. It's as if Bowie can't sonically distance himself from the singer-songwriting pretensions of the previous *Hunky Dory* version of Bowie. That said, it is a fabulous song, with another fine guitar break from Ronson. The "come on" exhortation at the end is almost coital in its repeated delivery. Live, it has always been a winner – a superb opener to many Spiders' shows, a reworked tour-de-force on Bowie's '78 tour, with Adrian Belew's guitar duelling with Simon House's violin, and even a surprise addition to several dates on the 2003-2004 Reality tour.

Ziggy Stardust

During the early Seventies, Bowie was so adroit at writing instantly recognisable and skilful pop/rock riffs, and nowhere is there a better example than on this, the title track of the album. Like Jimi Hendrix, Ziggy "played it left hand/But made it too far" and, in what many take to be a reference to the fans who helped provide Hendrix with the drugs that would eventually kill him, Bowie sings, "When the kids had killed the man/I had to break up the band". There is also a powerful sense of drama at the song's dénouement, when the band cuts off before the final "Ziggy played guitar" salvo. Performed as a brilliant final song on both the Heathen and Reality concert tours, its show-stopping final line, "Ziggy played guitar", has an almost epitaph-like quality to it.

Suffragette City

This is another "lost" Bowie single, which was coupled with 'Stay' and released in Britain to promote the hits compilation *ChangesoneBowie* in 1976. It was a complete flop, not even denting the lower reaches of the Top 75. That said, this tale of a hot and bothered Bowie fending off his male lover while his female one "said she had to squeeze it but she... and then she" remained a live favourite over three decades, and the "Wham bam thank you mam" is still naughty, but nice.

Rock 'n' Roll Suicide

Not content to wait for the *Diamond Dogs* material to be completed, RCA turned this, perhaps Bowie's most dramatic moment ever, into a minor hit single (UK number 22) and thus once again short-changed Bowie fans, many of whom would literally buy an EP of his selected sneezing at this stage. (Remember, 'The Laughing Gnome' had just sold well over a quarter of a million copies in the UK alone.)

'Rock 'n' Roll Suicide' is an effective parody of the sort of Las Vegas show business schmaltz Bowie found so execrable. Pounding away at the "Gimme your hands 'cos you're wonderful" line, he lashes out at the light entertainment "you were a lovely audience" rhetoric to great effect.

According to Ken Scott, Bowie's vocal was just two live takes: the first, quieter section, and then the second, belted-out finale. As perfectly as 'Five Years' sets the agenda, so 'Rock 'n' roll Suicide' ends the album with unbridled power and desolation. The final little orchestral flourish closes the curtain on a piece of genuine rock theatre.

THE THIRTIETH ANNIVERSARY EDITION

In 2002, *Ziggy Stardust* was again reissued, with a bonus CD (details below) and came newly refurbished with a booklet, timeline, exclusive photographs and, most importantly, excellently clear digital remastering. Those cross-speaker phasing strings at the end of 'Moonage Daydream' really have never sounded so good.

CD 2 includes 'John, I'm Only Dancing', one of Bowie's few overtly gay songs, and a number 12 in the autumn of 1972. Bowie assures his male lover that he is only flirting with the opposite sex. Bowie had famously admitted to being gay (although bisexual would have been more accurate) in an interview with *Melody Maker's* Michael Watts in January 1972. This admission not only secured him the tabloid publicity to make him a star, but also, very importantly, as the first instance of a male pop star being open about the gay side of his sexuality, helped others who felt themselves to be on the margins to take centre stage and admit their true orientation. Also included in this Thirtieth Anniversary edition is the great early Bowie pop song 'Velvet Goldmine', which, of course, would later provide the title to one of the few glam-rock movies of our time. The film itself, although undoubtedly amusing, was basically one long homoerotic romp, which is particularly ironic since the song itself discusses in coded terms the pleasures of the (heterosexually) fleshly. 'Holy Holy' is, of course, a well-known (and great) Bowie rocker, the B-sides 'Amsterdam' and 'Round And Round' are inessential, while 'Sweet Head', an average Bowie tune, is another sex-obsessed rocker.

CD 2: 'Moonage Daydream (Arnold Corns version)', 'Hang On To Yourself (Arnold Corns version)', 'Lady Stardust (Demo)', 'Ziggy Stardust (Demo)', 'John, I'm Only Dancing', 'Velvet Goldmine', 'Holy Holy', 'Amsterdam' (Jacques Brel/ Mort Shuman), 'The Supermen', 'Round And Round' (AKA 'Around And Around') (Chuck Berry), 'Sweet Head (Take 4)', 'Moonage Daydream (New Mix)'

PINK FLOYD

Dark Side Of The Moon

March 1973

By Andy Mabbett

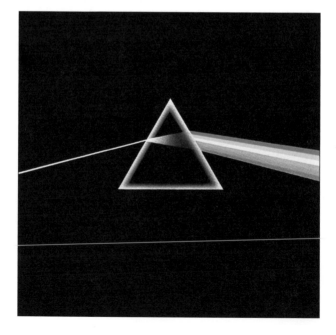

WITHOUT A DOUBT, this is Pink Floyd's BIG one. Statistically, it should be playing somewhere or other on the planet during every moment of every day, with a copy in one in five UK households.

The record's release was not the suite's début, however, as the very first performance, subtitled "A Piece For Assorted Lunatics", was in early 1972 and was abruptly halted by a power failure during 'Money'. The title Dark Side Of The Moon is a reference to the occult name for the subconscious. However, Medicine Head released an album of that name in late 1971, so the planned title was changed to Eclipse. When the Medicine Head album flopped, the original title was revived by the Floyd, but even they weren't sure exactly what to call their new, self-produced album. Original copies prefixed the title as The Dark Side..., as did the front of the first CD issue. However, later copies, and both the spine and disc of the first and latest CDs, all omit the troublesome definitive article.

Dark Side... was to be the first of a run of albums with all the lyrics by Roger Waters. The importance of his narrative was highlighted by the fact that this was the first Floyd album to have the lyrics printed on its sleeve (although the recent CD reissues of earlier albums have had lyrics added retrospectively). The idea of linking songs with themes of madness, ageing, work and death – worries that trouble every one of us – came about in a band meeting in Nick Mason's kitchen.

Recording started on June 1, 1972 and continued throughout that year, the first sessions to take place on Abbey Road's new 24-track equipment. The album's engineer was Alan Parsons, who was then earning £35 per week. After receiving an Emmy for his work on the record and going on the road as Pink Floyd's sound mixer, he built an entire career emulating Floyd's sonic soundscapes on his own albums. In the past, this has elicited some sharp comment from David Gilmour, but the hatchet appears to have been buried, as Gilmour contributed guitar to a track on Parsons' 2004 album, A Valid Path.

Even at this stage in the band's career, tensions were running high between Waters and Gilmour, and record producer Chris Thomas – who was managed by the same company as Pink Floyd, Steve O'Rourke's EMKA Productions – was brought in to arbitrate between the members during the final mixing. This was done in such a way that all the tracks, with the exception of the break between the original vinyl sides, before 'Money', segue into each other. The making of the album was later discussed by all four band members in the 2003 documentary, *Classic Albums: Pink Floyd - The Making Of The Dark Side Of The Moon*.

The impromptu spoken parts were obtained by Waters, who showed flash-cards to various crew members and studio staff. These had questions such as, "When did you last thump somebody?" or, "What do you think of death?" on them. The subjects' replies were recorded and extracts edited into the mix. One of the participants was Paul McCartney, although his contribution was considered too cautious to be used.

A quad version of the album (Harvest Q4SHVL 804), had some subtly different mixes (notably the spoken parts on the final two tracks, as heard on *Works*), but these were closer to the regular stereo version than other quadraphonic and mono versions in the Floyd catalogue. However, the quad mix was reissued in Australia on pink vinyl in 1988. A quad master tape, intended for vinyl pressings, was inadvertently used in the US for the first batch of CDs.

Despite only reaching number two in the UK and managing only one week at number one in the US, the album's chart performance has never been equalled, and probably never will be. Even taking into account a couple of minor breaks, it was in the US Top 200 for over 800 weeks – more than 15 years!

The album's saxophonist was Dick Parry, a relatively unknown session musician who was favoured for sharing the band's roots in Cambridge, where he had played in groups with Gilmour. He was an inspired choice, and accompanied them on tour for the next two years and again in 1994. For *Dark Side...*, he was, says Gilmour, asked to "play like the sax man in the cartoon band who did the theme music for Pearl & Dean's ad sequence at the cinema in those days".

Apart from Clare Torry's famous contribution (of which more below), backing vocals were performed by female session singers Liza Strike, Barry St. John and Lesley Duncan, plus veteran gospel performer Doris Troy. A pair of black women singers, Carlena Williams and Vanetta Fields, known as The Blackberries, joined the band for post-album performances of the suite. All in all, Pink Floyd performed the suite at least 385 times until abandoning it for almost 20 years after the 1975 Knebworth festival. The BBC recorded a superb performance at Wembley Arena (then the Empire Pool) in 1974 but, although this receives an occasional airing, sadly the band have refused requests for it to be granted an official release.

Dark Side... returned in 1994 for many of the dates on The Division Bell tour, and is included whole on the live P*U*L*S*E album and DVD. Waters performed the suite on each of the 100-plus dates of his tellingly-titled The Dark Side Of The Moon Live tour in 2006-8, and has thus performed it more times than any other band member. Nick Mason joined him on several dates, and some were filmed.

The original sleeve is one of the best – and best-known – in rock. A triumph of simplicity, it was designed by the Hipgnosis art team and drawn by George Hardie. Hipgnosis offered the band several alternative designs. The meeting, according to Hipgnosis's Storm Thorgerson, "took about three seconds, in as much as the band cast their eyes over everything, looked at each other, said in unison, 'That one', and left the room". The sleeve includes two deliberate mistakes: there is no purple in the spectrum, to simplify the design; and the rear sleeve showed the prism producing a converging spectrum – a physical impossibility, but necessary to allow opened out sleeves to be arranged end-to-end, forming a continuous design, or mandala, useful for in-store displays.

Vinyl copies came with two free stickers and two posters – one a collection of live shots, the other a night view of the pyramids at Giza. For some reason, both are different in American copies, while the Japanese edition came with a lavish booklet. The band had wanted everything to be presented in a box, but EMI vetoed this on the grounds of cost. Twenty years later they relented and a limited-edition boxed CD (EMI 7 81479 2) was released, using a digitally revamped master tape. The box also contained a new booklet, revised artwork and five "art cards". A year later, the new master was used as one of EMI's series of reissues. Shortly afterwards, the album became the first Pink Floyd minidisc (EMI 8 29752 8).

For all its brighter sound and glossy artwork, the 1994 reissue's packaging is inferior to that of the original album and the first CD. Not only is the comforting familiarity of the airbrushed prism on the front lost to a harsher version taken from a photograph of a real glass prism, but the live and pyramid shots (the original posters were adapted for the first CD's booklet) have been replaced and the photogram backgrounds are just plain tacky.

In 2003, the album's 30th anniversary was marked by the release of a hybrid Super Audio SACD with a 5.1 channel DSD surround-sound version remixed from the original 16-track studio tapes by James Guthrie. It featured new Thorgerson artwork, the front cover being a photograph of a stained-glass design based on the original. SACDs use a higher sampling rate than regular CDs, and so have higher quality and more fidelity to the original recording. The SACD content requires a special player, so a regular CD version is also encoded, on the same disc.

Fans were disappointed at Guthrie's somewhat conservative approach, feeling that he didn't make adequate use of the surround-sound capabilities, and were angered that he ignored the alternate guitar and vocal takes used on the vinyl quadraphonic version. A spine-chilling surround-sound DVD version, reputedly from the master tapes of the original Alan Parsons quadraphonic mix, with a low-frequency fifth track added (giving a 4.1 configuration, instead of the more common 5.1), was bootlegged in 2006, and could be downloaded on-line. Though the band rejected this mix in favour of Guthrie's, it's far superior, and the format can also be played on either DVD-audio or regular DVD equipment.

The album has been covered, wholesale, several times. In 2003, the entire album was performed, in reggae style, by a collection of acts on the Easy Star label, as *Dub Side Of The Moon* (Easy Star Records ES-1012, USA) with bonus tracks called 'Great Dub In The Sky' and 'Any Dub You Like'. In 2006, former Yes member Billy Sherwood devised and produced a version (Purple Pyramid CLP 1621-2, USA) with contributions by many notable artists, including Adrian Belew, Bill Bruford, Vinnie Colaiuta, Geoff Downes, Larry Fast, Steve Howe, Robby Krieger, voice actor Malcolm McDowell, Colin Moulding, Del Palmer, Steve Porcaro, Rick Wakeman, Edgar Winter, Dweezil Zappa and, notably, Pink Floyd collaborators Tony Levin and Scott(y) Page. As befits artist of such stature, they avoided making a slavish copy and added their own interpretations and embellishments, making it worth hearing, even for fans with numerous copies of the original. (Sherwood had earlier done the same thing with *The Wall*.)

A similar level of invention went into The Section's *The String Quartet Tribute To Pink Floyd* (Vitamin Records CD-8469, USA, 2003), an unhelpfully named, instrumental version of *Dark Side…* performed by said configuration, without taking the lazy option of using electric instruments, which has marred so many other "classical" Pink Floyd covers. No less enjoyable was the delightfully quirky *Dark Side Of The Moon A Cappella* (Vocomotion Records VOMO 0105, USA, 2005), credited to Voices On The Dark Side and rendered entirely by mouth, right down to the sound effects and percussion. They are among a host of "tribute" acts, including Dream Theatre, moe., Phish and The Squirrels, who have covered the entire suite live.

Speak To Me
(Mason)

Opening with a reassuring heartbeat, this introductory sound collage forms an overture to the rest of the suite, including sounds from the rest of the album, plus the manic laughter of road manager Peter Watts. (Trivia fans will be delighted to know that his daughter is the actress Naomi Watts.)

The piece's title was the catchphrase of the band's then tour manager, Chris Adamson, whose audible contribution includes the famous, "I've been mad for fucking years", which was much more prominent in live performances. Also heard is the "…even if you are not mad" spiel by Abbey Road Studios' doorman, Jerry Driscoll.

Roger Waters has since claimed that he devised the track and that Mason's credit (his only solo credit outside *Ummagumma*) was merely a gift, though its working title was "Nick's Section".

Although listed separately on the 1994 remastered CD, 'Speak To Me' and 'Breathe' are indexed as one track, as they were on the first CD issues. To confuse matters, the CD in the *Shine On* box set and the 30th anniversary version index them as two tracks.

Breathe
(or Breathe In The Air)
(Waters/Gilmour/Wright)

More naming problems occur with this song, which is sometimes listed as 'Breathe In The Air' and sometimes as just 'Breathe', for example on the remastered and 30th anniversary CDs (the copy in the *Shine On* box set managed to use both names). Perhaps the longer title is intended to distinguish it from another track called 'Breathe', on *The Body*, Waters' 1970 film soundtrack album recorded with Ron Geesin. They share their opening line and, with a little imagination, it is easy to hear how one may have mutated into the other. In contrast, the first line of the second verse is the title of a song that was originally a "hit" in 1939, when Flanagan and Allen sang it in The Crazy Gang's film *The Little Dog Laughed*.

A short section from a 972 rehearsal is on *The Making of...* DVD.

Until using it on the 1994 tour, Pink Floyd only ever performed the track as part of complete *Dark Side...* shows, but Waters used it as a stand-alone song during some concerts on his 1987 tour. At Live 8, 'Breathe' and 'Breathe Reprise' were performed, for the first time in their history, as one song.

On The Run
(Gilmour/Waters)

The title is Waters' representation of the stresses of being always on the go, whether as a touring musician or in any other career.

The piece was largely created on a VCS3 synthesiser. Waters is seen recreating the track at Abbey Road in the *Live In Pompeii* film, though by the time of filming the album was finished. Responsibility for the footsteps in the closing sequence was later claimed by engineer Alan Parsons. Roger the Hat, a Floyd roadie, is heard saying, "Live for today, gone tomorrow, that's me". An airport PA system (actually a studio recording from an earlier EMI comedy album) announces a flight to cities in Italy.

In pre-album concert performances, this part of the suite had been a completely different, guitar-based tune, 'The Travel Sequence', with a keyboard solo.

During concert performances, a large model aeroplane would descend on a wire over the audience, crashing onto the stage to explode in a ball of flame, while film of aerial shots was projected behind the band.

For some dates on Pink Floyd's 1987 tour, the plane was replaced by a giant bed, echoing the *Momentary Lapse* artwork. New, Storm Thorgerson-directed concert footage was introduced, with a man strapped to a bed, being wheeled along hospital corridors at ever increasing speeds until it burst through a pair of doors onto a runway and took off.

Time

(Mason/Waters/Wright/Gilmour)

This track is perhaps most famous for its cacophony of chiming clocks, recorded as a quadraphonic demonstration tape for EMI by Parsons, who suggested it for use on the album. The lyrics address Waters' concerns about ageing – remarkable for something written when he was just 28 – and his fear that life was passing him by, which was ironic for someone about to score such a massive success. David Gilmour and Richard Wright, the latter backed by the session singers, take alternate verses, with Wright's having the more mellow style. Gilmour's guitar solo is unequalled, remaining one of his all-time classics. Early live versions were much slower, with some awful harmonies (the term is used loosely!) between Gilmour and Wright.

Waters' line about "hanging on in quiet desperation" is borrowed from *Walden*, the 1854 autobiographical work by American Henry David Thoreau, in which he writes, "The mass of men lead lives of quiet desperation". After the song's final, pessimistic lyric, comes an extra verse, subtitled 'Breathe Reprise', which is missing from a bootlegged alternative take. The segment's working title was 'Home Again'. Gilmour performs a solo version, with acoustic guitar, on *The Making Of...* DVD, which also includes part of Waters' original demo as an extra.

A US single release has Nick Mason's opening Rototoms reprised at the end, courtesy of a deft piece of studio editing. The song is used on *Echoes*, complete with 'Breathe (Reprise)'.

Live performances were accompanied by back-projected film of animated clocks, which was eventually released as an extra on both *The Making Of...* and P*U*L*S*E DVDs.

The Great Gig In The Sky
(See description for credit)

This is surely the most seductive song about death ever. At Parsons' suggestion, Clare Torry was brought in to perform the almost painfully beautiful vocalese. She recorded several takes at different volumes and pitches, and the track is a compilation of these. Although she improvised her part in the studio, Torry was for many years not given the co-composer's credit that many now feel she deserved, receiving instead double the standard flat fee – a staggering £30!

Torry obviously didn't hold a grudge, though, as she reprised her performance on stage, both for Roger Waters' New York and London shows in 1987 and with Pink Floyd at Knebworth in 1990. She later earned a much larger sum when the track became the first Floyd piece to be officially used for a television commercial, in this case for Neurofen painkillers. After seeking permission from Wright (who, as credited composer, then held sole authority to say yea or nay), the agency concerned recruited Torry to recreate the original with session musicians, earning her a repeat fee every time it was screened. In 2004, she finally decided to take legal action to secure her due, and, in an ensuing agreement, which involved a gagging clause, was awarded a considerable sum of money, plus the right to be credited on future releases.

Early live versions, known as 'The Mortality Sequence', were fairly dire, comprising a speech by journalist and moral crusader Malcolm Muggeridge, a recital of 'The Lord's Prayer' and taped Bible readings, from the Book of Ephesians, with a keyboard accompaniment. The track returned to Pink Floyd's live set early in 1988.

On *Dark Side* CDs, 'Great Gig' cross-fades into the following track, masking what was originally the break between vinyl sides. The track is used on *Echoes*.

The "I am not frightened of dying" line is Jerry Driscoll's.

Money

(Waters)

The album's other great piece of musique concrète is the speaker-hopping rhythmic till-ringing that heralds its best-known song. This was created by carefully marking the original recording, cutting it into inch-long pieces and painstakingly reassembling it on the studio floor, so that the various tills and coins sounded right on the beat – a task that could have been accomplished in minutes had the band had access to a modern sampler and sequencer. The aggressive saxophone part was capably handled by Dick Parry. The spoken comments are all from Wings' guitarist Henry McCullough, apart from "crusin' for a brusin'", which was spoken by Patricia Watts, second wife of Peter.

Waters' reference to Lear Jets is ironic, considering that both Mason and Gilmour went on to qualify as pilots, the latter (who handled the song's vocals) at one time operating a company, Intrepid Aviation, to own, fly and promote his collection of classic aircraft.

'Money' was released as a single in the USA, using an edited version, a rarity only ever released in the UK on the vinyl-only compilation *Rock Legends* (Telstar STAR 2290). The single's chart success – it reached number 13 – changed the band's fortunes forever. It also changed their audiences, and they were never again able to play quiet passages without being drowned out by noisy fans unimpressed by the band's more tranquil moments.

'Money' is the most-performed piece in Pink Floyd's history, used as the encore throughout the 1977 Animals tour, played on both Gilmour and Waters' solo tours and at all Pink Floyd's subsequent dates. Gilmour has performed the track at over 780 concerts!

Waters produced a pseudo-live version for a single B-side in 1987, and Gilmour, when he appeared on Nicky Horne's Radio One show in July 1992, allowed the airing of a brief portion of Waters' original demo for the track, with the composer singing to his own crude, double-tracked acoustic guitar accompaniment. The demo is also heard on *The Making of...* DVD. Inevitably, 'Money' is on the *...Great Dance Songs* and *Echoes* compilations.

Us And Them

(Waters/Wright)

Richard Wright originally composed this tune as a simple piano piece for the *Zabriskie Point* film soundtrack, with a descriptive working title of 'The Violent Sequence'. It was given just a handful of pre-*Dark Side...* live airings in early 1970, including a gig the Floyd performed without their usual equipment, when it was stretched to 21 minutes long! Wright can be seen working on his piano part in the studio segments of *Live At Pompeii*. The song was released as a single in the USA.

Unlike the original, the album version is enhanced by Parry's saxophone, in a much more laid-back vein than his strident blowing on 'Money'. Waters sang early live versions, but Gilmour did the honours for the album, with Wright unusually providing the heavier singing on the angrier second and final verses. The anti-war, anti-hierarchy lyrics could have been lifted straight from *The Wall*, though roadie Roger the Hat's "short, sharp shock" may not have gone down so well there. The person who said he was "really drunk" was Wings' guitarist, Henry McCullough.

As well as being an occasional encore on the band's 1977 tour, 'Us And Them' was a regular in Pink Floyd's post-Waters concerts.

An early studio version has been bootlegged, with the sax solo mixed very differently and no echo on the vocals.

'Us And Them' is the fourth and final *Dark Side...* track on the *Echoes* compilation.

Any Colour You Like

(Gilmour/Mason/Wright)

This instrumental – a VCS3 synthesiser and guitar workout – is the only track in Pink Floyd's entire canon that the "other three" wrote together without Waters, while the latter was still in the band. The title is taken, indirectly, from Henry Ford's oft-misquoted remark, of his Model T, that, "Any customer can have a car painted any colour that he wants so long as it is black," though the band knew it as something often said by Chris Adamson. Working titles included 'Scat' and 'Dave's Scat Section'.

Brain Damage

(Waters)

This, the nearest thing to the album's title track (it's the only song to include the words "the dark side of the moon"), and the following song, represent Waters' only vocals on the album. The songs have always been performed as a pair, including the encores on Waters' 1984 and '87 solo outings.

In *Live At Pompeii*, Waters is seen pretending to overdub his bass part to a tape that already contains his completed vocals. Later, Gilmour is seen supposedly adding further layers of guitar. A 1972 version is one of the few post-Sixties Pink Floyd out-takes to have surfaced. Waters performs an acoustic version for *The Making Of...* DVD.

The lyric about "the lunatic on the grass" is taken from an unrecorded song Waters wrote during the *Meddle* sessions in 1971. Its title? 'The Dark Side Of The Moon'!

Eclipse

(Waters)

'Eclipse' demonstrates one of Waters' favourite writing techniques – when in doubt, write a list. This "list-o-mania" can be heard on most of his subsequent albums while still in Pink Floyd, as well as several of his solo works. The words were not written until, after a few live performances, the band realised that the suite needed some kind of ending.

The album closes with the heartbeat once more, behind which Jerry Driscoll cheerfully adds, "There is no dark side of the moon – matter of fact, it's all dark."

Or does it? The pages of *The Amazing Pudding*, the independent Pink Floyd and Roger Waters magazine, were consumed with debate for almost two years in the early Nineties over a piece of music that could be heard very faintly during the final heartbeats. Some claimed it was a figment of readers' warped imaginations, but something resembling a string orchestra playing 'Ticket To Ride' could definitely be heard at the end of Driscoll's line, on the remastered CD, if the volume was set very loud.

Other copies, such as the previous UK CD, did not seem to have this, but a whispering voice could be heard at 1'41". Explanations ranged from a Floydian joke to interference during mastering, and from the use of second-hand tape to a performance in an adjacent studio being picked up. All seem equally unlikely.

BOB MARLEY

(The Wailers)

Catch A Fire

May 1973

By Ian McCann

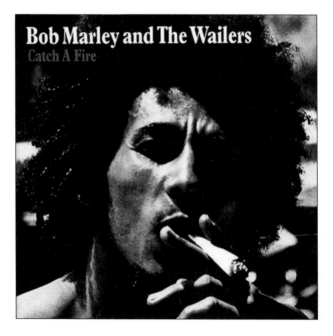

AFTER THE WAILERS' relationship with producer Lee Perry petered out, Bob Marley spent some time working on singles for his own label, Tuff Gong. At some point in 1972 Chris Blackwell, the Anglo-Jamaican founder of Island Records, sought Marley out and offered him a verbal contract. Some pundits claim that Blackwell originally wanted to sign Toots & The Maytals and settled for Marley instead, although this seems unlikely since Blackwell had already produced Toots and therefore had all the opportunity he needed to strike any deal he wanted.

Blackwell gave £4,000 to The Wailers to make this album. The trio of Marley, Peter Tosh and Bunny Livingston were now bolstered by The Upsetters' rhythm section of Carlton and Family Man Barrett, who had largely split with Perry, though both Bob and the Barrett brothers still worked with the producer occasionally throughout their careers nothing in Jamaican music is permanent. It also reputedly cost Island a payment to CBS and to song publisher Danny Sims, who also had points on several Marley Island LPs. Although most Jamaicans reckoned that Blackwell would see nothing for his money or Marley and co. again, his faith was justified, and in 1973, The Wailers released *Catch A Fire*.

Blackwell cleverly marketed The Wailers in the manner with which he had already achieved success for Island rock acts like Traffic, Cat Stevens and Fairport Convention. He presented them as an alternative to mainstream rock music, and doubtless their rebel image and Marley's growing locks, reminiscent to a white audience of the hippieish rock of the era, helped a lot. *Catch A Fire* drew reviews from cautiously favourable to ecstatic to bewildered from a UK music press that usually dismissed reggae as the province of skinheads (reggae review singles were forever available at bargain prices in London's second-hand stores), and The Wailers was suddenly a name to drop for the campus hip.

Island's marketing strategy had been very effective for their rock acts and the same style, ironically, would make a legend out of Bob Marley — famous in his own country for a decade, yet whom few white fans had heard of before 1973. Blackwell's company had tried to market reggae before with

Jimmy Cliff, who nearly became a major star at the time of the film *The Harder They Come* (1972) and had had a couple of huge chart hits in Britain ('Wonderful World, Beautiful People', 1969; 'Wild World', written by Cat Stevens, 1970).

The album was credited to The Wailers, which gives the lie to the common assertion that Island's insistence on Bob as the frontman split the band. In truth, Marley's name had often been used out front (such as on the Lee Perry-produced LPs), just as Peter Tosh's had (on several singles). The brief explanatory sleeve note manages to spell Peter and Bunny's surnames incorrectly (McIntosh was 'Mackintosh', Livingston was 'Livingstone'). It's also the only reggae album to come in a flip-up sleeve shaped like a Zippo lighter! (The Jamaican issue wasn't shaped, neither were the reissues.) Recorded at Dynamic, Harry J, Randy's and Kingston Studios, with which The Wailers were already familiar, and mixed in London at Island's own suite in Basing Street, where overdubs also took place, production credits went to Bob Marley and Chris Blackwell.

Catch A Fire was originally scheduled to come out as a rare LP on Island's Blue Mountain label, even given a suitable matrix, BML 2001, which appeared on the original stamper but was crossed off. This suggests that the project was to have been far more low-key than it subsequently became, even though the lone Wailers Blue Mountain single, 'Baby Baby We've Got A Date', garnered strong reviews in the UK music press – uniquely for a reggae single. At the time, Blackwell had a loose plan to make Blue Mountain Island's reggae division, although the idea was soon dropped when he decided that The Wailers might catch on with a white audience if they were marketed just as strongly as a rock band. It took time, but he was undoubtedly correct.

The first Jamaican pressing, catalogue number 19329 FG, featured the same mixes as the UK version on a Tuff Gong label apparently never used elsewhere, featuring a dread bashing a gong. It is a commonly held belief that Jamaican pressings of Marley LPs featured different mixes. They do not, although sometimes the mastering process may have left the sound slightly amended from the original: this was more likely to be a muting, rather than an enhancing, effect.

Band members: Marley, Tosh, Livingston, Aston Barrett (bass), Carlton Barrett (drums). Also on the sessions: Earl "Wya" Lindo, Tyrone Downie ('Stir It Up', 'Concrete Jungle'), Winston Wright, Glen Adams (keyboards), Alva Lewis (guitar), Willy San Francisco, Winston Wright, Chris Karen (percussion); Rita Marley and Marcia Griffiths (backing vocals).

The album failed to chart in either the UK or US but its influence among musicians, of course, belied its initial sales.

All songs written by Bob Marley unless otherwise indicated.

Concrete Jungle

Guitar solos like Roger McGuinn tuning up. A beat that doesn't reveal itself as reggae for a few bars. If you wanted to launch reggae on a rock audience that knew nothing about it, you did it like this. Although the mix is decidedly strange in places to reggae ears, it soon makes sense. The Wailers sounded better-produced than ever before, more confident, and suddenly altogether more adult. Scan the credits and by Tosh's name it says "guitar", but not lead. In fact it was Wayne Perkins, an American session musician, who put the licks on at Island's behest.

The other uncredited musician was John "Rabbit" Bundrick, an erstwhile Free member and, since the death of Keith Moon in 1978, the keyboard player of choice for The Who, both on record and on stage. Bundrick added keyboards and was part of the Johnny Nash band when Marley was first in Europe in the early Seventies (see 'Acoustic Medley' on *Songs Of Freedom*, and *Chances Are*). Exactly why these people were uncredited at the time is a mystery of marketing, but perhaps Island felt it would be confusing to have both a Bunny and a Rabbit in the same group!

The Wailers' thoughts on this at the time are unrecorded, although Marley later gave Perkins' work his approval and was reputedly present on at least one overdub date. The Jamaican session for 'Concrete Jungle' did not feature Family Man Barrett, with his protégé, a youth called Robbie Shakespeare, taking the bass role. The song is a defining moment for Marley: here's the wise sufferer's stance in a nutshell.

'Concrete Jungle' was a single on Island (WIP 6164, 1973), was collected onto *Songs Of Freedom*, and later appeared on *Babylon By Bus*.

Slave Driver

Here's where the album title came from: "Slave driver, catch a fire so you can get burned." The fantastic harmonies Wailers fans have, by now, become used to dominate this track, reinforced by a scratchy Tosh guitar. Marley's blood runs cold at the crack of a whip, which it must have done often since something akin to handclaps forms a whiplash whenever he mentions it. An instant classic, later covered in fine style by Dennis Brown (1977).

Also an Island single (WIP 6167, 1973), 'Slave Driver' appears on *Songs Of Freedom* and *Rebel Music*. A different version shows up on *Talkin' Blues*.

400 Years
(Tosh)

Tosh retreads a track from an earlier Wailers album, *Soul Rebels*. Here the tempo is slower and the attitude more laid-back and meandering, with a clavinet roaming around in the middle eight like a lost soul wandering the cosmos. The writing credit is still Marley on the original label, although the sleeve has it as Tosh, which is nearer the truth.

Stop That Train
(Tosh)

Tosh again remakes an old song (this time from *The Best Of The Wailers*) in a slower, gospellish style. Organ, credited to Tosh on the sleeve, sounds more like the work of a session man and adds to the churchified atmosphere.

An instrumental cut of the song forms the flip to the UK single 'Baby Baby We've Got A Date' (1973), both on the Blue

Mountain and later Island pressings. Tosh cut it yet again for the *Mama Africa* album (1983).

Baby We've Got A Date (Rock It Baby)

The Wailers' first single on the UK Blue Mountain (BM 1021) label as 'Baby Baby We've Got A Date', and on US Island as 'Rock It Baby' (both 1973) from the new Island deal, also pressed for Tuff Gong as 'Rock It Babe'. Obtrusive slide guitar from Wayne Perkins again, and uncredited female vocals (Marcia Griffiths and Rita Marley, most likely) provide support for the sort of "let's get together baby" song you'd expect from The Wailers' Leslie Kong period.

Stir It Up

Another one from The Wailers' rocksteady era remade. Johnny Nash had already had a hit with the song (CBS, 1972) and this precise, neat version, with what sounds like more dubbed guitar, has an ease that Nash didn't achieve. Later to appear on the *Babylon By Bus* LP and a favourite on The Wailers' first UK tour in 1973. Uncredited musicians also on the track: Ian and Roger Lewis (bass and guitar, both later in Inner Circle), Sparrow Martin (drums). Although the Barrett brothers were official Wailers members, Marley's musicians varied from day to day.

Unbelievably, considering its commercial potential, this version was not a 45 until 1976 and even then not an A-side (WIP 6309 UK, IS 089 US).

Kinky Reggae

'Kinky' was a bit of a catchword in early Seventies Jamaica, appearing on a good few records. Marley uses the word here to mean a general sexiness. Lyrically, this is another precursor to 'Natty Dread', with Marley wandering through various areas describing the people he meets, seemingly unable to decide whether he wants to live in a kinky part of town or not. The "right on" chorus was also common in reggae at the time.

'Kinky Reggae' was also central to the band's live set of the time, and a steamy live cut later turned up on the *Talkin' Blues* set (1991), as well as *Babylon By Bus* (1978) and as the flip to 'No Woman No Cry' (1975), on the UK single drawn from the same shows that produced the breakthrough *Lyceum Live!* set. The song has an unselfconscious air that became increasingly rare as Marley's fame grew.

No More Trouble

Bob rejects problems to a clavinet, more uncredited female vocals, and a bass line reminiscent of Isaac Hayes' 'Do Your Thing', another reggae cover-version favourite. Carlton Barrett's "one drop" drum style is particularly magnificent here; otherwise this slight song is the least interesting thing on the album.

This version also appears on a US 45 (Island 1215) and the *Songs Of Freedom* set. A live cut, segued into 'War', turns up on *Babylon By Bus* and *Rebel Music*.

Midnight Ravers

A rootsy one to close the album, with the sort of raw mix usually found on a Tuff Gong 45 rather than an album. As indeed it was (1972), with a magnificent instrumental version featuring a strange, flanged mix (which tips over into feedback) for the flip. Glorious harmonies on this version, and the apocalyptic vision of confused sexes and 10,000 horseless chariots must have seemed baffling to first-time Marley buyers not used to his Book Of Revelations imagery. A remarkable record any way you look at it.

DELUXE EDITION

DISC 1 - **The Unreleased Original Jamaican Versions**

'Concrete Jungle', 'Stir It Up', 'High Tide Or Low Tide', 'Stop That Train', '400 Years', 'Baby We've Got A Date (Rock It

Baby)', 'Midnight Ravers', 'All Day All Night', 'Slave Driver', 'Kinky Reggae', 'No More Trouble'

DISC 2 - **The Released Album**

'Concrete Jungle', 'Slave Driver', '400 Years', 'Stop That Train', 'Baby We've Got A Date (Rock It Baby)', 'Stir It Up', 'Kinky Reggae', 'No More Trouble', 'Midnight Ravers'

This Deluxe Edition more than lives up to its name and really is quite special. Despite its rather misleading title, Disc One was never actually released in Jamaica. Instead, it features the mix of the album that was sent to Chris Blackwell in London from Jamaica and demonstrates just what a wise investment his £4,000 had proved to be.

There have been many complaints over the years about the overdubs that were added to "sweeten" Catch A Fire, but there can be no denying that the musicians did the job that was required of them at the time, and they undoubtedly helped to make the sound more acceptable to a crossover audience. Perkins' guitar and Bundrick's keyboards filled out the sound but, here without their contributions, The Wailers' beautiful harmonies assume greater prominence and the overall sound is sharp, clear and stripped back to basics.

The two tracks left off the original album have become the stuff of legend over the ensuing years and it's not difficult to hear why, as 'High Tide Or Low Tide' and 'All Day All Night', two beautiful, yearning love songs, are as dense and committed as the other tracks that were included. Perhaps too many love songs would have detracted from the rebellious image that Island were working to establish for The Wailers in the early Seventies. Both albums are excellent and both work in their own right, so it's almost impossible to choose which is the "better" one. An essential purchase.

As well as the Deluxe Edition double CD series, all of Bob Marley & The Wailers' Island albums have been subsequently remastered (but not remixed) and re-released by Island/ Tuff Gong/Universal in the new millennium. Nearly all have additional bonus tracks added, in the case of Catch A Fire, 'High Tide Or Low Tide' and 'All Day All Night'

BRUCE SPRINGSTEEN

Born To Run

August 1975
(Original US release date)

By Patrick Humphries

I T WAS THE record nobody wanted. Columbia weren't exactly rubbing their hands at the prospect of a third album from Bruce Springsteen; the label was concentrating on new releases from their established and consistently best-selling acts like Chicago, Barbra Streisand and Paul Simon. Springsteen's previous two albums, *Greetings From Asbury Park N.J.* and *The Wild, The Innocent & The E. Street Shuffle*, and two singles ('Blinded By The Light', 'Spirit In The Night'), had sold less than 90,000 copies in total. This third album really would be make or break.

Springsteen himself knew how crucial his third album was; if he didn't deliver the goods, he was off the label. That knowledge weighed heavily, and he was reluctant to let his third record out of his grasp.

Two years into his professional career, Springsteen was still dogged by the "new Dylan" tag, despite having built quite a reputation as a unique live performer, with shows stretching from 75-minute showcases to two-hour spectaculars. Fans wanted something more representative of those breathtaking live shows than the flimsy-sounding albums currently available.

In August 1974, along with manager Mike Appel, Springsteen repaired to 914 Sound Studios at Blauvelt in New York State, where his first two albums had been recorded. The fruit of the 914 sessions were four separate mixes (some including strings and a female chorus) of a new song called 'Born To Run', which had been going down well in concert. However, Springsteen was unhappy with the technical quality of the studio and, on the advice of rock writer Jon Landau, who was already on his way to becoming an integral member of the Springsteen team, production moved to New York's Record Plant.

Springsteen seemed to have found a soul mate in the journalist, but the presence of Landau only widened the gulf between the artist and Appel. Ironically, in view of the differences that developed, the finished version of 'Born To Run' was a joint production between Springsteen and Appel.

Springsteen had a clear vision of how he wanted the finished *Born To Run* album to sound – like Roy Orbison singing the lyrics of Bob Dylan to a Phil Spector production. To his credit, he came within a whisker, but getting there was a nightmare. "The album became a monster," he reflected later. "It just ate up everyone's life."

Band personnel were a problem, too. E Street Band drummer, Vini "Mad Dog" Lopez, had just been fired and his replacement, Ernest "Boom" Carter, stayed only long enough to play on the album's title track, while pianist David Sancious quit to pursue a solo career. Feeling that his manager wasn't protecting him sufficiently from the label's indifference, Springsteen confided more and more in Landau. Gradually, the axis shifted, and Landau found his opinions sought on the actual recording of the album.

Landau did have some experience in record production, with albums by the MC5, James Taylor's younger brother Livingston and J. Geils Band to his credit. Appel was, predictably, less than happy with the situation: "I believe Landau had it in his mind all along, once he saw Springsteen and declared him rock'n'roll's future, to produce Bruce and eventually take over his management... The best I can say about Landau as a producer, prior to working with Bruce, was that he was a heck of a critic." The battle for the soul and future of Bruce Springsteen raged in the studio.

Appel recalled the stresses and strains in Marc Eliot's underrated Springsteen biography, *Down Thunder Road*: "Bruce had lost his direction, his energy, and to some extent his confidence. We'd been at it now for a year, deep in debt to the label, no enthusiasm up at CBS for us, continual personnel shifts, so when there were technical breakdowns, it was easy to start shifting the blame as to why things weren't happening."

It was only when DJs started playing leaked copies of the 'Born To Run' single that Columbia began to get behind the album. Springsteen had the songs – some of his best ('Born To Run', 'Thunder Road', 'Backstreets', 'Jungleland') – but the sound was eluding him. With costs rising above $50,000, the sessions, which had begun in the summer of 1974, dragged on and on into 1975.

Ever the perfectionist, Springsteen fell asleep at mixing sessions and chucked one finished master out of a hotel window because it hadn't captured the sound he was chasing. He knew everything rested on this third roll of the dice. Landau remembers being impressed by Springsteen's determination as the record company applied further pressure to rush-release *Born To Run*: "The release date is just one day," Bruce cautioned. "The record is forever."

However, now being a full-time member of Springsteen's inner circle, even Landau grew frustrated with the delays. He snapped when at one point Springsteen decided to scrap what had been recorded by substituting tracks taped at forthcoming live shows. "Look," chided Landau, "you are not supposed to like it. You think Chuck Berry sits around listening to 'Maybelline'? And when he does hear it, don't you think that he wishes a few things could be changed? C'mon, it's time to put the record out."

Provisional album titles included *American Summer, The Legend Of Zero & Blind Terry, From The Churches To The Jails, War & Roses, The Hungry & The Hunted*. But everyone knew that there could only ever be one title after they'd heard the single.

On its release, *Born To Run* cemented itself as one of the key albums of the Seventies. There were weak links – the jerky 'Tenth Avenue Freeze-Out', the uncharacteristically cinéma vérité 'Meeting Across The River' and the shallow 'She's The One'. But at its best, *Born To Run* conveyed an epic grandeur and big screen rock'n'roll that hadn't been heard since Phil Spector's teen symphonies of the early Sixties. The title track offered exhilaration and opportunity, while the rest of the album spoke of gritting your teeth to get through the day, while revelling in the freedom offered by the highway and street corner. Springsteen took everyday characters, incidents and locations, and transformed them into myth.

Columbia Records is believed to have laid out between $100,000 and $150,000 on promoting *Born To Run*, an unheard-of amount to spend on a relative unknown. But the sum would be more than matched by the hysterical press coverage that surrounded the artist around the time of its release.

The extent of Springsteen's celebrity became apparent late in 1975 when he became the first non-political figure to feature simultaneously on the covers of both *Time* and *Newsweek* magazines. Though in the minds of some critics, such blanket exposure only confirmed that Springsteen was nothing more than a media fabrication.

Appel was confident that his boy would remain on the straight and narrow: "If I had a weak artist, I'd be a nervous wreck because of all the attention. But I've got Bruce Springsteen. That's why I know the *Time* and *Newsweek* covers will be to our advantage... Hollywood couldn't have manufactured a better story. If there was any hyping, it was the press hyping itself. All I did was co-ordinate it. They came to us."

It had been a long, hard drive. *Born To Run* finally transformed Springsteen from East Coast cult to world star, but there was a heavy price to pay. Aggrieved by the way Landau had muscled in, Appel decided to take legal action, which effectively kept Springsteen from releasing a follow-up for three long years.

Rock had never sounded more exultant and celebratory and joyous than it did when Bruce Springsteen drove off down 'Thunder Road' and exulted: "It's a town full of losers, and we're pulling out of here to win." The album had taken its toll, but "The Boss" had survived.

In the UK, *Born To Run* reached number 36 in the LP charts when released there in October, becoming Springsteen's first chart album. It made number three in the US.

All songs written by Bruce Springsteen.

Thunder Road

At one point Springsteen envisaged *Born To Run* as a – gulp – "concept album". It was scheduled to have a "day in the life" theme, beginning with an alarm clock and an acoustic version of 'Thunder Road', ending up late in the day with a full band version of the same song. Mercifully, wisdom prevailed, and the album kicks off with a full-throated rocker. Car imagery rampant, Springsteen tore into 'Thunder Road' with all the tenacity of a terrier with a leg of lamb. Performed at virtually every E Street Band show since its release, the version that found its way onto *Live 1975 – 85* was a stark, stripped-down version, with Springsteen accompanied only by Roy Bittan's mournful piano. The Roy Orbison homage in the first verse was a further testament to the influence on Springsteen's work of those who had gone before. 'Thunder Road' was also the title of a 1958 film about bootlegging starring Robert Mitchum.

Tenth Avenue Freeze-Out

One of those Big Apple melodramas that Springsteen can churn out by the yard. Strong-fisted brass from Clarence Clemons (whose joining the E Street Band features in the third verse), plus top-rated session men the Brecker brothers and saxophonist David Sanborn. The song reappeared regularly during the 1988 tour to promote *Tunnel Of Love*.

Night

Back on the road again, 'Night' has similarities with 'Factory' from Springsteen's follow-up album, *Darkness On The Edge Of Town*. Outside the factory gates, the only freedom lies in the highway, and the life lived outside working hours, managing to survive until the weekend. Indeed, many of the terms of reference here will figure again prominently in 'Darkness On The Edge Of Town'.

Backstreets

'Backstreets' is one of those big songs that fuel *Born To Run*. This was Springsteen writ large, the sort of rock'n'roll record that hadn't been heard on the airwaves since they had bounced off Phil Spector's Wall Of Sound a decade before. The piano and organ of Bittan (rescued from the pit orchestra of *Jesus Christ Superstar*) usher in Clemons' sultry saxophone and Springsteen's raw-throated vocal. All the Springsteen hallmarks are here: the intense infatuation, the precision of location, the street gangs, the loyalty, the cars... A storming version from his 1978 Roxy residency appears on *Live 1975 - 85*.

Born To Run

Springsteen's sole entry in *The Oxford Dictionary Of Modern Quotations*. In his own words: "My shot at the title. A 24-year-old kid aiming at 'the greatest rock'n'roll record ever.'"

'Born To Run' is probably still the one song most associated with Bruce Springsteen, although incredibly, in 1975, it only ever reached number 23 in the American charts. Allan Clarke of The Hollies made history – and the first cover of a song by Bruce Springsteen – when he recorded the song in 1974, a full year before Springsteen's own version. Frankie Goes To Hollywood recorded the song for their début album, *Welcome To The Pleasure Dome*. Springsteen returned to the song during his 1988 tour, performing it solo, slower and stripped down, a reflection, 13 years on, of the now married couple. It was this version that finally made its UK chart début in 1987.

Few rock'n'roll songs can match the exhilaration and the sheer, resurgent magnificence of 'Born To Run'. It is the ultimate song of escape, of liberation from life's weary tedium, with a simple, four-note octave riff that takes the towering chorus towards a delirious, unforgettable high. And nowhere in rock is there a count-in as uplifting as Springsteen's manic charge into the final verse after Clemons' solo.

In 1994, in a poll conducted by *The Times* and Radio One, 'Born To Run' was voted the greatest song of all time, just beating 'Like A Rolling Stone'. In an interview with Radio One's Trevor Dann, Springsteen remembered writing it in Long Branch in 1974. He also admitted that there was no such thing as a "drone". Looking back on the song as it appeared on the *Live 1975-85* box, Springsteen told Dave Marsh: "The most important thing is the question thrown back at 'Born To Run' – 'I wanna know if love is real?' And the answer is yes.

She's The One

Jerky and staccato, an early version of the song included lyrics that later wound up in 'Backstreets', as well as filching from Springsteen's own 'Hey Santa Anna'. Released as the B-side of the 'Tenth Avenue Freeze-Out' single, 'She's The One' is a love song of fierce, possessive intensity, even if it's not up there with the all-time-best-ever Springsteen songs. "I wrote 'She's The One' because I wanted to hear Clarence play the sax in that solo. I sort of went back and wrote the words to it just 'cos I wanted to hear that beat and hear Clarence play that."

Meeting Across The River

Springsteen goes out and plays with the gangsters. A hand-held, black-and-white, film noir account of life on the wrong side of the tracks. Lacking the urgency of Lou Reed's 'Waiting For The Man', 'Meeting Across The River' is nonetheless a more considered depiction of a drug deal. Instrumentally sparse and stripped down, 'Meeting Across The River' is another uncharacteristic Springsteen song. At least he had the courage to try something different, but file next to 'Wild Billy's Circus Story'.

Jungleland

The inherent strength of the song lies in Bittan's piano and Clemons' saxophone, the foundations of another great Springsteen epic. Following on from the characters introduced on 'Incident On 57th Street', 'Jungleland' is familiar Springsteen territory – sleek machines sprint across the New Jersey state line, midnight gangs assemble, guitars are flashed like switch-blade knives. But there is a loneliness at the heart of this togetherness. For all the florid romanticism, there is a weary resignation in Springsteen's voice as he revisits the divided turf of Romeo & Juliet. This was Springsteen's opera out on the Turnpike. Listen carefully and in 'Jungleland' you can hear the wide-screen, Wagnerian rock-opera concept of 'Bat Out Of Hell'.

FLEETWOOD MAC

Rumours

February 1977

By Rikky Rooksby

THE PRESSURE OF continuous touring to support Fleetwood Mac's first album together (released in 1975) created enormous personal stresses, the consequence of which was that the relationships within the band all seemed to be fracturing while they recorded the follow-up. No one was speaking to each other and life in the studio was very tense. Mick Fleetwood's wife, Jenny (sister of Patte Boyd, who married George Harrison and then Eric Clapton), left California and returned to England. Stevie Nicks and Lindsey Buckingham split, and Christine and John McVie had broken up on the road. This lent a somewhat bittersweet humour to the photos on the back sleeve of *Rumours*, which depict members of the band embracing as if no one can remember who goes with whom. The front cover reprised the mysterious sphere from the first album and the quaint theatrical trappings. Stevie Nicks was now in full flight as the winsome California fairy in ballet shoes and drapes, the result of her "Rhiannon" stage persona.

Producer Richard Dashut recalled, "The band brought some great songs with them, but they needed arrangements and a unified sound. All I can say is that it was trial-by-ordeal, and the craziest period of our lives. We went four or five weeks without sleep, doing a lot of drugs. I'm talking about cocaine in such quantities that at one point I thought I was really going insane. The whole atmosphere was really tense, with arguments all the time and people storming in and out. To relieve the tension we'd look for sexual release, but even that didn't help much... The only refuge was in the music... At one point, things got so tense between us all that I remember sleeping right under the soundboard one night because I felt it was the only safe place to be."

In his account of the band's history, Mick Fleetwood says that "everyone made tremendous emotional sacrifices just to show up at the studio".

Recording took place at the Record Plant in Sausalito, California, and proceedings were apparently hampered by a number of unwelcome phenomena, including a tape machine that chewed up tapes, a piano that didn't want to be tuned even after four days (they tried nine pianos and eventually gave up on the idea), and a large number of sightseers who came over when word got out that Fleetwood Mac were recording there. The band would spend several days trying to get a drum sound for one track. Away from Sausalito the tapes sounded horrible, and the band ended up re-recording all the parts. A potentially lucrative spring tour in 1976 had to be cancelled (despite the success of 'Rhiannon', which had been released as a single) because the album was not completed to the perfectionist requirements of the musicians. The band had 10 days' rehearsal in June for a summer tour and hit the road.

The album was recorded under the working title *Yesterday's Dreams*, but John McVie changed it to *Rumours*. It sold a million copies in the first month of release, went on to top 20 million sales, spent 31 consecutive weeks at number one, and – has become one of the all-time best-selling albums. It spent an amazing 400 weeks in the UK Top 100. How can such success be explained?

Rumours had a commercial set of songs in a melodic soft-rock, radio-friendly vein. It had guitar solos that never outstayed their welcome, "unplugged" acoustic moments of crystal clarity, West Coast breezy harmonies in the grand Beach Boys/Mamas and the Papas/Eagles tradition, and three distinctive, strong lead voices. With a mix of male and female singers, the band could avoid drawing an audience biased towards one gender or the other. It was a 12-inch soap opera: given the treatment of the relationship themes, there was something to which everyone could relate. *Rumours* was a cut diamond with a thousand facets. However you held it up to the light, a glint would catch your eye. And breaking up never sounded so musical.

One odd track from the sessions, Nicks' 'Silver Springs', was held over and put on the B-side of 'Go Your Own Way'.

A deluxe version of the album (Warner Bros 8122-73882-2) was released in 2004 and contains 'Silver Springs', together with the following extra tracks on a second CD divided into two parts, 'Roughs and Out-takes' and 'Early Demos': 'Second Hand News', 'Dreams', 'Brushes (Never Going Back Again)', 'Don't Stop', 'Go Your Own Way', 'Songbird', 'Silver Springs',

'You Make Loving Fun', 'Gold Dust Woman #1', 'Oh Daddy', 'Think About It'; 'Never Going Back Again', 'Planets Of The Universe', 'Butter Cookie (Keep Me There)', 'Gold Dust Woman', 'Doesn't Anything Last', [Jam sessions] 'Mic The Screecher', 'For Duster (The Blues)'.

Rumours is also available as a DVD-A with 'Silver Springs' included, and there is a DVD documentary about the LP in the *Classic Albums* series (WEA/Rhino 1998).

Second Hand News

(Buckingham)

Rumours kicks off with this jaunty, acoustic-driven upbeat number, in which Nicks supplies the backing vocal and Buckingham plays sprightly harmonics on an open-tuned guitar. The image of "going down in the long grass" to "let me do my stuff" struck an erotic chord and made it a great party record. There's almost a jug-band quality to this. The title may have suggested that the singer was down and out but the mood was buoyant, and faded out on a few seconds of guitar lead. Short'n'sweet.

Dreams

(Nicks)

In which our Lindsey gains the coveted Peter Green award for gallant guitar conduct. This is Buckingham's finest hour as a guitarist, using a volume pedal on his lead fills to produce a moody accompaniment to Nicks' tale of what happens to those who make decisions they regret. The whole track is based on a mere three chords climbing up and back. There's a hint of strings, strummed acoustic, and John McVie is rock-steady on bass throughout. The lyrics allude back to the vision of 'Crystal' on the previous album, and the image of the players picks up the imagery of the theatre suggested by the sleeve. The essential ambiguity of the song lies in whether the singer is addressing herself in a mood of self-recrimination and weary wisdom, or whether she is addressing someone else and suppressing a whole ocean of grief. The line about being washed clean by the rain that appears at the end was another of those universal motifs that appeal to everyone. Romantic disenchantment is the best disenchantment of all.

'Dreams' ends on a high string note and a chilling couple of notes from Buckingham. One of the few tracks by the later Fleetwood Mac that approach the intensity of the best of the Peter Green era.

Never Going Back Again
(Buckingham)

This is a brief acoustic interlude fingerpicked for a folk feel. The guitars are capoed high for additional brightness, with occasional vocal lines from Buckingham and a little vocal support from the others. Once more, the lyrics are enigmatic: what was it that the singer was never going back to again? Buckingham was able to make good capital out of this live.

Don't Stop
(C. McVie)

Piano, strings and a gradual drum build-up establish an intense rocking dance track that can't fail to get the feet moving, and conveys an optimistic sentiment of looking forward to a better future. The vocal is shared between Christine McVie and Buckingham, who take a verse each and share the brilliantly catchy chorus. Buckingham turns in a neat economic solo in the middle just to spice things up. There are nice touches to the arrangement like the sudden stop towards the end; the repeated guitar note; and the occasional touches of honky-tonk piano. The coda fades on the advice, "Don't you look back".

John McVie: "I'd be sitting there in the studio while they were mixing 'Don't Stop', and I'd listen to the words which were mostly about me, and I'd get a lump in my throat. I'd turn around, and the writer's sitting right there."

As well as being the third single to be taken from the album, peaking at number three on the *Billboard* singles chart, the song is one of Mac's most enduring hits, used by US presidential candidate Bill Clinton for his first campaign. Upon winning the election, President Clinton persuaded the then-disbanded group to re-form to perform it at his inaugural ball in 1993.

Go Your Own Way
(Buckingham)

The tempo is sustained with this track, driven by a powerful drum rhythm during the verse. The chorus breaks into standard rock drumming and brings in the others for the harmony on the hook. There's some strong electric rhythm, and the mood see-saws between the promise of the verse – the singer offering his lover the whole world – and the chorus, which expresses the pain of telling her to go her own way and suffer the consequence of another lonely day. Buckingham builds the coda's intensity through a neat guitar solo, which slowly increases in pitch. It was obvious that this – probably the rockiest number on Rumours – would be a very strong number in the live set.

Songbird
(C. McVie)

To get this exquisite take, the band took a mobile into an empty auditorium at Berkeley University. Fleetwood said, "It should sound like Christine is sitting alone at the piano after a concert, when everyone has gone home." That was exactly how it came out. The rock of the previous two songs gives way to this beautiful, plaintive track with piano and chorus. The lyrics are generous and melancholy.

McVie sings to a departed lover, promising never to be cold, for love is both sharper and deeper even though the songbirds know the score – an effective use of a colloquial word in this context. There's an emotional simplicity and depth here, and the song is almost classically controlled in the way she decides to end the track without going for the obvious heart-wrenching twists. As a result it has dignity under pressure, and nothing of the fey romanticism that often weakens Nicks' songs. Christine's Perfect Hour.

The Chain

(Buckingham/McVie/Nicks/Fleetwood/McVie)

'The Chain' was created by splicing tapes of several different bits of music together. This is the only fully collaborative effort on the album, starting with some bluesy guitar, a bass thump and distant harmonised vocals. When the first chorus comes in, there's some lovely keyboard in the background and an effective vocal arrangement, where the hook line is echoed first by Nicks and then much higher with reverb by McVie.

The lyrics give open expression to hurt and pain in the "damn your love, damn your lies" lines. The sentiment is a powerful one. Once you said you would never break things up – but you did. There's a brief pause before McVie enters with a memorable bass riff, which became famous in the UK in the Nineties when it was used as the theme for televised Formula One Grand Prix racing.

Buckingham winds things up with a solo in the Neil Young mode of seeing how much mileage you can get out of a couple of notes. The band then bring in another harmony vocal hook. The lyric expresses the idea that the chain has become a way of linking lovers and is no bad thing, but, on a broader allegorical level, it could refer to the unbroken chain of circumstance that has held Fleetwood Mac together through thick and thin since their inception in 1967.

You Make Loving Fun

(C. McVie)

A phased electric piano gives this track a funky feel, despite the minor-chord opening. Christine McVie takes the vocal on a lyric that tells of fun, but the musical setting digs a bit deeper. The chorus features stunning vocal harmony arrangements, adding a ghostly back-up and some brilliant guitar work from Buckingham, who hits just the right notes quietly in the background of the verse and then comes in with a fine melodic solo after the first chorus. Equally great is his repeated guitar phrase at the back of the chorus. McVie's vocal on the last verse suggests she's trying to win back her man. The ending of the song is deeply plaintive, with the massed harmonies in counterpoint with some extraordinary lead guitar by Buckingham, who shows a wonderful melodic ear here.

I Don't Want To Know
(Nicks)

Acoustic guitars start off this dead-ringer-for-Cat-Stevens until the vocals come in, shared by Nicks and Buckingham. This is a simple, sprightly, uptempo, three-chord major song with hand claps, some nice touches and a simple, tight bass line. It sounds more upbeat than the lyric probably suggests, though the general state is one of confusion. Buckingham comes up trumps again on the guitar solo, making use of the top string as a pedal note while the other note moves around.

Oh Daddy
(C. McVie)

Written for Mick Fleetwood, the only father in the band, this opens very quietly with a synth-flute sound and two acoustic guitars, before the doomy first piano chord. In a lyric that speaks of mistakes made and regretted, Christine McVie admits that he's right and she's wrong. There are some stirring moments of sudden accented chords, John McVie's bass line moves around in a pleasing manner and there are nice guitar touches. The mood is not quite as naked as 'Songbird', but has instead a tone of self-criticism in a restrained performance and arrangement.

Gold Dust Woman
(Nicks)

There's a fade-in to this track with some strange, throaty, sitar-like sounds accompanying the acoustic guitars. It's another subtle arrangement, patient in the way in which it builds but lacking the atmosphere of 'Rhiannon'. Nicks uses her fey rapid vibrato, and is joined by Christine McVie and Buckingham on the chorus harmony. The lyric seems to issue a warning, anticipating the feel of Nicks' solo material. At one point there's a patented banshee wail by Nicks, dropping down the notes, leading to the coda, which sees her indulging her taste for the gothic by singing about black widows. This was take eight of a night's long, arduous recording session, and doesn't have the emotional or commercial appeal of some of the other tracks.

The Clash

April 1977

By Tony Fletcher

ECORDED AND MIXED in three sessions of four days apiece in February 1977, *The Clash* is more than just the definitive punk-rock statement; it's also one of the most exciting and enduring debut albums in rock'n'roll.

The primary reason for its immediate appeal is relatively obvious: there had never been anything like it before. The previous year, The Ramones' debut album had influenced British punks (including The Clash) with its speaker-shattering, stripped-down simplicity, but much of its sensationalism was wrapped in direct humour, and the New York band made no attempt to anger the political establishment. *The Clash*, on the other hand, from violent sleeve imagery through provocative song titles, presented itself as nothing less than a call to musical and class warfare. Rock fans up and down Great Britain, tired of aloof heroes playing elaborate compositions in vast seated halls – and these fans were often the same young people struggling with the monotony of school, or to find meaningful employment in an increasingly depressed economy – discovered with delight that *The Clash* spoke for them, as opposed to them.

Criticism from "elders" and "betters" only endorsed the record's appeal. For the thousands captivated by *The Clash*, the apparent repetition of subject matter served to render the largely unintelligible words emotionally coherent as a whole; the violent stance reflected in titles like 'Hate And War', 'White Riot' and 'London's Burning' was matched by a contagious emotional energy, the embodiment of punk's purist promise; the lack of musical skill served not as deterrent but inspiration for all who had previously cowed in respect to mid-Seventies guitar gods and their supernatural solos. *The Clash* set children against parents, pupils against teachers, even siblings against siblings. The Clash as a group often spoke of society in terms of "Us Against Them"; *The Clash* as an album delivered on that divide.

The reasons for the album's longevity lie just beneath the surface of its supposed simplicity. Though it was presented partly as a reaction to the overblown prog-rock operas of the mid-Seventies, *The Clash* was very much a concept album. The group members were frequently criticised for overstating their supposed social disenfranchisement, and it's true that they rewrote their personal histories to avoid any suggestion of prior security or comfort. But it's the very fact that they stepped beyond personal experience to speak, not just for themselves, but in the voice of the ultimate urban outcast, that renders the lyrics so eternally effective.

Mick Jones said in an interview, shortly before the group signed their record deal with CBS, "These songs couldn't be written in any other year," and he was right. Mark P, founder of punk fanzine *Sniffin' Glue*, then wrote of those songs, as they were heard on *The Clash*, that, "It's like watching my life in a movie." And he was right. *The Clash* will forever tell the story of the desperate, repressed young white male in the faltering, fragmented England of 1977 — and precisely because, in its nihilism, it dares not look further ahead than the present moment, it's never lost its impact as a cultural statement.

Musically too, *The Clash* is more sophisticated than originally perceived. Having unloaded their two most overtly voluminous and confrontational songs for their debut single, the group were now free to record those numbers that had real hooks, proper bridges, genuine choruses. That they downplayed any pop sensibility with vocal shouts, amplified feedback and atonal guitar solos have failed to prevent the tracks standing the test of time as great songs, pure and simple.

Finally, and crucially, *The Clash* embraced variety. It's there in the 13 Strummer-Jones compositions for those who have listened to *The Clash* often enough, but it's most pronounced in the six-minute rendition of Junior Murvin's 'Police And Thieves'. The Clash's audacious adaptation of this reggae number separated them from other punk groups, who wouldn't dare to (or more likely, simply couldn't) play black music, and hinted at future musical evolution. The Clash, both the group and the album, refused to be confined to the sound of the white riot.

Terry Chimes, who refused a full-time role due to philosophical differences, played drums on all 14 songs. He's credited, with more humour than malice, as Tory Crimes. Production is credited to Mickey Foote. The uncredited engineer was Simon Humphreys. CBS Records deserves credit for staying out of the studio, though that was not entirely altruistic: the album had barely been released before the label started trying to dictate proceedings. The American arm of CBS, meanwhile, in a magnified display of myopia, "passed" on the album. The Clash nonetheless seeped, and eventually flooded, into the States as an import, by which process it sold an unprecedented 100,000 copies. In the UK, The Clash was, for all its confrontational stance, a considerable commercial success, spending much of 1977 in the album charts and peaking at number 12.

All songs written by The Clash unless otherwise indicated.

Janie Jones

The opening song on The Clash features almost all the album's familiar ingredients: staccato guitars, lo-fi drums and bass, a chorus half-sung and half-shouted in three-person unison, and largely indiscernible lyrics. (On closer examination, the words glorify "rock'n'roll" and "getting stoned" from the perspective of a frustrated office employee, whose sexual relief is to be found with the title character.) Mick Jones' phonetic harmony towards the end of the two-minute anthem is the first appearance of a particularly popular and enduring Clash trademark.

Jones had originally written 'Janie Jones' in the first person, on the number 31 bus from his Westbourne Grove home to the band's Camden Town rehearsals, but Strummer balked at singing "I'm in love" with anyone. The perspective was switched to the third person − "He's in love with Janie Jones" − and the song's prominent placement as opening track suggests that the group recognised its atypical approach.

The real-life Janie Jones was a madam who had been British front-page newspaper fodder back in 1973. But by the time of the song's release, The Clash were attracting such a young audience that many didn't understand the reference. In that sense, too, 'Janie Jones' is something of an anomaly on an album that is otherwise very much rooted in the social maelstrom of urban Britain, 1976-77.

Remote Control

Written, primarily, by Mick Jones, following the farcical Anarchy In The UK tour of December 1976. The Clash had set off with The Sex Pistols, The Damned and, from New York, The Heartbreakers, on a schedule of 19 shows intended to introduce the nation to some new, streetwise rock'n'roll. On the eve of the tour, The Sex Pistols had their infamous expletive-ridden run-in with Bill Grundy on live TV, which provoked media hysteria and encouraged local councils to ban almost all the concerts under the pathetic pretence of "protecting" their constituents. The Sex Pistols rarely played in Britain again.

But 'Remote Control' cast a wider net than the "civic hall", complaining also about the lack of options in London after the pubs shut at 11 each night, and throwing in a veiled reference to the EMI board meeting after which that label dropped The Sex Pistols from its roster. That is on the occasions when the words can be heard: Strummer and Jones alternate vocals here, and prove that poor pronunciation was a band trait. Strummer defended the group's diction in an interview at the time of the album's release, stating, "Our music is like Jamaican stuff – if they can't hear it, they're not supposed to hear it. It's not for them if they can't understand it." 'Remote Control' is the only song on the album not to take any possessive perspective, which might explain its placement directly after 'Janie Jones'. From here on, all Strummer-Jones compositions on The Clash are sung in the first person.

Despite its sharp lyrics, 'Remote Control' betrays its relative youth with a hackneyed, glam-like opening riff, an uninspired guitar solo and tame drumming. That it was the softest song on the album naturally inspired CBS to release it as the album's second single, against the band's wishes and despite their belief that their contract granted them "complete control." The 'Remote Control' single (backed by a "live" rendition of 'London's Burning', in fact, recorded for a promo film) was a commercial failure, partly because The Clash urged their fans not to buy it.

I'm So Bored With The U.S.A.

Originally titled 'I'm So Bored With You', Mick Jones' long-standing anti-love song was quickly turned into an anti-American rant when Joe Strummer joined the group. The lyrics are quite advanced for supposed anti-intellectuals, aiming barbs at military adventurism (Cambodia), Washington intrigue (Watergate) and cultural imperialism (*Kojak*).

When The Clash embarked on a mutual love affair with America only a year after the album's release, they attempted to downplay the song's intent, though the lyrics were so direct there was little wriggle room. In reality, there was no need to apologise for directing some of their considerable anger in such an obvious direction, and American youth demonstrated equal ambivalence towards the USA by lapping up *The Clash* in those unprecedented import numbers.

'I'm So Bored' is driven by a singalong chorus, constant bass notes and a succession of hard-hitting guitar riffs – a perfect punk anthem. Throughout the album, the rhythm guitars are "hard-panned" (one to the left speaker, one to the right); this is the first number in which the effect is clearly in evidence.

White Riot

A different mix than the single; thicker, more dense, with the vocal pushed up front for once, and notably absent are the various sound effects. It all serves to render the song yet harder and more violent, the most uncompromising aural assault on the album.

Hate & War

Joe Strummer, 24 at time of *The Clash's* release, was old enough to remember the late-Sixties hippy ethos of "love and peace". He inverted it for this statement of mid-Seventies reality, which he then painted on the back of his boiler-suit jacket for emphasis. Many in The Clash's audience, too young to make the hippy connection, simply understood 'Hate & War' as an accurate summation of the world in which they were living. Mick Jones ended up singing lead on one of the album's most musically commercial yet lyrically nihilistic numbers, wherein the singer stubbornly refuses to quit town and instead promises to meet violence with more of the same. The wonderful crack in Jones' voice as he reaches for the high notes offsets the unfortunate closing reference to getting "beat up by any kebab Greek".

What's My Name
(Strummer-Jones-Levine)

The first Clash line-up temporarily included a third guitarist, Keith Levine (sometimes spelled Levene), who would later play in Johnny Rotten's post-Pistols band Public Image Limited. Levine's sole song-writing credit from his Clash period is 'What's My Name', which he shares with Strummer and Jones. (Paul Simonon, who came up with the band name shortly after Strummer joined, was still struggling to learn bass as The Clash was recorded, and therefore not granted any songwriting royalties.)

The lyrics of 'What's My Name' can be seen either as fictional Clash self-glorification, or as an example of the narrative being projected beyond group experience to represent that of society's real outcast. Either way, with its propelling tom-tom drums, phonetic harmonies, use of the f-word and simplistic singalong chorus, 'What's My Name' sounds like it was designed for the football terraces. In reality, and for all of Simonon's dressed-up past as a Chelsea skinhead, there was almost no interaction between punk rockers and football fans in 1977.

Deny

A "love song" of sorts for punks, in which the narrator forgoes traditional romance and admiration to accuse his girlfriend of deceit and deception. There's a reference to the 100 Club, home base for punk gigs at the time of the song's writing, and a none-too-subtle accusation of drug addiction. Vocal "oohs" and guitar riffs reminiscent of Mick Jones' early Seventies heroes Mott The Hoople reveal The Clash's commercial influences, while Strummer's vocal performance is among his most urgent on the album. As pure a pop song as anything on *The Clash*.

London's Burning

Written from the perspective of the 18th-floor balcony at Wilmcote House, the tower block overlooking the Westway where Mick Jones lived with his grandmother during the early days of The Clash – but then actually composed by Strummer in near-silence in his own squat while his girlfriend, Palmolive of The Slits, slept in the same room.

'London's Burning' is often considered of a pair with 'White Riot': each song places itself in west London, cementing the group's association with the Notting Hill and Ladbroke Grove neighbourhoods, and each expresses dissatisfaction with these surroundings through shouted choruses, crude verses and the barest of melodies, lending themselves to instant punk anthem status. Yet 'London's Burning' is also a companion to 'I'm So Bored With The U.S.A.', and as with that song's vast target, The Clash were in fact using "boredom" to mask an obsession.

Listen again and it's obvious that The Clash are genuinely excited by London's burning boredom. (Perhaps because, they grasped, they could now do something about it?) For all these reasons, 'London's Burning', though too musically simplistic to age well, would remain close to the group's heart, its title and imagery reworked through much Clash and post-Clash material.

Career Opportunities

For the three core members of The Clash, all of whom were on the dole through much of 1975 and '76, unemployment was a matter of choice: they viewed the meagre weekly dole cheque as the natural successor to their art-school grants. But as they discovered when they began playing in the north of England, employment was a matter of pride for many in the real working class, and the few low-end jobs on offer did nothing to inspire anyone's confidence in government policies as jobless numbers rose to figures unknown since the Thirties. (And then, in the Eighties under Margaret Thatcher, rose beyond them.)

'Career Opportunities', then, is one of those songs in which The Clash project themselves through their own experiences, and then descend down the food chain until they're representing the desperate man at the very bottom of the pile. He shares with The Clash a refusal to take the crap jobs – despite a final recognition that he may have "no choice" – and it's this defiance that marks 'Career Opportunities' as such an emphatic, enduring protest anthem.

Bolstered by Mick Jones' power chords, which owe much here to Pete Townshend's rhythmic style of playing, Strummer's voice is mixed high, as if this one time he wants every word to be clearly understood. The dropped "t's" on the phrase "let'er bombs" and a shouted "Oi!" perhaps over-play his narrator's working-class roots, but they may also be intended to downplay the song's commercial foundations. 'Career Opportunities' follows a classic pop pattern – intro, verse, chorus, verse, chorus, middle eight, verse, chorus, outro – all completed several seconds' shy of two minutes. Its prominent placement as opening track on Side two provides confirmation of the group's own belief in the track.

Cheat

Written during rehearsals for the album, 'Cheat' continued the nihilistic message of 'Hate & War'; taken together, the songs suggest The Clash's punk vision as inherently negative and violent. It's also worth noting that 'Cheat' encourages people to "learn how to lie" while, earlier in the album, the song 'Deny' berates a girlfriend for doing just that. But this is only a career contradiction for those who would assume every lyric to mirror Strummer and Jones' personal intent; from the perspective of the album's narrator, the dichotomy is part of his frustrating everyday life. A particularly strong middle eight leads into an extended back-to-basics Jones solo, bolstered by phased rhythm guitars that continue into a rare fade-out.

Protex Blue

Mick Jones sings lead on his only pre-Strummer song to make it to *The Clash* unaltered. As was the guitarist's particular punk skill, it's an anti-love song, concerning the era's predominant condom of the title. There's no sense of political correctness about using protection, just a typical male acknowledgement that, "I didn't want to hold you". (And a final verse in which the Protex has become the singer's sexual accompaniment for the night.) Stereo separation of both guitars, drums, classic Clash vocal harmonies, and a guitar solo all of four seconds long do much to propel the song beyond the ordinary.

Police & Thieves
(Murvin-Perry)

In 1976, with punk yet to make it onto record, Britain's only contemporary rebel music was Jamaican reggae. Given that both Simonon and Jones had roots in the heavily West Indian south London community around Brixton, and that all three members had moved into the similarly Caribbean-dominated Notting Hill, it's hardly surprising that the group lapped up reggae singles with almost as much enthusiasm as the local Rastafarians did. One of them was Junior Murvin's 'Police & Thieves', co-written by that singer with producer Lee Perry, which became a big reggae hit that summer, peaking at the Notting Hill Carnival, where it gained extra credence given the subsequent riot.

By the end of the year, The Clash were trying to turn a Bob Marley B-side, 'Dancing Shoes', into a punk song, but occasionally played 'Police & Thieves' for fun – and when Mick Jones had Strummer strike a power chord on the down beat, leaving himself free to accentuate the more familiar reggae up beat, the group succeeded in creating their own distinct version. It was soon worked up into a six-minute epic.

On record, the pared-down rhythm affords the kick drum

rare prominence; the group prove adept at instrumental drop-outs, as already practised on their own material, and the deliberately thin Mick Jones solo, repeating the melody of the verse, is a moment of back-to-basics punk genius. It all builds through a lengthy second half with unmistakably white rage.

"It was punk reggae, not white reggae," Strummer later observed. "We were bringing some of our roots to it." More than that, the recording served to drastically shift the mood of the album at the very moment it could have been written off as monochromatic; it formed a perfect counterpart to 'White Riot' and it helped bring the length of the finished record well above 30 minutes. More than anything, it demonstrated that punk's love of reggae was more than mere lip service, and influenced a number of white groups, young and old, to try incorporating black music into their repertoire.

The crossover success of The Police, the 2Tone label and British reggae acts like Steel Pulse and Aswad can all be traced back to this song. The favour was returned almost immediately in highly appropriate fashion, when Lee Perry wrote and produced a B-side for the new Bob Marley single, 'Jamming', called 'Punky Reggae Party'. It included the line "The Wailers will be there, The Damned, The Jam, The Clash..."

48 Hours

Another song written close to completion of the album, '48 Hours' offers an echo to the last sharp British street movement, the mods of the Sixties and their focus on the weekend. Again, The Clash were not singing from their own experience – as dole-queue veterans, they hardly knew where the working week ended and the weekend started – but from that of their audience, the same frustrated, lowly office employee of 'Janie Jones', screaming for his "48 Thrills".

Unstated in the song except in its frantic pace (96 seconds, the shortest song on the album) is the fact that punks, like mods before them, lived largely on amphetamine, and that it was not uncommon for bands and audience alike to stay up for 48 hours straight. It seems appropriate, then, that Jones claims the song was written in just half an hour, and it's worth noting that, in December 1978, he claimed, "I was so into speed, I don't even recall making the first album!"

Garageland

The final song on *The Clash* was also the last to be written. Significantly, it's the first occasion whereby The Clash sing about themselves as a band. Soon enough, this would become their calling card, an unfortunate inversion of the "everyman" persona that dominates the debut album. At the time of 'Garageland' the self-mythologising had yet to fully take hold, so while the inspiration for the song was personal – a damning review in NME by Charles Shaar Murray that concluded of The Clash, "They are the type of garage band who should be speedily returned to the garage, preferably with the motor running" – the lyric was broadened to include every band that ever aspired to make a noise for the sheer gleeful hell of it. ("Twenty two singers! But one microphone!")

With the twin guitars (again hard-panned) drenched in reverb, and Jones contributing occasional harmonica, one of the album's strongest melodies finds Strummer referring to the group's major record deal but, crucially, without the details that would have rendered the song specific to The Clash alone. Instead, in the final verse Strummer venomously disassociates himself from "the rich". Those who found this amusing given his father's diplomatic status and his public schooling perhaps missed the point. No one has a say in how they are born, but everyone has a say in how they choose to live as adults. Strummer had long ago made that choice, and on 'Garageland' he appears to be inviting every other dissatisfied middle – and upper-class kid to follow his lead, leave home and come join The Clash's revolution.

Many would heed the call and, though some would come to question their leaders' own allegiance, as its own answer to the album's unstated but constantly suggested question, "Which side are you on?", 'Garageland' provides *The Clash* with the perfect finale.

THE SEX PISTOLS

Never Mind The Bollocks, Here's The Sex Pistols

October 1977
21st Anniversary Edition in book cover
with photo booklet, released 1998

By Mark Paytress

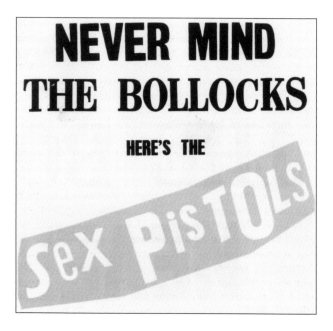

THOUGH IT'S BEEN reissued in countless editions, the latest, 21st-anniversary package of *Never Mind The Bollocks...*, coming with a booklet of vintage photographs and a disc cut from the original 1977 analogue master, is as good a place to begin as any. For this is the one and only album issued by the Pistols during their brief, momentous career. Including all four of the band's original A-sides, it's The Sex Pistols in a nutshell: everything else is decoration.

At least that's the theory. In fact, *Never Mind The Bollocks...* endured a difficult birth, and the results weren't always to the band's, or their original fans', satisfaction. That's why the group's early demos are so coveted. Whereas *Bollocks* was essentially a compromise between anthemic glam rock and riffing hard rock, the band's earlier, earthier studio excursions were ballsy, raw and ragged and, for many, represent the true sound of The Sex Pistols.

Rotten himself has fanned much of the anti-*Bollocks* feeling. Discussing the Pistols' legacy in December 1978, he said: "Fatty [guitarist Steve Jones] would lay down 21 guitar solos. That was nauseous. I didn't like the sound of that album. Well old-fashioned... I'd be left there making sure Chris Thomas didn't fuck us up and make us sound like Roxy Music and then find out that was exactly how Steve and

Paul wanted us to sound. So I'd completely fuck-up the mix and make it sound like a rock album should. The result was that Malcolm, Paul and Steve would sneak in the next day while I was asleep and remix it and not say anything. I won on 'Problems', 'Submission' and 'Bodies'... none of the others could even be bothered to listen to 'Bodies'."

Years later, in his autobiography, *Rotten: No Irish, No Blacks, No Dogs*, he'd changed his mind: "Chris Thomas did a hilariously good job as producer of *Never Mind The Bollocks*. I liked the idea of using him because I liked Roxy Music, although I knew we would never sound anything like them."

The group started work on the album in January 1977. By the time the final touches were being added in September, they were with a different record company, had a new bassist and had created sufficient interest to notch up healthy pre-sales orders of 125,000 copies. Inevitably the album debuted at number one in the UK LP chart. Less expected, though, was its enduring privileged place in rock history. In 1987, the mildly conservative US magazine *Rolling Stone* voted it number two in its greatest rock'n'roll album listing, and it's barely come down since.

Apart from the four singles, which were recorded when necessary, much of *Never Mind The Bollocks...* was taped at Wessex Studios with Chris Thomas and his assistant, Bill Price, during March and April 1977. By late June, a title, *God Save The Sex Pistols*, had been chosen and the running order was as follows: 'Seventeen', 'New York', 'Pretty Vacant', 'Holidays In The Sun', 'EMI (Unlimited Edition)', 'Liar', 'Problems', 'Anarchy In The UK', 'Submission', 'No Feelings' and 'Satellite'. With typical contrariness, it had been decided not to include the title track (of sorts), 'God Save The Queen'. (The Jamie Reid artwork for this proposed album is reproduced in the booklet of the new edition, alongside other variations.)

It appears that indecision gripped the project right up until the last minute, which was why the first 10,000 copies of the record include 11 tracks sequenced differently, with a 12th, 'Submission', slipped in as a one-sided 45 at the last minute.

A popular misconception about the album – and the band – is that Sid Vicious was a fully functioning member and perhaps second-in-command after Johnny Rotten. In fact, as Steve Jones and others have since confirmed, his contribution to this album was virtually nil – Jones recalls Sid playing bass on 'God Save The Queen' and 'Bodies', but he also remembers his lines being so inadequate that he had to overdub them himself. Although Glen Matlock had left the band before the bulk of the album was recorded, it's commonly assumed that he deputised as a session bassist on several songs.

The controversies don't stop there. Upon the album's release, on October 28, 1977, shops displaying the sleeve in their windows were prosecuted, prompting a court ruling on whether the word "bollocks" was indecent. Apparently, it wasn't, but that didn't prevent high-street shops like Woolworths, Boots and W. H. Smith from banning it.

Holidays In The Sun
(Jones, Cook, Rotten, Vicious)

By confronting taboos and courting controversy, punk invested rock music with an incendiary cultural effect that had been lost since the panics surrounding drugs, permissiveness and student revolution of the late Sixties. The swastika, the symbol that acts like a sore on the 20th century's other-wise smug notion of irreversible progress, became part of punk's armoury in its bid to court outrage. Designer Vivienne Westwood incorporated it into her designs, Siouxsie Sioux and Sid Vicious were widely photographed wearing swastika armbands, and the insignia appeared on many customised T-shirts during 1976 and 1977. The appropriation of this symbol of mass conformity was partly ironic, partly dumb: both appeared to be valid responses for a generation unwilling to pick up the pieces for the mistakes of their forebears.

Some commentators initially tried to label the band as leaders of a new "race hate" cult, but this failed to stick. The Sex Pistols had a Jewish manager, a reggae-obsessed frontman, and a mission to pierce the heart of conformist culture. By the time of their fourth single, 'Holidays In The Sun', in October 1977, several members of the group and its entourage had felt the full force of a media-inspired backlash that compelled young men of a pro-nationalist persuasion to attack them with knives and iron bars.

'Holidays In The Sun', written in Berlin during March, likened the popular penchant for package holidays to a trip to Belsen ("A cheap holiday in other people's misery!" was one of Rotten's finest vignettes), and the Nazi references continued with the sound of marching jackboots at the start of the song, and a "rea-son" chorus sung in the manner of a "Sieg Heil!" cry.

The object of Rotten's displeasure was exactly that kind of docile, conformist culture that provides fertile ground for fascist ideology to take root. But, as the Berlin trip proved, the working-class boy from Islington was hardly enamoured of this century's other great ideology, communism, either, describing those who lived east of the Berlin Wall as "down-trodden, dull, grey, military-minded bastards who live thoroughly miserable lives." Party politics existed outside Rotten's and, by proxy, The Sex Pistols' world view ("I don't understand this thing at all"). The Berlin Wall, the song's central motif, might have been where capitalism met communism head-on, but 'Holidays In The Sun' was less concerned with the battle between the two great ideologies than with the concept of the Wall as metaphor for the authoritarian boundaries found in any political system.

The most alarming aspect of 'Holidays In The Sun' was its reliance on a riff that sounded remarkably similar to that of 'In The City', released earlier that year by new wave retro-rockers The Jam. This didn't go unnoticed by the critics, who inferred that Glen Matlock's departure in the spring might have left the band wanting in the songwriting department. Something else that was soon picked up on was the sleeve, a witty Jamie Reid collage based on a brochure issued by the Belgian Travel Service; 60,000 copies of the single were hastily recalled to avoid a copyright infringement case. The single, which found Rotten's laughably exaggerated vocal hurtling towards self-parody and Steve Jones making up for the Jam riff with a head-drilling, Johnny Thunders-style guitar break, still managed a number eight chart placing.

'Holidays In The Sun', first attempted in the studio in May, was finally nailed at Wessex Studios on 18 June.

Bodies

(Jones/Cook/Rotten/Vicious)

Much of The Sex Pistols' work can be heard as an antidote to the Sixties "love-is-all-you-need" dream – which looked rather more misguided in 1976 than it had done back in the late Sixties. The Beautiful People, who once shed their clothes to reveal skin painted in exotic designs and colours, had grown old and jaded. Some had even died in their reckless pursuit of happiness. Few, barring a handful who fled to set up communes in the Welsh hills, were willing to countenance pipe dreams any longer. The generosity of spirit that had compelled a generation to explore the deepest recesses of its collective mind had given way to a new, more tangible concern for exteriors.

David Bowie showed the way: never mind who you might think you are, the only thing you can be certain about is the reality of the façade you present to the world. Punk took this a stage further, so that the façade resembled an authentic statement of the wider reality. A safety pin through the cheek said much about the nation's mid-Seventies self-loathing. And so, in a way, did 'Bodies', the fastest song The Sex Pistols ever recorded.

Song titles were crucial to the Pistols' oeuvre. In punk's harsh searchlight, we were in truth no more than "bodies", a functional conglomeration of skin, blood and bone that ate, fucked and died. And for every beautiful baby born into the world, another was being aborted. A popular piece of mythology that seemed to sprout up in every town during the punk era was the tale of the local punkette who'd arrive at gigs with an aborted foetus in her bag. Such tales inevitably got back to the Pistols camp, and provided Johnny Rotten – whose Catholic upbringing must have made him particularly sensitive to the subject – with the narrative for this most graphic of Sex Pistols songs.

Pauline, the "girl from Birmingham" in the song, was an avid follower of the band (and, it is said, an intimate of Steve Jones) who'd spent time in an asylum. She, too, had spun the "abortion" tale, and was once reputed to have turned up at Rotten's front door. The singer embellished the tale, darting cleverly from first to third person during the song, before its anguished, possibly anti-abortion concluding cry of "I'm not an animal... Mummy!"

But what ensured the song's immortality, both among fans and detractors, were the five "fucks" in the third verse. According to Tory MP Norman St. John Stevas, 'Bodies' "... is the kind of music that is a symptom of the way society is declining. It could have a shocking effect on young people." Jones and Cook might well have agreed, but for entirely different reasons, when they later cited it as their favourite Sex Pistols song. The fact that the Pistols kicked off their 1996 Filthy Lucre reunion shows with 'Bodies' confirms its exalted status.

'Bodies' was the last bona fide (i.e. Rotten) Sex Pistols studio recording, having been taped at the final *Bollocks* album session at Wessex Studios in August 1977. It was also one of just two songs to feature Vicious – although his bass-playing is tellingly low in the mix. The performance, the band's first studio work since escaping the 'God Save The Queen' backlash by touring Scandinavia, is suitably venomous, though the band were unable to premiere it live until December.

No Feelings
(Jones/Matlock/Cook/Rotten)

The community politics that grew out of the Sixties underground was in tatters by the mid-Seventies. Love was patently not enough. Even the fallacy of a united Sixties youth culture was ruthlessly exposed during the early Seventies, by which time any notional centre had obviously collapsed, leaving various subcultures to battle for supremacy among themselves. The cult of the Rock Superstar, detached and isolated, had been born with Bolan and Bowie. Punk took from the glam-rock idols the ideas of elitism and self-invention and brought them down to street level.

Narcissism was democratised. Elevation of the self was all that mattered, as Rotten plainly demonstrated on 'No Feelings': "You better understand I'm in love with myself, my beautiful self-ish."

Not everyone was invited to the self-love party. By extension, "No feelings, for anybody else, except for myself", burst into random acts of violence, a crucial element of punk rock that is sometimes overlooked as the pages of rock history acquire a yellowing charm. If punk grew out of a suspicion that the human spirit had become debased, then it was inevitable that its response would be ugly. When Rotten sang, "I'm so happy, I'm feeling so fine/I'm watching all the rubbish and wasting my time", there was no doubt that "rubbish" meant other people. They weren't just there to be eyeballed either: "I kick you in the head, you've got nothing to say"; "You come up and see me and I beat you black-and-blue". For years, rock had been unable to connect with anything as mundane – or as ludicrous – as real life. Like the work of emerging playwright Mike Leigh, punk attempted to get real – whatever the hell that was. Only, in 'No Feelings', Rotten forgot to include any jokes.

'No Feelings' began life as a gritty, New York-inspired Steve Jones riff, but it was Rotten's lyrics that transformed the song into a virtual punk manifesto. It was a credo that was fully reinforced in photographs. Compared with Rotten's steely stare and sardonic smile, Elvis' curled lip, Lou Reed's scowl and Iggy Pop's wide-eyed look were mere child's play. Had Steve Jones, Paul Cook or, for that matter Joe Strummer or Jimmy Pursey, been appointed "The Face of Punk Rock", its threat – and appeal – would have been perceived quite differently.

Playing its part in that was a bout of meningitis suffered by the 11-year-old John Lydon, which left him with poor eye-sight that goes some way to explaining the cold-hearted stare that gazed out from photographs. Johnny Rotten – the name, the face, the voice – is inseparable from punk rock.

'No Feelings' was one of three originals taped at the first Sex Pistols recording session, with Chris Spedding, in May 1976, and the band went back to it on several occasions. The arrangement stayed much the same over the course of the next year, and this definitive *Bollocks* version, produced by Chris "Wall Of Sound" Thomas, was taped at Wessex Studios in April/May 1977.

The version of 'No Feelings' that turned up on the B-side of the withdrawn A&M edition of the 'God Save The Queen' single was produced by Dave Goodman at the band's Denmark Street rehearsal studio in July 1976.

Liar

(Jones/Matlock/Cook/Rotten)

When punk opened its collective mind, it found not truth but paranoia: it was the subculture that mistrusted everybody and everything. Having grown up amid the spectre of unfulfilled Sixties dreams, the generation born in the first decade of rock'n'roll was now returning to bite the hands that overfed.

'Liar' was aimed at no one and everyone. It scowled where before it might have shrugged: "I'm nobody's fool," sang Rotten, "I don't need you, don't need your blah-blah". This generation had stopped listening.

The song, an early Rotten/Matlock collaboration written during a barren spell in summer 1976, was reduced to the status of an occasional encore song after Matlock's departure, which says much about its low-priority status. Solid rather than invigorating, 'Liar' nevertheless tempted a fine vocal out of Rotten, even if his lyrics were uncharacteristically short on memorable one-liners. In fact, the central lyric motif, the chorus of, "You're in suspension", bears no relation to the song's general thrust. A more likely source for it was the terraces at Highbury, where John Lydon used to follow the fortunes of his local football team, Arsenal FC. Liars don't get suspended: footballers do.

God Save The Queen
(Jones/Matlock/Cook/Rotten)

Even more than 'Anarchy In The UK', this song must go down in history as The Sex Pistols' finest moment. It was the song that disrupted the cosily imperialistic celebrations for the Queen's Silver Jubilee by placing a safety pin through her nose for the sleeve, by launching the infamous Sex Pistols boat trip down the Thames that ended in several arrests, and by provoking gangs of Her Majesty's most loyal subjects to take up bars and bottles and hunt down the perpetrators of the record that, contrary to popular opinion, didn't call the Queen a moron. It was her ever-obedient, dumbly adoring public to whom that noun was addressed.

With apologies to those not old enough to have been playing records back in June 1977, 'God Save The Queen' has never sounded quite so good as it did when it first slid out of its royal-blue sleeve and the heavily compressed 45rpm vinyl single hit the turntable. Mastered at great volume, it roared its displeasure at the pompous pageantry by presenting its very own State Of The Nation address. Its conclusion was loud and clear: "No Future".

Although this latest analogue-edition of *Bollocks* is intended to minimise the compact disc format's tendency to metallicise musical sound, and while the opening chords still attack like few other rock singles do, 'God Save The Queen' never quite sings as it should do. Maybe it's the "you-had-to-be-there" thrill of taking a spanner to the royal fawn-fest that's missing. Perhaps it's a measure of the record's lasting historical importance that it's impossible to recapture the history-in-the-making effect that 'God Save The Queen' had during the summer of 1977.

Britain's most notorious group taking on its most revered figurehead in her moment of glory. Kind of inevitable, wasn't it? If Malcolm McLaren is to be believed (though there is a mountain of evidence to suggest that he shouldn't be), Johnny Rotten, the acknowledged author of the lyrics, was adamant about titling his new song 'No Future'. It was, after all, written months before the Jubilee hype got going, in October 1976, during a break in the 'Anarchy' sessions with Dave Goodman. Rotten, of course, is too scornful of McLaren's claim that he retitled the song to bother to argue.

What's not in dispute is that the riff that gave the song its right royal attack was born when Matlock tinkered about on a studio piano, later transposing it to his bass guitar. Cook took the tempo of the song down a bit. Jones turned in one of his finest performances, economical but fiercely effective. But the star of the show, more than ever, was Rotten. His sarcastic, contemptuous performance made every line count. His witty, hippy-baiting, "We mean it, maaan", his immaculately ironic "We love our Queen", those sarcastically rolled "r"s ("made you a mo-r-r-r-on!") and the cheerleading "No future!" finale never fail to please.

According to Rotten, he had the words already prepared (written, according to his autobiography, on his kitchen table while waiting for some baked beans to cook) before Matlock had written the song's defining riff, but never imagined they'd find the music to match. He was wrong – the ferocity of the sound easily matched Rotten's spumatic assault on a "great" British institution.

There are several reasons why 'God Save The Queen'

remains the ultimate Sex Pistols cut, but the one that everyone overlooks is how the double-act of Jones' power chording and Cook's effortless accompaniment conspired to create the rock equivalent of laughter. Unlike much of the Pistols' work, which is muscular rock writ large, 'God Save The Queen' sounds like it's taking the piss even before Rotten picks up the mike. When he does, a stream of incendiary phrases dribble from his insurrectionary tongue.

The opening line turned the public's jaundiced view of punk rockers as comic-book dullards back on itself: "God save the Queen / The fascist regime / It made you a moron / A potential H-bomb". No, Rotten suggested, the morons are those who remain obedient to a system where a quirk of birthright dictates who holds the wealth and power in the country. That, in Jubilee year especially, few even questioned this anomaly is exactly the kind of "potential H-bomb" that provides a breeding ground for fascism. Unlike conventional left-wing politics, hopelessly wedded to a romantic view of the working classes, punk's bullshit detector left no room for pussyfooting around. Blind ignorance is dangerous whichever side of the fence it sits on. And there was plenty of it about in 1977, according to the song that used the Queen as a hook from which to dangle a wider message of warning: "God save the Queen / We mean it, maaan / And there is no future in England's dreaming." The outro, several rousing ensemble choruses of "No future", sounded like a burial rite.

This punk-inspired anti-national anthem placed the red-top press in a quandary. It was a story that was a gift to sensationalise, and therefore shift more papers, but a strange semi-silence seemed to engulf the record and the band's accompanying activities. It was as if, out of reverence to the Royal Family, newspaper editors had decided to deprive the party-poopers of the oxygen of publicity. This coincided with a feeling that the band had already enjoyed enough free publicity at the tabloids' expense.

The music press filled the gap admirably, offering blanket coverage of the infamous Thames boat trip on June 7, when 11 partygoers, including Malcolm McLaren, Vivienne Westwood and Jamie Reid, were arrested. The idea was brilliant: hire a pleasure boat called *The Elizabeth*, pack it with a crowd of friends, journalists and Virgin Records employees, and have The Sex Pistols play a short set as the vessel – flying a banner that read "Queen Elizabeth Welcomes The Sex Pistols" – sailed merrily down the Thames. Oh, and when they reach the Houses of Parliament, get the band to play 'Anarchy In The UK'. Inevitably, the captain got jumpy and, when he prematurely docked the boat by the Embankment, a posse of police officers and dogs were neatly on hand to greet them in a manner reserved not for royals but for rogues.

This was merely the high point in a series of controversies that surrounded 'God Save The Queen'. Ever since it was publicly unveiled as 'No Future' at a gig at Hendon Polytechnic on October 19, 1976 (when Rotten sang his words from a sheet of paper), Matlock had been unhappy with the lyric content. According to Rotten in his autobiography, Matlock feared the song would get the group branded as fascists: "I agreed with him... to get rid of him," recalled the singer.

The band persevered with the song, recording it at a Christmas session with Mike Thorne for EMI (apparently a five-minutes plus version, complete with lengthy break and longer fade-out), and further road-testing it during a short series of gigs in Holland in January 1977.

At the last of these, a show at the Amsterdam Paradiso club on January 7, Matlock refused to encore with the song. From that moment, his days in the band were numbered. The band's resident Sixties aficionado (and therefore someone too steeped in traditional rock values for the new breed) was outed by Rotten in the press as "a mummy's boy", showed himself as too competent at another round of recording sessions later that month, and was essentially persona non grata by February. Although Matlock still insists he left the band by mutual consent, Malcolm McLaren used the situation to the band's advantage in a telegram to NME that announced that Matlock had been sacked. Apparently, the bassist was no longer in The Sex Pistols because: "He went on too long about Paul McCartney. EMI was enough. The Beatles was too much."

The next controversy stirred up by the song was the band's

week-long tenure with A&M Records, the label set up by easy listening trumpeter Herb Alpert, which, by the mid-Seventies provided a home for acts like Rick Wakeman, Peter Frampton, Supertramp and The Carpenters. The label, which had been courting the band since January, pipped CBS and finally signed The Sex Pistols to a two-year deal on March 9, repeating the feat a day later outside Buckingham Palace for the benefit of the press. But an altercation in London's Speakeasy nightclub involving Matlock's rowdy replacement Sid Vicious and rock DJ Bob Harris, prompted the label to terminate the contract a week later.

The group pocketed a £75,000 cheque to add to the £40,000 already procured from EMI. This necessitated the withdrawal of some 25,000 copies of the freshly minted 'God Save The Queen' single, which had been recorded just days earlier, with Jones apparently handling bass duties. (Cook and Jones had spent a fruitless two days attempting to teach Vicious the bass line at the Denmark Street rehearsal studio to little avail. Little wonder that Clash bassist Paul Simonon was also briefly considered for the role.)

The delay in releasing the single suited the band, who'd struck a new deal with Virgin on May 13, with the record released two weeks later. Even before the limited coverage of the boat trip, attempts were made to snuff out the single. Apart from a couple of spins by DJ John Peel, something of a law unto himself at Radio 1, the BBC refused to play a record that was one of the most eagerly awaited in years. Meanwhile, high street chains like Boots, Woolworths and W.H. Smith declined to stock it. The attempted blackout didn't stop there. When 'God Save The Queen' charted at number two, suspiciously one spot behind old fart Rod Stewart's 'I Don't Want To Talk About It', shops declined to acknowledge its existence by leaving the position blank on their Top 20 wall displays.

In contrast, the music press, now all firmly behind the new punk explosion, which they hoped would revive rock's flagging fortunes, almost universally declared it Single Of The Week.

Prior to 'God Save The Queen', Scottish MP Willie Hamilton

was the only visible thorn in the monarchy's side. As Jubilee Week subsided, the papers finally began to acknowledge The Sex Pistols' latest record. On June 12, the *Sunday Mirror* declared open season with the headline: "Punk Rock Jubilee Shocker".

Rotten defended the song. "The single is nothing personal against the Queen. It's what she stands for... a symbol." He added, "She's probably just like everybody else but watching her on telly, as far as I'm concerned, she ain't no human being. She's a piece of cardboard that they drag around on a trolley, and she does it blindly, because she's in a rut."

Within the space of a week, members of the group's entourage were attacked in three separate incidents. First, Jamie Reid was left with a broken nose and a cracked bone in his leg after an attack by four youths. Then Rotten and Chris Thomas were set upon in the car park of a Highbury pub, prompting the almost gleeful tabloid headline: "Rotten Razored". When Cook was set upon with bars and bottles outside Shepherd's Bush tube station, McLaren and the group decided to take the heat out of the moment and hastily organised a tour of Scandinavia. And thus the skins of The Sex Pistols were saved.

Problems
(Jones/Matlock/Cook/Rotten)

Like 'Seventeen', 'Problems' was one of the earliest Sex Pistols originals, dating from a late 1975 rehearsal when Jones and Matlock forged together fragments from two other songs. The lyrics, as usual, were Rotten's, and reflected what he later said was "about how I felt being in the band". Earlier in the decade, the struggling David Bowie resorted to irony when he titled his fourth album *Hunky Dory*. Rotten and The Sex Pistols were far less coy: 'Problems' epitomised the "punk" world view in a single word, and angered the culprit with a second "you". Sufficiently unburdened by the troubles of the world ("To people like me, there is no order"), punk hedonism could go about its business: "There's too much fun in being alive."

In 1980, John Lydon admitted that 'Problems' was his favourite Sex Pistols song. Judging by the amount of times it was recorded, and the fact that it was the band's set closer for much of 1976, it was popular with the rest of the band, too. 'Problems' was one of three originals taped at that first Chris Spedding session; the version on *Never Mind The Bollocks* dates from the April/May 1977 Wessex sessions.

Seventeen
(Jones/Matlock/ Cook/Rotten)

The cult of youth was a vital ingredient of punk rock. The musical rebels of the Sixties, such as Bob Dylan, The Rolling Stones and The Who, were approaching middle age, and their music was designed to be heard from a distant seat in an arena, not in a sweaty club that smelt of beer and amyl nitrate. No one's certain when the phrase was first coined, but the Great Divide during 1977 pitted the new wave against the so-called 'Boring Old Farts' – hairy, bearded and usually wearing vast expanses of flared denim. 'Seventeen' opened with a typically sardonic barb from Rotten: "You're only twenty-nine, got a lot to learn". The rules had changed. Time was no longer on the side of the elders.

'Seventeen', or at least its basic structure, pre-dated Rotten's arrival. While other songs from this period, such as 'Kill Me Today' and 'Concrete Youth', were discarded, this track, written by Jones with some input from Matlock, survived. But Jones' tentative lyric, which included the line, "I'm all alone, Give a dog a bone", didn't. Complaining that he couldn't read the guitarist's handwriting, Rotten wrote a new set of lyrics for the song, inspired, it is said, while the band rehearsed a version of The Small Faces' 1968 hit, 'Lazy Sunday'.

Sometimes known as 'Lazy Sod' or 'Only Seventeen', 'Seventeen' was transformed into an anthem for the burgeoning dole-queue culture that had been fostered by the decade's series of economic crises.

A version of the song recorded by Dave Goodman at Denmark Street in July 1976 suffixed the opening, "You're only twenty-nine" line with the words, "But when your business dies, you will not return". Because McLaren, the small-time entrepreneur with big ideas for his King's Road boutique SEX and for The Sex Pistols, was 29 when the song was written, this is widely regarded as an early slight to the manager. By the time the band returned to the studio in April/May 1977 to tape this definitive *Bollocks* version, "business" had been altered to "mummy" – though, presumably, not out of any new-found deference to McLaren. Rotten's claim that, "I just speed", a fact confirmed in March 1977 when he was fined £40 for possession of a small quantity of amphetamine sulphate, remained intact.

Unsophisticated, even by the band's standards, 'Seventeen' was not one of the Pistols' more enduring recordings, being little more than a one-line joke thanks to its, "I'm a lazy sod" chorus. In December 1978, Rotten was particularly uncharitable about it, describing it as, "The most abysmal song I've ever heard. That was Steve and Paul. It appealed to their basic instincts or something. God, and is it basic."

Anarchy In The UK
(Jones/Matlock/Cook/Rotten)

In one of the Pistols' first music press write-ups, in NME, Neil Spencer's review of their February 1976 Marquee support slot quoted Steve Jones as saying: "Actually, we're not into music... we're into chaos," That quote, more than anything else, set the tone for The Sex Pistols' career; it gave them something to live up to. From that moment on, the band's elitist fan following was invaded by a mix of rock music malcontents and a boisterous crowd more au fait with pubs and football terraces than the rock circuit.

'Anarchy In The UK' was always likely to become the band's first single from the moment Jones suggested they needed a theme tune. According to legend, Matlock duly obliged, and by the end of the rehearsal session, Rotten had scribbled down a set of words that formed the basis of the lyric.

Much later, Jordan, the flamboyant shop girl at SEX who did much to advance punk's sartorial dimensions, claimed that artist Jamie Reid had more than a hand in the lyrics, which, given his politicised background, is quite possible. That said, 'Anarchy' was a manifesto of doubtful conviction. Recognised anarchists might well have questioned the group's debt to the politics of Bakunin and Proudhon, and could easily claim that the mood of the song owed more to the popular definition of the word, i.e. a rowdy situation. After all, the closing call-to-arms was not, "To the barricades!" but a typical Friday night closing-time call: "A-get pissed, destroyyyyah!" (In June 1977, Rotten claimed the record was about "musical anarchy. I don't think you can be a political rock'n'roll band. It's a loser stance.")

However, the song's tone suited the playful, Situationist International (SI) approach to politics, which had influenced both McLaren and Reid in the late Sixties. In fact, the song – and with it the entire Sex Pistols episode – seemed to be the material offspring of McLaren's manifesto for his 1968 film about Oxford Street: "Be childish. Be irresponsible. Be disrespectful. Be everything this society hates."

However much help and encouragement Rotten may have had from the two former art-school malcontents, there's no doubt that whatever words spilled out of his mouth, it was the way he sang them – taunting, accusatory and with an abandon rarely heard in British rock – that more than lived up to the Pistols' bad-boy billing. When the power chord roll-call (not unlike The Who's 'Anyway Anyhow Anywhere') subsided, Rotten made his great rock'n'roll entrance with just two words, "Right!... Now!" followed by a dirty old man cackle that leather-faced *Carry On* star Sid James would have been mighty proud of.

The Sex Pistols' greatest weapon had been declared; for the next few years, countless rock hopefuls would ape Rotten's style, rolling their "r"s and braying as if they had a huge chip on their shoulder. It was the aural equivalent of being gripped by the collar and forced to look into the face of a future dystopia.

After declaring himself to be Public Enemy No. 1 ("I am an Anti-Christ!"), Rotten unleashed a litany of anti-social attitude, interspersed by a roll-call of anxiety-inducing acronyms (MPLA, UDA, IRA) to a surprisingly sluggish backing that teetered under the weight of a wash of guitars. It was everything Jones had asked for: a song that summed up the band's "fuck-the-system" approach, strong enough with which to open (and often close) their shows, and memorable enough for audiences to go home energised by what sounded like a virtual call-to-arms. Little wonder that after the Pistols debuted the song at Manchester's Lesser Free Trade Hall on July 20, a host of bands – including Joy Division – formed according to the new template. One month later, after the band performed it on their first television appearance, on Granada's *So It Goes* – it was obvious that 'Anarchy In The UK' was going to be the first Sex Pistols single.

Dave Goodman produced the first version of 'Anarchy' at the band's Denmark Street rehearsal room in July, and it was Goodman who were their first choice as producer after they signed to EMI. The team was installed in the professional confines of Lansdowne Studios on October 11, 1976, but after four days' recording, no one was satisfied with the results. While the perfectionist Goodman worked his way round the mixing desk, the band, bored by the endless retakes and waiting around, began to deface the studio walls. The finished take was rejected by EMI, and staffer (and perhaps the sole resident Sex Pistols enthusiast) Mike Thorne suggested that established producer Chris Thomas might rescue the situation. (McLaren had a hunch that Syd Barrett, Pink Floyd's errant and long-retired songwriter, could be tempted out of his madcap world to work with the band, a notion that made better copy than sense.) Because of Thomas' work with Roxy Music, the band relented and the new team was packed off to graffiti the Wessex Studios walls for a week.

'Anarchy In The UK' eventually cost EMI the best part of £10,000 to record, but it was to cost them considerably more in the weeks ahead, when the company was pilloried by the press in the wake of the Pistols' notorious foul-mouthed appearance on the *Today* live TV show. The confusion over the producers spilled onto the record itself. The first 2,000 copies, issued in November in an appropriately matt-black sleeve, credited Thomas as producer of both sides. In fact, the flip, 'I Wanna Be Me', was a Goodman production, as subsequent pressings correctly stated.

'Anarchy In The UK' wasn't the first punk record – The

Damned's 'New Rose' pipped it by a matter of days – but it was one of the most short-lived. When EMI was forced to bow to public opinion and fire the group, the single was deleted in January 1977. As a consequence, the shops were flooded with imported copies of a 12" edition, issued by the French-based Glitterbest label, with whom McLaren had set up a separate deal.

Equally short-lived was the 'Anarchy' tour. Nineteen dates appeared on the tour poster – a Union Jack adorned with safety pins, clips and burn holes – but due to the moral panic that swept the nation in the wake of the Grundy episode, The Sex Pistols were able to play just three of them. Councils hastily arranged meetings to ban the group and, when they did play, as in Caerphilly in south Wales, more people attended the candlelit demonstration outside the hall than turned up to see the band. New York new wavers The Ramones were originally booked to play the tour, but quit after an argument over who should receive top billing.

The Clash and The Damned, plus The Heartbreakers, fronted by one-time New York Dolls' guitarist Johnny Thunders, joined The Sex Pistols to travel the length and breadth of the country, searching for places to play. (Because The Damned agreed to break ranks and perform in a town where The Sex Pistols had been banned, they were soon kicked off the tour.) For a while, the lurid headlines, and the national debate that quickly followed, suggested that anarchy, or at least something equally unwelcome, had indeed been let loose in the country.

Submission

(Jones/Matlock/Cook/Rotten)

Aside from the title, with its dark hints at sexual power play, 'Submission' is the rogue element in The Sex Pistols' *Bollocks* portfolio. Written at the suggestion of Malcolm McLaren, who wanted a song that would help publicise his and Westwood's SEX shop, Rotten instead mangled the manager's song title, turning it into "a submarine mission". In time, the song's real function was to give both band and audience a breather

during the live set, although its mid-tempo pace (the riff was
The Kinks' 'All Day And All Of The Night' slowed down)
earned it a place on *Bollocks* too.

Most rock music post-1967 seemed to exist in a vacuum,
referring only to itself and barely acknowledging the
existence of a world beyond the record player or the concert
hall. Punk, which introduced a short, sharp shock of reality,
helped change all that, and McLaren – a schemer and ideas
man rather than a musical purist – was crucial in altering
perceptions.

'Submission' might have worked better if it had been a
musical calling-card for SEX, because the more punk rock
referred to the outside world, the more powerful it became.
The shop had been crucial both to The Sex Pistols' story
and to the ideas that clustered around punk, making it a
cultural, rather than simply a musical, revolution. McLaren
and Westwood, already lovers, took over the premises in
November 1971, shortly after McLaren bowed out of his
Goldsmiths College arts course without completing his degree.
Situated at the unfashionable end of the King's Road, suitably
known as World's End, their Let It Rock shop at No. 430
quickly acquired a reputation among born-again Teddy boys,
who purchased their retro fashions to an accompaniment of
vintage rock'n'roll records on the jukebox. Even at this early
stage, McLaren was fascinated by the concept of a subculture
that lived out its own lifestyle, as opposed to atomised,
anonymous music fans.

Impatient and eager to learn more, McLaren and Westwood
transformed their shop a year or so later into a haven for
bikers, Too Fast To Live, Too Young To Die, before moving
into fetish clothing in April 1974, when it was rechristened
SEX. This was when things began to accelerate. Matlock
became a Saturday shop boy, Jones, a regular customer since
1972, began to interest McLaren in a group he was playing
with, and one day in August 1975, in walked John Lydon.

When the Pistols took off during 1976, the band were often
pictured in Westwood's designs – fetish T-shirts (including the
infamous one depicting two "undraped" cowboys), straight-
legged cord trousers and Teddy boy-style jackets. When

McLaren was interviewed by Jon Savage for *England's Dreaming*, the definitive book on The Sex Pistols and punk rock, he said that he wanted 'Submission' to advertise his shop because, "I was out to sell lots of trousers." In the event, he, or at least Westwood, did anyway. Late in 1976, Westwood invented the "bondage trouser", a garment to which Rotten soon took a fancy. The shop then changed its name to Seditionaries, and Westwood probably earned more from her punk clothing (especially the hugely popular "Destroy" T-shirt) than McLaren (or, for that matter, the band) originally did from The Sex Pistols.

'Submission' was one of the few things Rotten and Matlock ever agreed on. Even then, the song was born out of an argument between the pair, at rehearsals in the Roundhouse during the winter of 1975/76. That was when McLaren made his suggestion and gave the pair £20 to write a song over a few beers. The riff was agreed upon because the pair both discovered that they liked The Doors, whose 'Hello, I Love You' was based on The Kinks' "All Day And All Of The Night'.

The song was first played at a February 1976 gig in Welwyn Garden City and, while a handful of studio takes exist, the album version dates from the April/May Wessex sessions. 'Submission' made a surprise appearance on the B-side of the American 'Pretty Vacant' single.

Pretty Vacant
(Jones/Matlock/Cook/Rotten)

EMI wanted The Sex Pistols to record 'Pretty Vacant' as their follow-up single to 'Anarchy', and it's easy to understand why. It's the most conventional, and certainly the most commercial, song on the album. It's also probably the band's best-known recording. Perhaps to take the heat out of 'God Save The Queen', 'Pretty Vacant' became the third Sex Pistols single, in July 1977, and became the only bona fide Pistols 45 to win a slot on BBC-TV's long-running chart show *Top Of The Pops* (albeit in promo video performance rather than live on the show).

Unlike 'Anarchy In The UK' and 'God Save The Queen', which both sent shivers down the nation's collective spine, the message of 'Pretty Vacant' was more "lovable rogue" than lynchable renegades. Well, blow me if The Sex Pistols aren't just a bunch of regular ne'er-do-wells, revelling in their "I'm daft, me!" culture that was as British as fish'n'chips. " 'Ere, you 'eard that new Sex Pistols record? Pretty Vay-cunt. Ha ha." Why, it even came with a three-note intro hook and a chorus that Matlock customised from Abba's 1975 hit 'SOS'. It was 'Pretty Vacant' that took the fear factor out of punk rock; from the moment it charted, the revolutionary dreamers had lost the battle for punk's true meaning.

'Pretty Vacant' has Matlock's pop heart written all over it. No one, not even Rotten, now disputes that the song is virtually all his. To prove his point, when Matlock went out with his new band, the power-pop combo The Rich Kids, during the winter of 1977/78, 'Pretty Vacant' was the centrepiece (some would say the highlight) of the band's set. In turn, Matlock has since admitted that the song was largely inspired by events in New York, which he heard first-hand from Malcolm McLaren on his return from a spell out there managing The New York Dolls.

"The idea for it ['Pretty Vacant'] came from a poster that Malcolm had brought back from the States," Matlock told Clinton Heylin, author of a book on *Never Mind The Bollocks...*, "a small handbill for a Richard Hell Television gig with the titles of several songs scattered across it." One of the titles was '(I Belong To The) Blank Generation'. "As soon as I saw that I thought – that's the kind of feeling that we want to get across in our songs."

The first truly great song written by the band, 'Pretty Vacant' was one of three tracks recorded at the first Sex Pistols demo session with Chris Spedding, and it was committed to tape on several occasions after. Once again, the album version was recorded at Wessex Studios in April/May 1977, and is probably one of the songs that feature Matlock as a session-playing bassist.

Meanwhile, his replacement, Sid Vicious, was already in hospital, having taken the song's message to heart. Already locked in a self-destructive relationship with US punk/groupie Nancy Spungen, and lacking any of Rotten's perceptiveness and knowing arrogance, Vicious epitomised the notion of the "vacant" punk. In that respect, of course, he was a far less troublesome customer than Rotten, which was no doubt why McLaren had ambitions (alas unfulfilled) to make him the Pistols' front man in the wake of Rotten's departure.

New York

(Jones/Matlock/Cook/Rotten)

'New York' is one of the most pointedly contemptuous songs the Pistols ever wrote – and everything suggests that the finger was pointed in Malcolm McLaren's direction. The tension, and increasingly the rivalry, between the svengali and his most valuable charges was a testament to a central-punk rock maxim: confrontation is good. But more than that, 'New York' virtually enshrines a secret history of The Sex Pistols.

One of the first rock shows the teenage Jones and Matlock saw was The Faces at Wembley Empire Pool in 1972. The support band was The New York Dolls. "It was about the time their first album was out [sic]," Jones later told Fred and Judy Vermorel for their book *Sex Pistols: The Inside Story*. "And then I saw them on the old telly, like, and I was fucking really knocked out by them. It was mainly their attitude, I think: they were just all falling about all over the place, all their hair down, all knocking into each other... And they just didn't give a shit, you know." Jones was referring to the Dolls' appearance on BBC TV's *The Old Grey Whistle Test*, giving a performance that prompted the bearded and semi-comatose presenter, Bob Harris, to admonish them with the immortal phrase, "Mock rock".

Prior to this, in August 1973, McLaren and Westwood had flown out to New York to exhibit their Let It Rock designs at the National Boutique Show. While there, they socialised with the Dolls, as well as with the Andy Warhol entourage, and made at least one trip to Max's Kansas City. While in the Big Apple, McLaren also encountered Richard Hell, already sporting what became the punk look with short, tousled, randomly cut hair and ripped clothes. When the Dolls toured Europe late in the year, McLaren stayed close by their side, even accompanying them on a riotous trip to Paris. Taking his cue from Warhol, New York's patron of the gutter, McLaren seemed to think the band were so bad they were great.

By November 1974 he was back in New York and attempting to manage The New York Dolls, whose fortunes had plummeted during the intervening 12 months. But putting them in red patent leather and making them play in front of hammer-and-sickle backdrops pretty much killed off the Dolls for good and, by May 1975, McLaren was back in London – not with Richard Hell, whom he wanted to make into a star, but with Dolls' guitarist Syl Sylvain's white Les Paul guitar, which he gave to Steve Jones. By late 1975, when the newly formed Sex Pistols were practising on an almost daily basis, Jones was learning his roughly hewn guitar skills from the two New York Dolls albums and Iggy & the Stooges' fearsome *Raw Power*. The future sound of The Sex Pistols was being forged out of the current sound of New York.

Johnny Rotten has always been reluctant to recognise New York's contribution to The Sex Pistols and punk rock, partly to dismiss McLaren, partly because to acknowledge anything other than your own contribution devalues it. True, Rotten was far more important to punk than a bunch of cross-dressing decadents out of Queens, but the fact that he felt compelled to write a put-down says a lot about his competitive nature. After spitting out lines like "You think it's swell playing Max's Kansas-ah / You're looking to pull, you're acting flash-ah", he reserves his most potent weapon, his cruel, pitiless laugh, for the break.

Two Dolls tracks, 'Looking For A Kiss' and 'Pills', are name-dropped during the song, although less obviously, Rotten also smuggles in a reference to one of his own key influences, Captain Beefheart. 'Japan In A Dishpan' (he subtly alters "in" to "is") is a track from Beefheart's 1970 album, *Lick My Decals Off, Baby*, a classic of avant-rock, which was something Rotten briefly aspired to with his next project, PiL. In fact, it was Rotten's affection for "outside the mainstream" music – Can, Miles Davis, Peter Hammill, dub reggae – that gave The Sex

Pistols a twist lacking in other punk groups, whose heritage was usually more humdrum.

If 'New York' was a slight in the direction of McLaren and his failed anti-heroes from America, it has also been suggested that the song, written early in 1976, had another inspiration. On February 12, The Sex Pistols supported Essex pub rockers Eddie & The Hot Rods at the Marquee, a performance that climaxed in the band hotfooting it after some of the main act's equipment had been destroyed. Just over a week later, at Welwyn Garden City, 'New York' appeared in The Sex Pistols' set list for the first time. Apparently, the Hot Rods were regarded as "being above their station" and, like the Dolls, were no better than the old fart bands they'd set themselves up in opposition to.

In 1978, Johnny Thunders recorded his own sarcastic response to 'New York' (included on the guitarist's debut solo album, *So Alone*). Titled 'London Boys', it featured the playing of two grown-up London boys, Steve Jones and Paul Cook.

EMI (Unlimited Edition)

(Jones/Matlock/Cook/Rotten)

After the band's headlining performance during the first night of the 100 Club Punk Festival on September 20, 1976, the race was on to sign The Sex Pistols. The A&R men had obviously decided there was some mileage in this punk-rock thing after all. With Polydor also making loud noises in the direction of Glitterbest, the management company recently set up by McLaren to conduct the band's affairs, EMI was forced to move quickly.

Mike Thorne, who'd witnessed an earlier show at the 100 Club, had already taken EMI's top A&R man, Nick Mobbs, along to the band's showcase at the Screen On The Green cinema in Islington on August 29, but Mobbs, reluctant to embrace the new, was unimpressed. In the light of the publicity generated by the 100 Club Punk Festival, however, he decided to cast his personal reservations aside. On September 29, the pair travelled to Doncaster to see the band again. Mobbs changed his mind; on his return, he went to see his superior, Bob

Mercer, and by October 8, EMI had secured the Pistols on a two-year contract. The label didn't get 'Pretty Vacant', the single they wanted, but the band wasted no time in picking up their £40,000 advance.

The Pistols' December 1 appearance on the *Today* show had provoked a media onslaught. That was great for the band, establishing them as the first genuine rock'n'roll bad boys in years, but for EMI, an establishment corporation, the furore raised some serious questions. Ultimately, these all boiled down to one thing: should the label save face and drop The Sex Pistols from its roster (which at the time included Queen, Steve Harley, Marc Bolan and The Beatles' catalogue)? Or should it sit tight and wait for the controversy to die down? On December 6, just five days after the broadcast, the label was scheduling the group's second single for February 1977, with an album to follow in April. A day later, at a fiery AGM meeting, the Chairman, Sir John Read, admitted that he had been both upset and annoyed by the band's antics. He also suggested that EMI was reconsidering its position.

The band's fate was probably already sealed by this time, but the label chose not to make any declaration until the New Year, when the heat had been taken out of the situation. In a press release dated January 6 and headed "EMI and The Sex Pistols", it stated: "EMI feels it is unable to promote this group's records internationally in view of the adverse publicity which has been generated over the past two months, although recent press reports of the behaviour of The Sex Pistols appear to have been exaggerated." It was declared that "EMI and The Sex Pistols have mutually agreed to terminate their recording contract".

The Sex Pistols wasted no time in turning the situation to their advantage, boasting about the £40,000 advance they walked off with and — as it was revealed on *Never Mind The Bollocks...* months later — immortalising the episode in song. In fact, 'EMI' was the only new track recorded at the Gooseberry Studios sessions with Dave Goodman at what turned out to be Matlock's last official appearance as a Sex Pistol, late in January 1977. The version that ended up on the album, though, was recorded a couple of months later with Chris

Thomas at Wessex Studios.

'EMI' burst immediately to life with a strident Steve Jones riff. Rotten could barely contain his glee as he launched into the band's old label, rolling his "r"s more caustically than ever, and augmenting his taunts with the odd riddle or two ("Don't you judge a book just by the cover/Unless you cover just another"). It was unheard of: bands rarely mentioned their record companies – business was a dirty word in the rarefied world of rock artists – let alone wrote entire songs that badmouthed them, and so memorably, too ("Eee-emm-aye-ah!").

This was The Sex Pistols striking a blow for the common people against the establishment. It was a victory the band would savour and – why not? – indulge in the odd bit of self-mythologising. Even though 'Anarchy In The UK' had only managed a lowly number 38 chart placing, the group blithely claimed that, "Too many people have the suss/Too many people support us". With the press witchhunt briefly muted, the Grundy affair, the outcome of which had taken the Pistols' camp by surprise, was here immortalised as, "The day they wish that we had died".

Yes, The Sex Pistols, at least in the insurrectionary mind of Rotten, would be "ruled by none... Evah, Evah. EVAAAH!" In truth, the lyrics were more imaginative than the song, which climaxed in a glam rock-inspired call-and-response singalong before Rotten's witty denouement of, "Hello, EMI... goodbye, A&M", followed by that irresistibly British comic turn, a raspberry. It was never better fun being a Sex Pistol than when the band wrote and recorded 'EMI', which they debuted live at the Notre Dame Hall, London, on March 21, 1977

MICHAEL JACKSON

Thriller

December 1982

By Geoff Brown

A FTER THE SUCCESS of Off The Wall, artistic as much as commercial, Michael Jackson became something of a session animal. Short of erecting flashing neon lights that read "These Pipes For Hire", he could not have got more in the way of background vocal business. Projects included individual tracks on albums (all released in 1980-82) by Stevie Wonder, Diana Ross, Brothers Johnson, Quincy Jones, Donna Summer, Minnie Riperton, sister LaToya Jackson, Kenny Loggins (late of Loggins & Messina), Dave Mason (late of Traffic), crossover country star Kenny Rogers, songwriter Carole Bayer Sager and Joe "King" Carrasco. On the Ross album Silk Electric, he wrote and produced 'Muscles'; on LaToya's eponymous effort for Polydor, he produced and co-wrote 'Night Time Lover'.

In between this action he was coerced into recording another Jacksons set, Triumph, which saw a marked diminution in his contribution, outstripped only by the diminution of his nose. Yes, even before Off The Wall, the sustained teasing by his brothers and father had finally fattened the cosmetic surgeons' wallets. Jackson's profile changed in other ways. With the increased sales of his albums came increased media attention and the desire for titbits of "inside" information with which to titillate readers, listeners and viewers. His media profile was raised. Here was an area over which he could exercise little control. He was not comfortable with interviews, did not give great quotes, and so, throughout the Eighties, the media focused on the cloistered lifestyle, the menagerie and a burgeoning reputation as Genuine Oddball.

What hurt even more than the cosmetic surgeon's scalpel was the rejection by the National Academy of Recording Arts And Sciences. It nominated 'Don't Stop 'Til You Get Enough' for only two Grammies, awarding it one and ignoring Off The Wall entirely. Rewards and awards were important to Jackson. Moreover, it was clear that the album was one of the biggest sellers of the year and was also a tastemaker. By any criteria, it was a winner. To top it, Jackson and producer Quincy Jones reassembled substantially the same crew, but rather than guests with jazz, soul or (Stevie) Wonderlove chops – Larry Carlton, George Duke, Phil Upchurch, Wah Wah Watson,

Marlo Henderson – they also hired rock-orientated players in order to give the music a less subtle sound and feel. The set's original title, *Starlight*, seems singularly inappropriate.

Again, Jackson wrote a good proportion of the material – four of the nine tracks – with three more from Rod Temperton, including another title track that tapped straight into the singer's fascination with movies. However, the alteration in Jackson's writing was the critical factor. It was as though he'd been in therapy to teach him how to express anger. All of the songs he wrote are about conflict, although one of them is clearly light-hearted in intention.

The result, *Thriller*, provoked a vinyl, tape and CD feeding frenzy the like of which had not been seen since the emergence of The Beatles, when singles were still the stock-in-trade of the pop music industry, and certainly has not been equalled since. (In 1964, The Beatles had 11 Top 10 hits in the US; in 1983, when singles were mostly important adjuncts to album sales, Jackson had seven Top 10 hits.) Sales were boosted by several marketing coups.

As noted, seven of the nine tracks were hit singles, each one hoovering up more album sales. Videos with high production values were shot to promote the singles and Jackson eventually broke through MTV's racial barrier. After three hit singles, his appearance on the *Motown 25: Yesterday, Today, Forever* NBC TV special – in which the moonwalk dance was seen by an estimated 47 million viewers – gave the album yet another boost. By June 1983 *Thriller* had sold 10 million copies worldwide, over seven million of them in the US. This was serious business in an industry suffering a recession. In fact, the album's success in pulling buyers into the record stores was helping the sales of other acts.

When the dust finally settled, Michael Jackson's second Epic solo album had sold a staggering 51 million copies. And he got his Grammies. At the Awards ceremony, actor Mickey Rooney, one of the presenters, joked early on, "It's a pleasure doing The Michael Jackson Show", as the singer collected Album of the Year, Record of the Year (for 'Beat It'), Best Pop Vocal Performance, Male, Best Rock Vocal Performance, Male (for 'Beat It'), Best New Rhythm & Blues Song and Best

R&B Vocal Performance, Male (both for 'Billie Jean') and Best Recording For Children (for narration and vocals on E.T. *The Extra-Terrestrial* based on the Steven Speilberg movie). *Thriller* engineer Bruce Swedien won the Grammy for Best Engineered Recording (Non-Classical), and Quincy Jones and Jackson picked up Producer Of The Year (Non-Classical). In the US, the TV audience for the Awards was 60 million. In the week following the broadcast, *Thriller* sold another million copies in the US alone.

All songs written by Michael Jackson unless otherwise stated.

Wanna Be Startin' Somethin'

Written by Michael at the time *Off The Wall* was being recorded, there are obvious rhythmic parallels with 'Don't Stop 'Til You Get Enough' in the busy percussion section and David Williams' guitar. But there's a shift towards synthesisers (Greg Phillinganes and Bill Wolfer) as carriers of the rhythm. The real change is in the tenor of the lyrics – there is anger at gossips' vicious tongues, at treachery and cunning of false friends. The singer hurls insults ("you're a vegetable") and introduces Billie Jean, always talking, a motor-mouth, "tellin' lies and rubbish".

There's practical and moral advice offered too – if you can't afford to look after and raise a child, don't get pregnant, otherwise you'll find yourself stealing or the baby "slowly dyin' ". The song ends on a hopeful note – look to your personal pride, believe in yourself – buoyed up by a joyful African chant. The track was the fourth single, released in June 1983, backed with The Jacksons' 'Rock With You', a number eight UK hit and number five US hit.

Baby Be Mine

(Rod Temperton)

The first of three Temperton songs opens with a drum fill closely reprising the start to 'Rock With You' and grooves merrily into a mid-tempo love song of irrepressibly sunny disposition. In spite of the presence of a small regiment of synthesiser players/programmers (six of them, actually), drummer Ndugu Chancler keeps the track grounded, giving it a pop swing, particularly in the bubbly choruses. Oddly, it appeared only as a B-side to 'I Just Can't Stop Loving You'.

The Girl Is Mine

After the success of 'Girlfriend', the song Paul McCartney wrote for Jackson, a rematch was perhaps inevitable. At the time, McCartney's career was not at its perkiest and the critics were, as ever, condemning him for not being John Lennon. So Jackson's invitation to duet on this pleasant stroll through an AOR melody offered a welcome return to very familiar territory.

Although Jackson wrote it, 'The Girl Is Mine' sounds like the sort of song McCartney writes in his sleep. This is credit, again, to Jackson's aforementioned "sponge"-like quality, the way he can absorb people's styles. (Subsequently, Jackson and McCartney worked together on 'Say Say Say' and 'The Man', both of which appeared on McCartney's *Pipes Of Peace* album.) Although it is supposedly an argument between two friends over a girl's affections, she might not be flattered by the mild, jokey tones adopted here, which suggest that at the end of the day no woman is going to come between their friendship.

Far from the strongest track on the album, it was the first to be released as a single. "We really didn't have much choice," Jackson explained in *Moonwalk*. A duet between McCartney and Jackson would be playlisted unto oblivion and perish through over-exposure soon after the album came out. "We had to get it out of the way", by releasing it up front as a single. Not an outstanding advertisement for the album, it nonetheless reached number eight in the UK and was a number two US hit. It's MOR winsomeness is similar to McCartney's collaboration with Stevie Wonder on 'Ebony & Ivory'.

A few years later, while McCartney was visiting Jackson's LA home, the latter asked him how best to invest the massive fortune *Thriller* had earned. "In song publishing," replied the former Beatle, who had lately acquired most of Buddy Holly's song catalogue. Jackson took McCartney's advice to heart and promptly bought ATV Music, which owned Northern Songs, the Lennon/McCartney catalogue. They have not recorded together since.

Thriller
(Rod Temperton)

There obviously comes a time when trying to find something new to say about a work that has sold over 50 million copies seems just a little fatuous. This is that time. Does anyone not know about this track? Has anyone in the radiocentric world not heard it? Or 'Billie Jean' or 'Beat It'? Written by Temperton as a homage to horror movies, 'Thriller' creaks open with a door that could use some oil, echoing footsteps, a howling wolf and a howling wind. The dance groove, rolling in like fog on the moors, resolves into an evenly paced 4/4, driven solely by synthesisers and only Williams' guitar hinting at funky syncopation.

Jackson again sings with a harder edge – as he'd done on 'Wanna Be Startin' Somethin'' – but the crowning glory is the fruity closing recitation, or "rap" as it is inappropriately named on the sleeve, using the resonant, haunted tones of the late, great Vincent Price, the well-known horror icon. Jackson felt moved to treat seriously the laughable accusations that 'Thriller' implied approval of occult practices and to issue an official denial. This, too, may have helped to shift more copies. The fifth single off the album, it was a number 10 UK hit.

Beat It

Jackson gets pragmatic and kicks down the doors of MTV by cutting a straight, lumpen 4/4 rock track laced with an unbelievably fussy and flashy rock guitar solo courtesy of Eddie Van Halen. It clearly belongs on a different track but, hey, if it gets exposure on MTV, who's to care? Steve Lukather and Paul Jackson add further rock riffing. Lyrically, we find Jackson in his alter ego guise as Ice-J. He cuts the macho pull of the gang's colours but stresses the advisability of getting out before the kid becomes just another statistic. It was released as a single while its predecessor, 'Billie Jean', was still climbing the charts and ensured an almost complete takeover of the airwaves. It was a number three UK hit, a US number one.

Billie Jean

At one point this song was to be retitled 'Not My Lover', because Quincy Jones thought listeners might confuse the object of Jackson's ire with Billie Jean King, the tennis player. A celebrity of Jackson's stature is, as a matter of course it seems, plagued by a number of damaged or deluded people who think they have some claim on or against him. (And some may even be right.) The character filing a paternity suit in 'Billie Jean' is a composite of these lost souls, he admitted in *Moonwalk*.

Sung in an aching, angry voice with the full range of gasps, squeals and catches, the lyric is delivered in the style of one giving evidence under cross-examination, the passion of the story and the plea of innocence increasing from the plaintive to the bitterly declamatory as the track progresses. Dean Parks' terse guitar solo manages to say a lot with a few notes through the sheer bite of his playing. 'Billie Jean' reached number one in both the US and UK.

Human Nature

(Jeff Porcaro & John Bettis)

After the anger and aggression of 'Beat It' and 'Billie Jean', the mollifying effects of a sensual mid-tempo pop ballad are not to be sneered at, and this delightful tune by John Bettis and Steve Porcaro exactly fits the bill. Porcaro's Toto lay down a billowy wash of LA studio sounds and Jackson's voice is at its most breathy and feverish, as city streets call him to their night life. And if you think that the song, ostensibly about the joys of singles dating, sounds strangely at odds with the preceding track, you are not alone. Lovely sound though.

P.Y.T (Pretty Young Thing)
(James Ingram & Quincy Jones)

'Human Nature' ends with Jackson waking up, touching "her" shoulder, hearing the call of the street again. Almost immediately he's in the next track, huskily whispering how good she makes him feel, so let's be off into the city night. Subliminal connections like this are what's expected from a canny producer like Jones.

'P.Y.T' is a sharp little dancer, co-written by James Ingram, one of the best singers in Jones' circle, and Jones himself. Satisfactory enough in its pop-soul way, there is less to it than at first meets the ear. Cute and quite catchy, its attraction is its fizzy drive, courtesy of Ndugu Chancler's drums, but aside from the oft-repeated 'P.Y.T.' hook of the title, melodically there is not much to linger in the memory. The dance market was enough to turn it into a number 11 UK hit.

The Lady In My Life
(Rod Temperton)

The final *Thriller* track is a Temperton ballad and a very interesting one at that. It is one of the few occasions in which Jackson tries to take on the mantle of "Lurve Man" à la Teddy Pendergrass. This is not apparent during the first two verses and choruses, and one only gets a hint of it in the bridge. But after Paul Jackson's chords lay out and Louis Johnson starts poppin' his bass guitar, we suddenly find ourselves in the presence of Jackson, shirt open to the navel, extrapolating in increasingly urgent fashion about what he's going to give "his lady" and whereabouts he's going to give it to her (i.e. "all over"). Hey! He done growed up.

PAUL SIMON

Graceland

September 1986

By Chris Charlesworth

I N THE SUMMER of 1984, as he faced the problem of furthering a critically successful but commercially waning career, Paul Simon received a gift from his friend Heidi Berg that set him on the road towards what many critics believe to be his masterpiece. The gift was a bootleg tape from the townships of South Africa called *Gumboots: Accordion Jive Hits No. 2*, and it changed his musical direction radically.

Simon spent the rest of the year seeking out similar black African music and, thoroughly inspired by his researches, went to South Africa in February 1985 to spend 17 days recording with local musicians in Johannesburg's Ovation Studio.

Graceland, however, was not recorded solely in South Africa, nor did it consist only of South African music, nor was its subject matter African-oriented. The album was recorded in New York, Los Angeles, London and Louisiana as well as Johannesburg, and included tracks with Cajun and Hispanic backing musicians.

While South African mbaqanga and mbube rhythms dominate the music, adding a unique flavour hitherto largely unknown in America and Europe, the songs actually fuse South African elements with American pop, thus rendering the unknown more palatable to ears already tuned to Paul Simon. The majority of the tracks were backed by musicians from the townships, and the experience of writing for and in such a different musical tradition was obviously a liberating experience. While the concerns Simon chose to write about are those of an American writer – and he is too honest a writer to wish or be able to renounce his cultural heritage – his open response to other cultures loosened the bounds of his songwriting and seems to have enabled him to find a new language, both musically and lyrically.

The release of *Graceland* was met with as much political criticism as artistic acclaim. In 1986, South Africa was still ruled by the minority National Party, and the essentially peaceful "velvet revolution" (to borrow a description more usually applied to Eastern Europe) that followed from the release of Nelson Mandela, and Prime Minister De Klerk's recognition that apartheid was no longer sustainable, was some years away. Sanctions still applied, and a major focus of the anti-apartheid movement was on high-profile sporting and cultural events. Although the principal purpose of the boycott as it affected musicians was to prevent middle-of-the-road or pension-seeking rock dinosaurs cashing in at the notorious white playground of Sun City, Simon had clearly broken the letter of the sanctions regulations. *Graceland* thus stirred up more controversy than Simon, eternally quiet, diligent and uncontroversial, had attracted in his entire career.

In vain did Simon plead that, far from offering succour to the oppressor, he had been popularising (and rewarding handsomely) some of the very "victims" the sanctions were intended to benefit. He had wandered into a political minefield. To those who argued that any breach of sanctions was unacceptable – and this position is understandable both in theory and as a propaganda weapon – any counter-argument based on artistic grounds was irrelevant. In the final analysis, however, the artistic merits of *Graceland* figure more substantially in the history books than the fierce denunciations that were, in the event, soon overtaken by the accelerating march of progress.

The album was a massive commercial success, especially in the UK where, after reaching number one, it lingered in the charts for almost two years. In America, where radio stations are traditionally less attuned to styles of music that don't comply with their rigid formatting process, *Graceland* reached number three, though it stayed in the Top 200 for 97 weeks, eventually selling four million copies.

All songs written by Paul Simon.

The Boy In The Bubble

The growl of accordion with which the album begins states immediately that this is a different Simon product. With a nod to the *Gumboots* bootleg that had sparked his first interest in South African music, Simon lets his musical co-writer, the accordionist Forere Motloheloa, signpost the direction the album would take. It is a direction that, in its dense, churning rhythms, owes little or nothing to the blues, to Chuck Berry, or to the American folk and Tin Pan Alley traditions in which

Simon had made his reputation.

The subject matter – the horrors and insubstantiality that underpin the "days of miracle and wonder" – is less of a radical departure from Simon's previous work, but he brings a vividness to the lyrics (the juxtaposition of "the bomb in the baby carriage", for example), as well as a "serious playfulness" (witness the alliteration of "the boy in the bubble and the baby with the baboon heart"), which clearly shows the extent to which this new music had irrigated Simon's imagination. His lyrics add an ironic counterpoint to the upbeat, cheerful swing of the music, but it is not his purpose merely to moan about the awfulness of life on "a distant constellation that's dying in a corner of the sky". He is more knowledgeable, more compassionate and more of a poet than that, and if you doubt the poetic qualities of the song, try achieving in other words the same concise effect as Simon does in the final lines – "these are the days of miracle and wonder, and don't cry, baby, don't cry".

"'The Boy In The Bubble' devolved down to hope and dread," Simon told *Rolling Stone*'s David Fricke. "That's the way I see the world, a balance between the two, but coming down on the side of hope."

'The Boy In The Bubble' was released as a single in the UK, where it reached number 26 with the help of a stunning video, which, in 3D, placed Simon in the jungle, surrounded one minute by wild animals and the next by state-of-the-art technology.

Graceland

Joy and sorrow; history and today; America and Africa – in the album's title track, Simon brews a medley of contrasting ingredients into a song as fine as any he has written. The bubbling, insistent, sinuous playing of Baghiti Khumalo on fretless bass and Ray Phiri on guitar provides a perfect counterpoint to the American music the song celebrates – the Mississippi Delta, home of the blues, memorably defined as "shining like a National guitar"; Elvis Presley, whose Graceland home is the object of the singer's pilgrimage; and The Everly

Brothers, early influences who repay the compliment with their backing vocals on the fade-out.

But the song is no mere trip down nostalgia lane. Simon's concerns, and those of the "poorboys and pilgrims with families" who share his journey, are contemporary. The singer is not only divorced ("the child of my first marriage" accompanies him) but also a recent loser in the game of love (the bittersweet phrase, "She comes back to tell me she's gone" tells of a fresh, unhealed wound). Nor is his sympathy reserved for his own misfortunes. His "travelling companions are ghost and empty sockets"; he empathises with the "girl in New York City who calls herself the human trampoline".

The jaunty music, with its traces of rockabilly, might seem callous and insensitive set against the lyrics, with their clear-eyed view of the emotional detritus of modern life, and such a contrast is just the sort of thing Simon excelled at earlier in his career. Simon's purpose, however, is not to express pity — either for himself or for the other casualties "bouncing into Graceland". The happy accident of Presley's choice of name for his famous and magnificent abode allows Simon to play with the religious notion of redemptive grace. Though not previously, nor here, a religious writer, Simon presents music itself as offering a form of salvation. "Maybe I've a reason to believe we all will be received in Graceland," he concludes.

Bob Dylan expresses a similar belief in the redemptive power of music in 'Mr Tambourine Man'. It's curious to observe that, though written at a much earlier stage of his career, it too, like 'Graceland', reflected a distinct change of style from the writer's previous work.

I Know What I Know

This collaboration with General M.D. Shirinda and The Gaza Singers is a lighter piece, contrasting the Shangaan voices of South Africa with the febrile chatter of the New York party scene. The song itself stands as a tribute to Simon's self-confidence in his new work. He can afford to quote the party girl's put-downs ("She thought I was alright ... in a sort of a limited way for an off-night", and, "There's something about you that really reminds me of money"), as well as his own feeble chat-up line ("Aren't you the woman who was recently given a Fulbright?"). The repeated line, "Don't I know you from the cinematographer's party?", brilliant in its scansion and rhythm, neatly encapsulates the empty socialising of the New York arts crowd.

Simon, while clearly not averse to attending such parties, is not the prisoner of that scene, and has no illusions about the permanence of fame and reputation. He is, at this stage of his life and career, his own man. "I know what I know, I'll sing what I said, we come and we go, that's a thing that I keep in the back of my head."

Gumboots

As the title indicates, this song is another tribute to the accordion-based music that had triggered Simon's initial interest in the sound of Soweto. Backed this time by the Boyoyo Boys, he tackles a subject perennially popular with poets and songsmiths – love. Among the challenges this subject presents is the difficulty of finding anything new to say but Simon rises to this challenge. Three vignettes that show different ways of failing to communicate are separated by a chorus, which elegantly sums up a feeling every lover has suffered at one time or another. "You don't feel you could love me but I feel you could". The song ends with a repeat of the opening two lines, as if to make the point that this is a process that goes around and around forever.

This was the first song that Simon heard on his bootleg tape. It is the style of music favoured by mining and railroad workers in SA; 'Gumboots' are the heavy boots they wear at work.

Diamonds On The Soles Of Her Shoes

Unlike the previous songs on the album, which were initially recorded in Johannesburg, 'Diamonds...' was recorded entirely at The Hit Factory in New York, when Ladysmith Black Mambazo were in town for an appearance on *Saturday*

Night Live. Curiously, the song opens, unlike the "African" songs, with a verse in Zulu. It also features the popular West African star Youssou N'dour, as well as our old friends Baghiti Khumalo and Ray Phiri.

Ladysmith Black Mambazo open the song a cappella, before the familiar bouncing beat kicks in and establishes a cheerful, danceable groove driven headlong by the startling bass guitar of Baghiti Khumalo. The lyrics themselves are somewhat obscure. The rich girl whose non-standard footwear provides the title seems to be involved both with the singer, who takes her for granted, and, doubtless on the rebound, with a poor boy whose "ordinary shoes" can only walk her to a doorway on Upper Broadway.

Maybe there are metaphors here, or subtle allusions to New York street life, or a surreal reworking of the 'Down In The Boondocks' theme. Maybe Simon is just having fun – "and I could say 'oo oo oo ...' as if everybody knows what I'm talking about".

You Can Call Me Al

Rumour has it that this song had its origins at a party Simon hosted at which he met the composer Pierre Boulez for the first time. As he was leaving, Boulez called Simon "Al" and the hostess, his then wife Peggy, "Betty".

Whether or not this is true, the song itself has moved a long way from such a simple social misunderstanding. Its theme is an old Simon favourite – alienation. The three verses depict various instances – the man who feels "soft in the middle [though] the rest of my life is so hard"; the man who, having lost his wife, his family, and his role model, finds "my nights are so long"; the man lost in "a street in a strange world".

Now, though, merely depicting social alienation is not sufficient for the revitalised Simon. As in 'Graceland', he offers redemption from such angst. This time it is not music but friendship that provides the means of salvation – "if you'll be my bodyguard I can be your long lost pal". A penny whistle solo by Morris Goldberg (a white South African based in New York) offers plaintive support to the music of

Baghiti Khumalo and Ray Phiri, underlining the fragility of human relationships that Simon so frequently sees and so sympathetically describes.

'Al' was a number four hit in the UK, helped by an unusual, slightly surreal, video, whose principal attraction was its stark simplicity in the age of big-budget, often pretentious, rock videos. Shot with one stationary camera on one set, it featured Simon's friend, the actor Chevy Chase, appearing as Simon, playing a Fender bass guitar, while Simon himself appears dressed similarly in the same location, almost as a guest in his own video.

Under African Skies

If 'Graceland' offers the possibility of redemption through music, then the subject of 'Under African Skies' is its achievement – "after the dream of falling and calling your name out, these are the roots of rhythm and the roots of rhythm remain".

Set to a lilting "walking rhythm" and backed by Linda Ronstadt's beautiful descant, which seems to echo to the very skies Simon sings about, the song opens and closes with a pen-portrait of "Joseph" (a name undoubtedly suggested by that of his collaborator Joseph Shabalala, but perhaps more accurately to be taken as symbolising an African Everyman). In a few deft lines, Simon sketches both man and continent. Listening to the words and the music together, it is impossible not to sense the vastness of the skies under which Joseph walks.

The middle verse, which shifts curiously from Simon's own, masculine gender ("my nursery door") to the feminine halfway through, contains his clearest statement of the redemptive power of music – "give her the wings to fly through harmony and she won't bother you no more".

Homeless

Co-written with Joseph Shabalala, the leader of Ladysmith Black Mambazo, 'Homeless' is unlike any of the other songs on the album. Sung entirely a cappella, showcasing the remarkable range and power of Shabalala's ensemble, the lyrics, alternating between Zulu and English, have no discernible narrative structure, consisting mainly of phrases rather than complete sentences. The theme, as we shall see, is African.

Simon has said that, "[We] wrote in English and Zulu, starting the piece in the middle and working outwards to the beginning and end". The crux of the song, therefore, is the verse beginning, "Strong wind destroy our home, many dead tonight it could be you". This song is not about homelessness as a social problem affecting affluent western societies (not least London, where the song was recorded at Abbey Road Studios). This is the homelessness of massacre victims in a society where political violence rages. The haunting power of the key repeated chorus – "We are homeless... moonlight sleeping on a midnight lake" – works not just literally but as a metaphor for the political dispossession of the black South African majority.

The song ends with a verse in Zulu that translates as: "We would like to announce to the entire nation that we are the best at singing in this style". What, in another context, might simply be an amusing example of a performer's egotism becomes a statement of defiance. We do not accept, Ladysmith Black Mambazo proclaim, the subhuman status to which our oppressors wish to condemn us. We do not merely deserve better – we are better.

Crazy Love, Vol. II

With 'Crazy Love, Vol. II' Simon reverts to the music and the themes that dominate the album. Guitarist Ray Phiri's band, Stimela, provide the backing for the interwoven stories of Fat Charlie and the singer, both of whom seem to be in the throes (sic) of divorce. (It may be conjectured that this is the "second volume" of the title, divorce being an established stage in the lifecycle of American love affairs.)

The chorus lines ("I don't want no part ..."), repeated with subtle rhythmic variation after each of the song's three verses, show Simon rejecting the "craziness" of a life "on fire ... all over the evening news", and telling his ex that this time "the joke is on her".

Initially recorded in Johannesburg's Ovation Studios, the song was completed at The Hit Factory in New York. Morris Goldberg, the penny whistler on 'You Can Call Me Al', makes another appearance, this time on soprano sax.

That Was Your Mother

As if to make the point that this is a Paul Simon album, not a World Music curiosity, Graceland ends with two songs rooted in specifically American musical traditions. The first of these was recorded in Louisiana with backing from those doyens of the Cajun scene, Good Rockin' Dopsie & The Twisters.

Opening with the robust accordion of the great Dopsie himself (Alton Rubin Sr.), and thus linking the song to the *Gumboots* accordion-based style that originally inspired the album, 'That Was Your Mother' is a jolly romp, sung by a father to his (implicitly grown-up) son, recalling the circumstances in which the son's parents met. The singer reminds his son (whom he loves, despite his being "the burden of my generation" – a pun Simon uses to great poetic effect) that, though he might now be a parental authority figure, he was once a young man "standing on the corner of Lafayette", looking for some action. It is an observation few children relish hearing or are capable of fully understanding.

It is a mark of Simon's maturity that he can use this subject, and in a song of such danceable brio. (Irony is added by the presence in The Twisters' line-up of two of Dopsie's own sons.) It is also remarkable that, in such a seemingly simple song, he simultaneously takes the "child's" position vis-à-vis a musical "parent" and pays homage to Clifton Chenier, founding father of Cajun music and "the King of the Bayou".

All Around The World Or The Myth Of Fingerprints

The final song is perhaps the bleakest on the album. The second "American" track, this time backed by Tex-Mex stars Los Lobos, it also features the accordion – David Hildago establishing a rocking tempo, which, with the long and beautiful "oo oo oo" vocal melody, belies the unvarnished grimness of the song's lyrical content.

If the chorus is melancholy (the sun getting first "weary" and then "bloody" before setting, the lack of any answer to the question, "What's a better thing to do?" in "the black pit town", and the universality of this condition "all around the world"), then the verses positively drip with ennui. The first verse, in the voice of the cynical, faded "former talk-show host", defines "the myth of fingerprints" – far from being unique, as criminologists affirm, "I've seen them all and man, they're all the same". The second verse uses the image of an army post – that it is abandoned only adds to the world-weary tone – as a classic example of the crushing of individuality, in this case of the army's new recruits. The third verse largely repeats the first but, with no need to repeat his definition of the myth, Simon ends with a bleak conclusion – "that's why we must learn to live alone".

U2

The Joshua Tree

March 1987

By Bill Graham

THE UNFORGETTABLE FIRE had primed people to expect the unexpected from U2, and *The Joshua Tree*, delivered after a 30-month gap, again found them confounding predictions. Where *The Unforgettable Fire* sprawled and veered off into the realms of the unconscious, *The Joshua Tree* was concise and often as politically specific as U2 would ever get. If *The Unforgettable Fire* was an album of breadth, pushing the boundaries, *The Joshua Tree* was an album of depth, working within the constraining disciplines of the song.

Much had happened to the band during those two years and more. *Time* magazine would soon call them "rock's hottest ticket". Their show-stealing performance of 'Bad' at Live Aid meant U2 had ceased to be the secret and private property of their fans. Rock's biggest underground band had exploded overground and, as a result, they'd starred on Amnesty's Conspiracy Of Hope tour. It's entirely possible they would have already entered the megastar bracket if *The Unforgettable Fire* had contained a couple of other radio-friendly singles to follow 'Pride (In The Name Of Love)'.

Meanwhile, they were still hungry for new ideas and experiences, with Bono to the fore. With his wife, Ali Hewson, he'd volunteered for charity work in Ethiopia – the only Band Aid and Live Aid participant besides Bob Geldof to actively investigate what was happening there. He was also exploring areas of music that had not previously interested him.

Bob Dylan was one catalyst. When Dylan had played Slane Castle in 1984, Bono had guested on an encore and then talked with him and Van Morrison for an informal *Hot Press* interview. This relationship with Dylan would develop. Some months later, the writer met Bono in a Dublin nightclub; the latter went home early in the morning to receive a phone call from Dylan. But then U2 – and Bono especially – were always the sons who wanted to learn from the wisdom of the fathers; they'd already struck up chummy relationships with Bruce Springsteen and Pete Townshend.

At their first meeting, Dylan had disorientated Bono by talking about his own debt to Irish music, especially The Clancy Brothers, the prototype Irish ballad group, who'd played Greenwich Village in Dylan's early folk days. Till then,

U2, with the partial exception of their country and Elvis fan, Larry Mullen, hadn't been much interested in any Irish or American roots music.

Like all the young bands of their generation, they'd reacted against the prevailing Irish trends of the Seventies. From their perspective, Irish music seemed archaic, too nationalist and an obstacle to new ideas. In their early days, they'd also been rightly unimpressed by the clichéd blooze-rock bar bands then littering the Dublin scene. But now Bono entered a phase where he would duet with Clannad on 'In A Lifetime', write 'Silver And Gold' and recruit Keith Richards and Ronnie Wood to perform it for Little Steven's Sun City project.

The band from the south of Ireland would now dive into the American Deep South. The experience would teach Bono how to explore and reconcile the divide between the secular and the spiritual in his soul. Blues and rock'n'roll too often used Biblical imagery, and Bono's reading would also now turn to American literature, with Flannery O'Connor a particular favourite. In consequence, his lyrics would become far less vague and he would start to write in narrative idioms.

They would also understand better how to relate Christianity to social justice. Outsiders still often related Christianity to the reactionary televangelists of the Moral Majority, but U2 would find an escape from that trap. Touring for Amnesty and through Bono's travels in Ethiopia and Central America, they would encounter the radical Christian and Catholic aid charities dealing with poverty and oppression in the Third World.

Again, this was a particularly Irish response. Per capita, the Republic had been by far the largest contributor of donations to Live Aid. In response to the Troubles in the North, much Irish political and religious idealism had been deflected into Third World relief agencies like Concern. *The Joshua Tree* would be the one album by a major act that even noticed, let alone started to investigate, the larger and more painful issues surrounding Live Aid.

They were already signalling their changes before the album was released. In January 1986, they premiered an intentionally rough version of 'Trip Through Your Wires' on

RTE's *T.V. Gaga* show. Their short Conspiracy Of Hope set was débuted at the Dublin Self Aid show in May, and included Eddie Cochran's 'C'mon Everybody' and a vicious version of Dylan's 'Maggie's Farm'.

But none of this would have mattered if they hadn't mastered the art of songwriting. Methods changed. Previously, U2 material was usually worked out at band jams; now Bono and The Edge often brought basic song ideas to the rhythm section of Adam Clayton and Larry Mullen. With Nineties hindsight, it can all seem funny-peculiar. Only on their fifth album, into their second contract, had U2 learned proper, joined-up songwriting. Could any act expect such a long and lucrative apprenticeship now?

But other working methods remained unchanged. Again Daniel Lanois and Brian Eno produced, though the Canadian now took a more influential role. Again, much work occurred outside the studio, this time with an Amek console at The Edge's and Clayton's houses. The original band was still detectable on tracks such as 'Where The Streets Have No Name' and 'In God's Country', but they'd shed their first skin. U2 now underplayed and left spaces; The Edge was no longer required to layer overdubbed curtains of sound to fill every gap.

Indeed, it's remarkable how easily they slipped into their new identity. The album skilfully pastiches a variety of Top 40 rock styles of the time. There are hints of The Police and Lou Reed, traces of Rod Stewart in the rock ballads, and Jimi Hendrix and Led Zeppelin enter the band's vocabulary for the first time on 'Bullet The Blue Sky'. Dylan, too, is a new presence, palpable on 'Trip Through Your Wires'. Yet U2's own distinctive voice wasn't drowned out by their borrowings. *The Joshua Tree* is unmistakably classic U2, since these new influences release rather than imprison the band.

And then on the second side, when listeners might have been starting to suspect U2 were getting too radio-friendly, they strike out again in new directions with the gorgeous World Music lilt of 'One Tree Hill', and then, crucially, with the savage 'Exit'. This was a key song in U2's future development, since now it seems so obviously the first ancestor of the jagged sound and songs of bleak spiritual doubt on *Achtung Baby*.

For some time, Bono had been speaking of his ambition to make a record with all the diversity of The Beatles' *White Album*. This album lacks the sprawling anarchy of The Beatles' record, but it's the first conclusive evidence that the best young live band of their era had graduated as masterful pop mimics in the studio. With *The Joshua Tree*, U2's recorded work finally catches up and even outstrips their live reputation.

Bono is one major reason. Beforehand, while he might dominate on stage, he didn't always focus on record, especially since he was often a laggard struggling with the lyrics. But on *The Joshua Tree*, he knew his themes and targets. His lyrics leave the dream time for often harsh, daylight realities. This extra substance in the songs led to a new emotional authority and accuracy in his singing.

This individual and collective evolution between albums also shows how and why U2 have endured as a creative as well as a commercial force. Round about 1987, the Second British Invasion began to peter out. Its acts either fell foul of lifestyle problems, or produced soundalike albums or records whose attempted change of direction was unconvincing. Till then, U2 had often been associated with a pack of Big Music bands, notably Simple Minds, The Waterboys, Big Country and a very reluctant Echo & The Bunnymen. With *The Joshua Tree*, incidentally the first platinum million-selling CD in America, U2 launched themselves into their own solitary stratosphere.

They'd also won because they were still refusenik romantics, the last gang in town who still believed that rock shouldn't limit its horizons to private pleasures and problems. U2 didn't want rock to be a lifestyle accessory; they still insisted it might just involve some public dimension, some raising of communal consciousness. Despite the Reagan years, there were still some optimists who shared those beliefs.

However, let's not exaggerate the idealism in U2's audience. The hit singles, and their new welcome into Top 40 radio, also won the band another new audience of Young American teens who weren't necessarily appreciating them for their philosophy.

Really, U2 had been surfing a wave since Live Aid. As

so often happens, a band can seize their time. Their Irish optimism, curiosity and adaptability gave them a special empathy with America, while their humanism tuned in to a new generosity. But equally importantly, the chance for their breakthrough arrived just as their recording and songwriting skills reached maturity.

The Joshua Tree was the summarising symbol of the album. It was the name of the Californian desert town where Gram Parsons went drinking and fixin' to die; it's also the name of the desert's most resilient cactus. Even in the worst drought, life and the waters of salvation could still be found.

The album sleeve caused some ambivalence. Were these Irishmen in their cowboy clobber Mexican emigrants or lost gringos? Were they play-acting in a spaghetti Western or some more serious drama? And had the Irish the right to plunder and play with American images and music? In the aftermath of this album, those questions would hit U2 in the solar plexus.

Not surprisingly, the album sailed to the top of both the UK and US charts.

All songs written by U2.

Where The Streets Have No Name

For the opening track, the band fed their fans' sense of anticipation with a slowly swelling keyboard intro over which The Edge, Clayton and Mullen set a frantic, soaring tone for no less than one minute and 46 seconds before Bono arrives. With The Edge's skittering guitar, the first track is familiar U2, though the mood's far more sunlit than the autumnal weather of *The Unforgettable Fire*. But where were those "streets with no name"? There were two usual answers: the streets of both America's cities and of the derelict, abandoned ghost towns of the desert. It could also be a reference to the cities and towns of highland Ethiopia, where streets are also numbered, not named. You don't write lines like, "Show you a place/High on a desert plain/Where the streets have no name" about the canyons of Manhattan.

I Still Haven't Found What I'm Looking For

The first song that shows what a leap U2 (and Bono) had made. From one superficial perspective, it's a smart job of pop hackwork, pretty standard American radio, rock-ballad fare with the appropriate degree of uplift in the chorus to inspire the Yanks. But it's far more than just another stadium rabble-rouser to be played during the breaks in American football matches. The band's rhythms are far more supple and cultivated than your average bouffant HM band of that period; there's a spring and bounce in Larry Mullen's offbeats that those whitebread bands never played. Again, U2's Island background gave their music an extra flavour.

Besides, its religious theme hardly suited a half-time anthem. On *The Unforgettable Fire*, Bono had moved beyond dogma to explore the quest for faith, but here he isn't hiding behind codes, metaphors or Brian Eno's cloudy production, but has fashioned a spiritual song that even agnostics could admire.

Faith becomes not an act of blind obedience and death-delivering dogma – I don't believe this song could have been written by an Irish Catholic, disillusioned, lapsed or otherwise – but a constant struggle, with hope the ally in the search for renewal. In other hands, its themes could have been black and pessimistic, but the melody and performance of 'I Still Haven't Found What I'm Looking For' are free from despair and welcome the spiritual challenge ahead.

Moreover, Bono's witness – "I believe in the kingdom come/And all the colours bleed into one" – was inclusive, not exclusive. Not surprisingly, it appealed to Americans' own restless and shape-shifting religiosity.

With Or Without You

A masterful pop song that reveals how U2 had learned the lessons of emotional restraint. Bass and drums pad in, and what sounds like keyboards is The Edge unfurling his Infinite guitar, a gizmo invented by Michael Brook, with whom he'd worked on the *Captive* soundtrack. Again Bono's theme of self-surrender is familiar but his vocals are measured, no longer hurtling over the brink. Likewise, the band now had the emotional experience and technical expertise to build a performance. Now they simmered and the kettle didn't squeal.

Like 'I Still Haven't Found...' it's also proof that U2 had reinvented themselves as a quality pop band. The basic design might have come from Sting's bottom drawer, but here U2 had taken a contemporary and familiar style and invested it with their own character.

In another sense, this is also U2's first real adult love song. Being "with or without you" are equally tormented emotional states. As the song unfolds, there's tension and a quality of detachment and deliberation in the early verses – "a bed of nails/she makes me wait" – which makes the catharsis of the later choruses far more intense. "And you give and you give and you give yourself away", Bono sings, caught in that peculiarly suspended state of ego loss where love can dissolve the sense of self. Somehow, this writer could never quite understand why the singer was so regularly accused of egotism when so many of his lyrics concern egolessness.

It's tender and, above all, vulnerable. "She's got me with nothing to win and nothing left to lose" Bono sings before the last chorus, and the restraint is underscored by the final instrumental reprise. Other bands might have climaxed with a romantic storm but U2 instead close with the calm.

Bullet The Blue Sky

Very simply put, 'Bullet...' was the result of two discoveries. The Edge found Jimi Hendrix, and Bono experienced the Central American conflict when he travelled to San Salvador and Nicaragua through the good offices of Amnesty International. With it, the album moves from personal to political themes. Bono has always claimed the song was inspired by an incident in San Salvador when he witnessed government planes attacking a band of peasants.

Again, the Irish context is important. The Nicaraguan and the other Central American conflicts received far more coverage in Ireland than in Britain. The Irish identified with the

Nicaraguans, whom they believed were being bullied by the larger power of America. Many radical Catholic missionaries served in Central America, and the since-discredited Bishop Casey was present at the mass where El Salvador's Archbishop Romero was killed by government forces. Some years later, Nicaragua's rebel President, Daniel Ortega, would visit Ireland and meet U2, a private, unpublicised encounter set up by Michael D. Higgins, Ireland's Arts Minister at the time. There is a further Irish link in that Amnesty's American chapter was led by Jack Healey, an Irish-American who was formerly a Franciscan priest.

But the track also dramatises an internal conflict between the US's own angels and demons. The ugly Americans "peeling off those dollar bills" were the agents of religious imperialism, the fundamental sects who influenced the conservative forces in the region, and Bono's lyrics contrast the burning crosses of the Ku Klux Klan with the liberating spirit of John Coltrane's *A Love Supreme*, the man who "breathes into a saxophone". Ultimately the song pivots on its ambiguous final line. "Outside is America", but which face is it showing? With 'Bullet...' , U2 had learned they must deal with both the promise and the threat.

U2 had sometimes flirted with hard rock but they'd always been wary lest they be trapped by its formulas. But on 'Bullet...' they sidestepped its pitfalls. The Edge went back to the music's more enterprising Sixties origins in the styles of The Who, Led Zeppelin and especially Jimi Hendrix, when all the feedback furies usually served a tune, not a laboured riff, and the music hadn't completely lost the flavour of the blues.

Again, 'Bullet...' distanced U2 from their British Big Music contemporaries and showed they were capable of a far wider range of styles. And just as The Smiths were emerging, with Johnny Marr inaugurating a new school of guitar-playing that deleted Keith Richards and The Clash in favour of The Byrds and The Velvet Underground, The Edge was swimming against the tide of the new fashion. But it made sense. Any guitarist who married rhythm and melody like The Edge was destined to tangle with R&B playing and the legacy of Hendrix.

But if 'Bullet...' broke new ground, it's also a blueprint,

since the version is superseded by the epic live performance developed for *Rattle And Hum*.

Running To Stand Still

The fifth and final track on what was easily U2's best side of vinyl to date. 'Running To Stand Still' remains their finest Dublin anthem, returning to the "seven towers" of Ballymun, the housing development close to Bono's home that was also the site of Roddy Doyle's TV drama series, *Family*.

There, heroin had become a different escape route from the one U2 had been sufficiently lucky and talented to take. But if this ballad is suitably mournful, it's also flecked by an uncannily sympathetic compassion that refuses to cast stones at the woman who's the victim of junk. Heroin, too, can be a temporary transcendence, but the meaning of the melody is that there are other rivers to take out of hopelessness.

Appropriately, the music takes a lead from the Lou Reed songbook, but there's also a trace of Van Morrison and shades of the Bruce Springsteen of *Nebraska* in Bono's keening and harmonica playing. And yet again U2 show their new versatility, since the essentially acoustic performance is basically dominated by Bono and The Edge, with Larry Mullen taking only a brief cameo drum part.

Red Hill Mining Town

Here, the original vinyl version turned over to a far more disparate second side. 'Red Hill Mining Town' is the album's third ballad, but it contrasts with both 'I Still Haven't Found…' and 'Running To Stand Still' in that it's the most cluttered and literal, least mysterious and open-ended track on the album. The blocked harmonies in the chorus give the impression of a band striving too ambitiously and conventionally for effect. Their detractors wouldn't be completely out of order if they deemed it a scarf-waving variant of 'Sailing' written for the National Union of Mineworkers.

A pity they miscalculated, since the melody is undeniably potent and infectious. Furthermore, the song was born from fine intentions, a meditation on the social wreckage caused by the attack on mining communities that left so many unemployed and with uncertain futures.

It was the song on the album least played live. One can only wonder how it might have developed if they'd filleted its excess weight.

In God's Country

The album's second return to a more standard and familiar U2, 'In God's Country' is probably most significant as the last song the band recorded in their original trademark style. And even here Clayton's rumbling counterpoint bass figure before The Edge's guitar break is a mark of their progress.

It's also a companion piece to 'Where The Streets Have No Name', since Bono's back in the desert again, though this time the emotional landscape of "sad eyes, crooked crosses" is more identifiably American. But really, this is U2 cruising, a starter, not a main course. And though Bono's lyrics are clichés, they're saved by the fact that he did Bono better than anybody else.

Trip Through Your Wires

Débuted on RTE as a throwaway, 'Trip Through Your Wires' was intended to present a new, informal U2, a band of buskers who were now supping from the same brew as Dylan, the new folk-friendly Waterboys and The Hot House Flowers. But the studio version is indecisive. U2 seem uncertain whether to opt for carefree spontaneity or develop the song's basic idea, and the combination of Clayton's foursquare bass and Mullen's packing-case Glitter Band drums doesn't embellish it much either.

Bono's dualism about women as angels or devils re-emerges, but can be accepted in the context of 'Trip Through Your Wires' as an unsteady, stumbling drinker's song. His harp's fun too, but this was a far more convincing carouse in its later live version.

One Tree Hill

This was dedicated to the memory of Greg Carroll, a New Zealand Maori who'd worked hardly a year as Bono's personal assistant. Taking Bono's bike to run an errand on a rainswept Dublin night, he crashed into a car and was killed instantly. Happening just as the band were starting to record the album, the death of Carroll, who'd speedily become a much-loved member of the team, was a shattering experience for U2 and their close-knit organisation.

They gave him a celebration, not a lament. The Edge found a loose-limbed guitar melody with both an African and a Hawaiian tinge, and the surge of the playing and Bono's imagery fused to recapture Carroll's sea-going Maori heritage. Furthermore, the lyrics, with their reference to traditional Maori burial ceremonies on One Tree Hill (a suburb of Auckland), indicated that the band's faith didn't exclude an empathy with others' beliefs and rituals. Their Christianity wouldn't plaster over the universal archetypes of mourning.

And yet despite its moving vocal coda, 'One Tree Hill' isn't sombre. It celebrates the life of the spirit, not its extinction. Greg Carroll would not be diminished in death.

Exit

For anyone who was really listening, 'Exit' should have exploded the myth of U2 as the nice guys of rock. Never had they shown such a vicious streak or produced such a withering track. The Edge's sheets of sound return, but now they're not glistening but gorged with anger. Far more than even 'Bullet The Blue Sky', his playing is scratching at the prison bars of polished good taste.

But then, up till this track, U2 had preached alternatives to violence and evil; their music preferred to be inspirational, not confrontational, and had never really wrestled with those beasts in the bottom-most pit. But 'Exit', the wildest card in The Joshua Tree, is both a complete reversal of their previous public artistic character and a crucial clue to their later development that many missed.

Around this time, the writer remembers Bono talking

about another Dublin rock singer, Simon Carmody of The Golden Horde. Carmody had the violence all singers needed, but did he, wondered Bono, have the understanding to channel it? Certainly on 'Exit', Bono the singer ceased being afraid of calling upon his own furies, dramatising that condition of fanaticism where dogmatism verges with psychosis and a man will go "deeper into black, deeper into white" and kill with "the hands of love".

For the first time, the singer was owning up to the dangers of the dualism implicit in Christianity. The track's also notable as the first time U2 strayed onto the ground previously monopolised by their Lypton Village associates, The Virgin Prunes. The similarities aren't only spiritual. The Edge's elder brother, Dik, very briefly an early member of U2, also played a far more scalding and discordantly feedback-drenched guitar style with the Prunes.

But again, only a committed believer could have got inside the skull of the protagonist of 'Exit'. On the succeeding tour, performances of the song would grow ever more fraught and purgative. A year later, an American accused of murder would claim the song drove him to that drastic deed.

Mothers Of The Disappeared

The Joshua Tree is easily U2's most global album, with Bono, the band's foreign correspondent on assignment in Ethiopia, Central America and New Zealand. Now their Amnesty contacts supplied them with an Argentinean theme for the closing track.

Throughout the Seventies and until the middle of the Eighties, the Argentinean military junta had arrested many of its student opponents, who were never seen again, dead or alive. An organisation of the bereaved, literally called Mothers Of The Disappeared, was formed. When democracy returned in the wake of the disastrous Falklands/Malvinas war with Britain, they campaigned for the disclosure of the full truth and the trial of those who had kidnapped, tortured and killed their children.

The track continued the tradition of '40' and 'MLK', for

how long would the Mothers of the Disappeared sing their song? Again the lament works on a drone with Bono testifying "we hear their heartbeats". But its intro, with Eno's percussive treatment of a piano, is more experimental, and the shadows of this lament are punctuated by a barbed guitar interjection.

NIRVANA

Nevermind

September 1991

By Mark Paytress

THREE SIGNIFICANT EVENTS took place between the release of Nirvana's previous album, *Bleach* and the recording of *Nevermind*. Nirvana had been tempted away from Sub Pop, the small but aspirational independent record label that put Seattle on the map. They'd signed a lucrative deal with corporate heavyweight Geffen, which meant they could spend considerably more time (and money) working on a second LP with a name producer. And the merry-go-round of drummers that had seen several hopefuls occupy the hottest seat in the band had been resolved with the recruitment of Dave Grohl.

None of these changes could guarantee a hit record, let alone one that would redefine the sound of rock for the new decade. In fact, the most exciting thing about the continued ascent of *Nevermind* during the winter months of 1991/92 was that it seemed so unexpected. In the UK, dance music seemed to have many of the best musical ideas; in the States, rap and hip-hop danced on the cutting edge. After a mid-Eighties post-punk malaise, epitomised by the limp spectacle of Live Aid, rock had regained some of its disorder at the fringes, with grunge in the States and the short-lived "shoegazing" phenomenon in the UK. However, there was nothing at its commercial heart to suggest that it had regained its ability to enrapture in its time-honoured, high-spirited tradition.

Then Nirvana's *Nevermind* appeared, a blast of indie-forged dynamics made palatable to a wider audience via Kurt Cobain's fast-blossoming talent for applying pure pop bodywork to a souped-up grunge engine. Assisted by the dynamic Dave Grohl, his gangly on-stage foil, Chris Novoselic, and the commercial nous of producer Butch Vig and engineer Andy Wallace, Cobain found himself at the helm of the finest rock machine to make headlines, enjoy critical favour and find commercial success since The Sex Pistols.

Over two years had passed between the release of *Bleach* and the arrival of *Nevermind* in the shops. Irrespective of the major changes already outlined above, Nirvana continued to build upon their small but jealously guarded fan base. They had picked up pockets of support via some steady touring (including several notable festival appearances), some friends in high rock-critic places, and the occasional record. Cobain was every inch the Seattle slacker (unkempt and unwilling to play the game), Novoselic the student who seemed happy to slum it for a bit, and Dave Grohl the all-American kid who cheerfully went along with it all. In essence, Nirvana were a disparate trio that seemed destined for a year or two of cult celebrity before falling victim to the inevitable ebbs and flows of fashion.

Although often compared to both around the time of *Nevermind*, Nirvana were more Sex Pistols than Beatles, more charismatic frontman and his chaos-creating chums than a union of like-minded souls smiling their way to stardom. Less of an issue by this time were the band's roots in metal riffs of the most mind-crunching variety. Just months after *Bleach*, Cobain had warned of an imminent change of emphasis, telling a reporter that, "There won't be any songs as heavy as 'Paper Cuts' or 'Sifting' on the new record. That's just too boring. I'd rather have a good hook." On the face of it, that might have been a recipe for disappointment: plenty of bands get by with good hooks, but few have either the muscle or the individuality to make them count. There wasn't more than the merest suspicion that Nirvana would ever be one of those.

The first major step on the road to *Nevermind* was taken during one week in April 1990, when Nirvana travelled to Smart Studios, in Madison, Wisconsin, to work with one of the most rated producers of the new "grunge" era. Butch Vig was a failed power-pop wannabe who'd seen his vintage gear-filled studio become a beacon for the new breed of noise-makers. Killdozer, Laughing Hyenas, The Fluid, Smashing Pumpkins and Tad had all benefited from Vig's ability to make rock records sound like rock records ought to sound. He was a rarity in the modern producer's world in that he didn't go in for the ubiquitous "big-haired" soundboard experience.

At the time of the initial Vig sessions, Nirvana were still thinking in terms of delivering their second Sub Pop album, provisionally entitled *Sheep*, and drummer Chad Channing was still in the band. Despite the fact that so much change was just around the corner, most of the performances recorded at these heavily bootlegged sessions bore a remarkable similarity to those that ended up on *Nevermind*. Even Grohl later conceded that he basically repeated most of Channing's original drum parts.

The Smart sessions bore out Cobain's new hook-orientated statement with a vengeance. Nirvana's music was rarely hookless, often making a rant-along meal of the singer's one-line choruses, but the new material was crafted on a quite different level of sophistication. Tracks recorded with Vig in April 1990 included 'Pay To Play' (which became 'Stay Away', later issued in this original form on the DGC *Rarities* CD in 1994), 'In Bloom' (which received an early airing later that year on the Sub Pop Video Network *Program One* video, issued by Atavistic), 'Dive', 'Lithium', 'Sappy' (alias 'I Hate Myself And I Want To Die'), 'Polly' and 'Imodium' (which became 'Breed').

What had started life as a second album for an indie label was, by September 1990, regarded simply as a demo tape with which to court potential new backers. By then, Nirvana had shed Channing at the end of a spring tour of America. After a short spell with Mudhoney's Dan Peters holding the sticks, the band recruited Grohl ("the drummer of our dreams", said Cobain) from Washington DC hardcore band Scream. Nirvana, who'd looked on as local heroes Mother Love Bone, Alice In Chains and Soundgarden all signed up to major labels, were also growing impatient with the cottage-industry-with-attitude that was Sub Pop.

The catalyst for change was Sonic Youth, pathmakers for grunge whose wilfully experimental edge had prevented them from achieving the success they deserved. But they had signed to a major, and bassist Kim Gordon had recommended Nirvana to Mark Kates, Director of Alternative Music at Geffen's DGC subsidiary. He caught the band in action that autumn supporting Sonic Youth and, after fending off approaches from Capitol, Charisma and Columbia, announced in January 1991 that Nirvana was to sign to Geffen. The label had offered a $287,000 advance, which was smaller than Capitol's reputed $1 million but built in a higher royalty. The deal was finally inked on April 30, 1991.

No one questioned the choice of material for the band's

first major-label album, which was to be based on the songs cut with Vig at Smart the previous year. There were, however, doubts concerning the appropriate choice of producer: Geffen preferred to see an experienced, commercially aware pair of hands on the controls, like Scott Litt or Don Dixon (both had smoothed R.E.M.'s passage into the mainstream), though the band were happy to stick with Vig. At one point, it looked like Dixon was going to get the job, with Vig engineering, but eventually Geffen let the band have their way.

The label booked Nirvana and Vig into the Sound City Studios, in the sleepy Los Angeles suburb of Van Nuys. The studio was, by then, somewhat unfashionable, but had seen better days in the Seventies, with Tom Petty, Foreigner and Rick Springfield all having recorded major albums there. The biggest ghost of all was that of Fleetwood Mac, who'd recorded their record-breaking *Rumours* album at Sound City, taking rock into new, sleepier AOR pastures in the process. This amused the band and Vig. Cobain later described the studio as "a time machine".

The band met up with Vig in May 1991, and spent a week in rehearsal prior to the recording. The producer was also handed a tape that included material likely to feature during the sessions. Many he already knew from the Smart demo, but a couple of new songs, 'Smells Like Teen Spirit' and 'Come As You Are', caught his ear, despite the distorted sound quality of the primitively recorded cassette.

The *Nevermind* sessions, which lasted six weeks in total, were completed in a convivial, almost carefree atmosphere, the kind that history seems to have excised from the Nirvana story. The band goofed around with Alice Cooper, Aerosmith and Black Sabbath covers, but when it was time to get their heads down, they worked hard and efficiently, often up to 10 hours a day. The basic tracks were laid down in a matter of days, with much of the studio time being spent laying down overdubs – a problem the band had rarely encountered during the making of *Bleach*. A nightly bottle of Jack Daniel's, plus a jar of Hycomine cough syrup for the singer, helped to see them through.

Vig wasted no time in mixing the material, but Geffen

wasn't happy with the results, which were said to have lacked power, particularly in the drum department, and drafted in Andy Wallace, an established mixing engineer who'd previously given Slayer's *Seasons In The Abyss* album an accessible sheen. He boosted the drum sound by adding digital reverb, and whacked the guitars and bass through a flanger. He then compressed the lot, so that the results would sound punchy and dynamic on radio. Hey presto, a more inviting album and, by the way, your budget for the record has just doubled. It was one of the best investments Geffen ever made: the entire album had cost the label around half-a-million dollars from start to finish but, within two years, it had grossed in the region of £50 million – and that was before Cobain's death gave sales an inevitable new boost.

Cobain later remarked that he was embarrassed by the production, likening it to a Mötley Crüe record. But he was typically self-deprecating when it came to characterising the band's new sound for the record company press biog. "Our songs have the standard pop format," he told them, "verse, chorus, verse, chorus, solo, bad solo." And in an echo of his original handwritten bio for *Bleach*, he concluded: "All in all, we sound like The Knack and The Bay City Rollers being molested by Black Flag and Black Sabbath." The emphasis was now on pop being consumed by rock, rather than the other way around, which had been the case with *Bleach*. Some critics took the results far more seriously, wondering whether we were witnessing the emergence of a new, industrial-strength version of The Beatles. But first there was Nirvanamania.

Geffen had envisaged *Nevermind* as the first strike in what was going to be a lengthy campaign to take the band from indie cult status to a popularity approaching R.E.M. proportions. That was the daydream. Within three weeks of the album's release, on September 24, 1991, *Nevermind* had far exceeded its projected sales of 50,000 by shipping 200,000 copies, more than Sonic Youth's major label debut, *Goo*, had sold in two years. In a similar period, *Bleach* had sold just 40,000.

Hitting the *Billboard* chart on October 12 at number 144, the album's ascent was slow but certain. By the start of November, it nestled just outside the Top 30; by the end of the month, it had reached the Top 10; and on January 12, 1992, Nirvana had done the seemingly impossible, clambering over U2, Metallica and Michael Jackson to top the US chart. In the UK, Nirvanamania was slower to catch on, and less explosive in chart terms when it did, but *Nevermind* was still a regular fixture in the Top 30 for months, reaching a high point of number seven.

Many reasons have been put forward in an attempt to explain just why Nirvana and *Nevermind* broke so big. MTV getting behind one of the songs, 'Smells Like Teen Spirit', was certainly a crucial factor in earning the band almost instant crossover appeal. And radio quickly got behind the album, so much so that journalist and biographer Gina Arnold quipped that Nirvana had indeed become an AOR band – Always On The Radio. But these factors refer merely to the power of the communications industry. While that's all-important – no exposure, no sales – it doesn't necessarily guarantee a hit.

Although both band and label claimed to have been taken by surprise by the soaraway success of the album, the bleached-out grunge, the punk-meets-metal, the artful blend of melodies and rage, were all deliberately concocted in the studio with a view to potential markets. *Nevermind* was a multipurpose album that marked the coming of age of America's alternative rock scene, given a recent boost by the Lollapalooza tour. It regenerated a metal scene that was fast sliding into ineffective, poodle-haired posturing. And it breathed new dynamism into the melodic rock mainstream.

Although Nirvana could predict which musical currents their music might reach, there was no doubt about the message behind the cover artwork, which was similarly stunning and memorable. Depicting the five-month-old Spencer Elden swimming towards a dollar bill on a fishhook, it played on the indie-versus-major debate, symbolising the group's willingness to take the corporate cash, while doubling as a general comment on a money-obsessed society. The retention of the baby's penis (Geffen was in two minds whether to airbrush it away) signalled some kind of victory. And the band's new T-shirt, bearing the, "Flower-sniffin' kitty-pettin' baby-kissin' corporate rock whores" legend, poked self-conscious fun at their own new-found respectability. The laughter wouldn't last.

All songs written by Kurt Cobain unless otherwise indicated.

Smells Like Teen Spirit

(Kurt Cobain/Chris Novoselic/Dave Grohl)

The original album sleeve credited Cobain as the lyricist and the band for writing the music. By 1993, when the music was published in book form, Cobain had reneged on his benevolence, leaving just this song as a group composition. That was just as well for Novoselic and Grohl, because 'Smells Like Teen Spirit' was and remains one of those rare songs that seems to define an era. It almost felt like that on first hearing, and the fact that everyone else seemed to share that view helped make it the fastest-spreading virus of late 1991.

Recalling the origins of 'Teen Spirit' and other *Nevermind* anthems, Cobain said, "At the time I was writing those songs, I really didn't know what I was trying to say." Scrutinise the lyrics and you'll see exactly what he means, as seemingly unrelated phrases jostle to be sung, heard, yelled and scrawled onto banners at concerts, but rarely understood. What Cobain had succeeded in doing was to find a writing style that echoed the ultimately contradictory appeal of his music – intangible yet memorable, pleasurable yet inextricably bound up with some kind of inner pain.

These contrasts were built into 'Smells Like Teen Spirit': its central guitar motif, its measured, finely tuned course from coasting verses into expansive choruses, could hardly have sounded more life-affirming. Lyrically, though, the mood couldn't have been more different: boredom, guns, pretence, a reluctant smile, and the climactic refrain of "a denial" encapsulated Cobain's dichotomy perfectly.

The song was inspired by a slogan scrawled on Cobain's bedroom wall in North Pear Street, Olympia, by another paramour, Bikini Kill's Kathleen Hanna, one night late in 1990. 'Kurt Smells Like Teen Spirit' was meant to be a sly dig, Teen Spirit being nothing so threatening as an underarm deodorant aimed at young women. But the phrase stuck,

Cobain subconsciously (apparently) retrieved a riff from an old Boston hit from 1976, 'More Than A Feeling', and the track was formulated during the band's regular rehearsals in Tacoma that winter.

Later on, Cobain acknowledged another debt, telling *Rolling Stone* magazine in January 1994 that, "I was trying to write the ultimate pop song. I was basically trying to rip off the Pixies... We used their sense of dynamics, being soft and quiet and then loud and hard." While traces of that quiet/loud, soft/hard dynamic could be found on the band's earlier work, it was on *Nevermind* that Nirvana perfected the trick. But there was no doubt that listening to the Pixies' 1988 *Surfer Rosa* album (produced by Steve Albini) after recording *Bleach* left its impact.

When Nirvana debuted the song in Seattle in April 1991, there was little suggestion that 'Smells Like Teen Spirit' would soon be rotated on MTV an unprecedented 10 times a day. Or that its possible meanings would be debated by everyone from ciderheads to champagne-supping yuppies. Or that 'Weird' Al Yankovic would parody it, and Tori Amos would record an opportunistic "lounge" version of the song. By the time Nirvana returned to the UK to promote both the single and the album, Cobain was bored enough with the song to sing it an octave lower for BBC-TV's *Top Of The Pops*, undercutting much of its power in the process. (He also changed the song's intro to, "Load up on drugs and kill your friends".)

Months later, the band would tease audiences by playing the first few bars of the song before launching into something else. The irony of the line, "Here we are now, entertain us", was impossible to maintain once superstardom called.

In Bloom

'In Bloom', the fourth single lifted from *Nevermind*, was one of the songs originally demoed with Vig at Smart in April 1990. That version so impressed Sub Pop that it was issued on the Sub Pop Video Network *Program One* several months later, in order to promote the band (who, unknown to the label, were already intent on leaving).

It's not difficult to imagine 'In Bloom' performed Bleach-style, with the band going at the song hell-for-leather. Here, though, Vig and the band's original arrangement, and Wallace's delicate post-production work, gave the song room to breathe, while Dave Grohl's harmony during the chorus accentuated the track's anthemic qualities.

Lyrically, 'In Bloom' poked fun at the small-town dude, the one who sings along to all the pretty songs, who happily shoots off his gun, but who dares not stop and think about his life: "He knows not what it means". While recording the album, around the time of the bombing of Baghdad, Novoselic remembered having "such a feeling of us versus them. All those people waving the flag and being brainwashed. I really hated them. And all of a sudden they're buying our records, and I just think, 'You don't get it at all'." The in-concert mass chorusing along to 'In Bloom' (a favourite with Courtney Love, apparently) must have been a double-edged pleasure for the band.

Come As You Are

Unusually conciliatory in its subject matter, 'Come As You Are' was the song that Geffen envisaged would open up Nirvana to a new mass audience once 'Teen Spirit' had paved the way. As it turned out, the track sounded like a tame and strangely subdued follow-up, which seemed to grow in stature in the aftermath of Cobain's death: inevitably, a line like, "And I swear that I don't have a gun" would hold new meaning, as would Cobain's plaintive "memory" hook.

The heavily flanged guitar sound, which gave the impression that the song had been recorded underwater, united the track with the album sleeve, a connection that was pursued in Kevin Kerslake's promo video. Cobain, who often made reference to his watery, swimming-in-opposite-directions Pisces star sign, was drugged at the time, but water – often symbolic of emotional turbulence – was becoming a recurrent theme in several of his songs.

Nirvana were the victims of a couple of lawsuits during their short lifespan, but Killing Joke's claim that 'Come As You

Are' had been based on a riff from their own 'Eighties' was rejected by the courts.

Breed

Music analysts would characterise *Nevermind's* first three songs as "moderate rock" (check the sheet music for proof). But there was no way that 'Breed', a pile-driving, *Bleach*-on-speed offering, could ever fall into that category. Even the spartan lyric suggested this was a throwback to the band's debut album.

That wasn't far wrong, because the song was one of the earliest titles destined for *Nevermind*, written while the band were touring Europe with fellow Seattle labelmates Tad. It was Tad's hefty frontman, one Tad Doyle, who initially inspired the song, which was originally called 'Imodium' after the anti-diarrhoea medicine the singer was forced to consume during the tour. It retained this title when the band first taped it with Vig in April 1990, and might well have made it onto disc that way had a second track not been named after a medicinal treatment.

Lithium

That song was 'Lithium', named after a treatment for depression, and later the cue for audiences to raise their lighters to show their communion with the track's central hook: "Yeah, yeah, yeah, yeah!" No surprise there: without Cobain's grainy rasp, and a musical twist midway through the song, 'Lithium' might easily have slotted onto any soft metal compilation.

That gibe doesn't do justice to the song's genuine beauty. The melody was neatly forged from a bare minimum of notes, while the lyric, one of the album's best, poetically negotiates the thin line between madness and the search for faith.

According to Cobain, 'Lithium' was "probably" inspired by the time he spent living with the family of his friend, Jesse Reed, during the summer of 1985. The Reeds lived a full, born-again Christian lifestyle, and the details of religious observance in the song are likely born of the experience.

Another song first taped with Vig in 1990, 'Lithium' became the third single taken from Nevermind and had the dubious honour of later being recorded by the original Nirvana, the psychedelic late-Sixties UK edition, who reformed in the early Nineties.

Polly

Many of Cobain's earliest songs drew on real-life situations, often simply depressing, sometimes, like 'Paper Cuts', macabre and gruesome. 'Polly', which was written around the same time as much of Bleach, fell into the latter category, telling with some genuine insight the horrific local story of the rape and torture of a 14-year-old punkette by the inappropriately named Gerald Friend.

Told from the rapist's standpoint, Cobain's lyric gets into the criminal's mind, teasing out a series of 'justifications': "It isn't me/We have some seed", "the will of instinct", and finally, "I want some help to help myself". The full horror was brought home by the stark arrangement, featuring Cobain accompanying himself on acoustic guitar, which was the original Smart Studio demo, albeit in remixed form.

As if the song wasn't harrowing enough, 'Polly' itself was later sung by two men while raping a woman shortly after the release of Nevermind, yet another depressing burden for the songwriter to bear. Cobain nevertheless didn't shy away from playing it – though few could ever hear it again without an additional layer of disbelief.

Territorial Pissings

Despite the muscular hard rock of the band's early records, Kurt Cobain was never short of some punk-inspired rhetoric. Here, at last, was the song to match it: fast, furious and a match for almost anything released during the punk era. A regular cue for some onstage mayhem, 'Territorial Pissings' gained further infamy in 1992 when the band tore into it during an appearance on a British television chat show hosted by

Jonathan Ross. This totally unscripted move left the presenter visibly shaken, and the same could probably be said of his audience, shocked by a rare injection of televisual spontaneity. Nirvana's future in the UK was assured.

The song's distinct lack of gloss was down to Cobain's insistence that he plug his guitar directly into the mixing desk, despite Vig's reluctance. This was a common punk-rock production tactic, which gave the guitar an overloaded sound. Coupled with a vocal that was audibly being cut to shreds with each successive verse, and some magnificent drumming from Grohl, 'Territorial Pissings', recorded in one take, remains a truly definitive Nirvana performance that deserved to have been issued on single.

The song's central lyric phrase, "Gotta find a way", seemed to fit the exuberant desperation of the performance, with its references to paranoia and Cobain's desires to be an alien. Those concerns also connect to the oddly comic intro, where Novoselic tunelessly lampoons a line from the old Youngbloods' hippie anthem, 'Get Together', which gives way to Cobain's thrashy three-chord charge.

Drain You

'Drain You' welcomed back the happy, chart-bound production sound that characterised much of *Nevermind*, and for whoever sequenced the record, it couldn't come soon enough, bounding in almost as soon as the final cymbal of 'Territorial Pissings' fades. If there is an air of familiarity about the song, it's because the verses are built on the same chord structure to 'Smells Like Teen Spirit', although the vocal is less equivocal in its celebratory tone. This isn't always reflected in the lyric, which charts the symbiotic relationship between two babies/lovers, who are seen to be governed not merely by love but by mutual dependency, even naked self-interest.

Cobain later said that he felt the song was every bit the equal of 'Teen Spirit' – and its appearance on the flip of that single, and in live form as a bonus cut on 'Come As You Are', seems to bear this out.

Lounge Act

One of the lesser-known songs on the album, 'Lounge Act' grew out of a jam based around a cheesy bass line cooked up by Novoselic. So cheesy, in fact, that the song that built up around it was so titled because the bassist's line was laughably reminiscent of an inoffensive hotel bar band.

By the time the song was completed, it sounded more like an Americanised version of British, punk-inspired catch-a-wave acts like The Police: bouncy, energetic – and thoroughly inoffensive. It was by no means Nirvana's finest moment, though Cobain's lyric gave some insight into the difficulties he faced maintaining relationships while giving total commitment to his creative vision.

Stay Away

If Cobain's lyrics tend to avoid the pitfalls of embarrassment that is often the lot of the hapless rock lyricist, that is largely down to his scatter-shot approach, a stringing together of (often insightful) phrases that give the impression of being chemically induced. There is little anecdotal evidence to support this, save for the fact that Cobain's insecurity as a writer would have been overcome by mind-unlocking influences.

The curt couplets of 'Stay Away' seem to suggest this more than most songs. "Every line ends in rhyme/Less is more, love is blind", and, "Throw it out and keep it in/Have to have poison skin" could have come from the pen of any doodling dreamer. But the vision of Cobain in his pyjamas, cup of tea by his side, agonising over lines like those – though by all accounts he did agonise over his lyrics, which further suggests the need for "unblocking" agents – doesn't ring true.

'Stay Away', which first surfaced as a riff on the 1986 pre-Nirvana Fecal Matter demo, had one of the longest gestation periods of all Nirvana songs. By 1990, it was ready – as 'Pay To Play' – for Vig to record at the Smart Studios sessions, at which stage the song featured slightly different lyrics, more feedback and a coda. By the time it was recorded for *Nevermind* as 'Stay Away', it had been transformed from a put-down of an unscrupulous practice initiated by concert promoters during the Eighties, to a partial critique of rock band infighting.

Less sophisticated melodically than much of the *Nevermind* material, and lacking the relentless onslaught of 'Territorial Pissings', 'Stay Away' was another of the album's more anonymous tracks – though it would have been difficult to say that had it appeared on any other album at the time.

The original Vig recording of 'Pay To Play' eventually turned up on the *DGC Rarities Volume One* various artists compilation in 1994.

On A Plain

The few seconds of tune-up noise that introduced this song were deceiving: 'On A Plain' was one of the album's real moments of glorious power-pop release – upbeat, instantly memorable and even rejoicing in a call-and-response chorus (of sorts). Even Cobain was moved to sing an uncharacteristic "I can't complain".

The only trace of angst in the song came with the admission that, "I love myself better than you/I know it's wrong, but what should I do?" In fact, the lyrics comprised a few hastily dashed-off lines, written immediately prior to the recording session, which made it clear that Cobain had grown exhausted having to find words to fit his tunes. How else does one read a song that opens with the words, "I'll start this off without any words", and closes with, "Then I'm done, then I can go home"?

Something In The Way

This was one of the last tracks to be written for *Nevermind* and, placed at the end of the album, it encouraged the listener to leave with a quite different impression of the supercharged rock band they'd been listening to for the previous 40 minutes. Rock tradition often dictates that albums' parting gestures are either rip-roaringly typical of the artist's style or, if different, then indicative of a bold new direction being staked out. Certainly, there was more from where 'Something

In The Way' came from on Nirvana's next studio album.

The song was an exercise in self-mythology, with Cobain revisiting his brief period of homelessness in Aberdeen late in 1985. Forced to leave the flat he shared with Jesse Reed, and mindful of overstaying his welcome at the Novoselics' family home, Cobain spent a few nights sleeping under the North Aberdeen Bridge (which crossed the Wishkah river), surviving on wood fire for heat and cheap red wine for fortification. There is something about the romance of the drifter's life, free from responsibility and with civilisation in the distance, that suggests Cobain's decision to rough it wasn't entirely an involuntary one.

Whatever the truth, he got a great song out of the experience, again a latecomer to the *Nevermind* sessions. Never intended to be so sparse, 'Something In The Way' nearly didn't make it onto the record, after endless attempts to find a satisfactory band arrangement proved inconclusive. It was only when Vig asked Cobain to play the song for him on an acoustic guitar in his control room that the arrangement became clear: Vig taped Cobain's performance there and then. The band's overdubs, and a mournful cello part played by Kirk Canning, were added later.

Endless, Nameless

In 'Something In The Way', Nirvana had chosen to end the album in an uncharacteristic manner that may or may not have suggested that some drastic musical changes were afoot. But through a clever piece of digital trickery, they were also able to have it both ways, hiding a "secret" bonus track some 10 minutes after 'Something In The Way' had finished. (Soon afterwards, it seemed as if every other new CD release came with a "hidden" track.)

Sometimes called 'The Noise Jam', 'Endless, Nameless' came about at the end of a none-too-successful session for 'Lithium'. The sound of three musicians practising primal therapy through their instruments, this largely wordless jam (Cobain shrieks something like, "I think I can/I know I can" for a short while) wasn't entirely spontaneous; the group had been playing something like it for several months. And just as similar onstage free-for-alls ended with the sound of equipment being trashed, so, at somewhere around 19.32 on the track, Cobain's guitar can be heard disintegrating.

Just to confuse their new-found pop fans, Nirvana selected 'Endless, Nameless' to back the 'Come As You Are' single – a move that was also welcomed by early purchasers of *Nevermind*, who were cheated out of the song. And perhaps its belated appearance meant that Nirvana were having second thoughts that their next album would be more hardcore?

ABBA

Abba Gold
Greatest Hits
September 1992

By Carl Magnus Palm

THE ULTIMATE FLAGSHIP of the Abba catalogue is this incredibly successful compilation album. On original release in 1992, *ABBA Gold* helped spearhead the Abba revival that is still going strong more than two decades later. With over 30 million copies sold, *ABBA Gold* is the biggest hit album Abba will ever enjoy and its enormous success should at the very least put it in the Top 20 biggest-selling albums of all time.

After several years of down-market compilations issued by budget labels – all of them selling quite well, nevertheless – *ABBA Gold* was the first release after PolyGram bought Polar Music from Stig Anderson in 1990. The reason that two years elapsed before the new owners released anything was because they had to wait for all the licenses around the world to expire, so that they could issue a CD that would have true global impact. It was fortuitous for, following the growth of an underground interest in clubland – not least in the gay community – 1992 was the year when Erasure topped the UK charts with their Abba-esque EP of cover versions, while Björn Again (a cover band formed in Australia in the late Eighties) were enjoying immense success on the global live circuit. After a decade out in the wasteland of the terminally uncool, Abba were suddenly hot, hip and happening again.

The packaging of *ABBA Gold* was the subject of careful market research, concluding that the CD should not feature any pictures of the group on the front cover but focus on the simple, classic logo. This would help ensure that Abba were viewed not as a kitschy nostalgia phenomenon, but as a classy, timeless popular music act. It was the correct strategy: on release, the album shot to number one almost everywhere.

In 1999, when the première of the musical *Mamma Mia!* – based on Abba's songs – and the coincidental 25th anniversary of the group's Eurovision Song Contest win pushed them back in the spotlight, *ABBA Gold* was remastered and reissued, and was soon back at the top of the charts. A further repackaging in 2002 – commemorating the 10th anniversary of its original release – failed to set the charts alight, although the upgraded artwork was sorely needed to give the entire package a look worthy of its status as a prestigious catalogue item. Abba's

30th anniversary in 2004 kicked the album back in the charts again, with a double-disc edition (Polar 981 929-7; the second disc was a DVD collection of videos) reaching the Top Five in the UK.

All songs by Benny Andersson and
Björn Ulvaeus unless otherwise indicated.

Dancing Queen
(Benny Andersson/Stig Anderson/Björn Ulvaeus)

'Dancing Queen' was perhaps the one Abba track that saw the longest journey from initial recording sessions to completion, and then to final release. The first recording took place on August 4 and 5, 1975, and the last known overdub was made a full four months later. Then, it took until August 1976 before it was finally released as a single. But there can be little doubt that the results justified the means, for 'Dancing Queen' stands not only as one of Abba's very best – and best-known – tracks, but is now widely acknowledged as one of the all-time classic singles in the history of popular music.

When Ulvaeus and Andersson first entered the studio with engineer Michael Tretow and the session musicians on that August day, all they knew was that they had a song with the working title 'Boogaloo' and that they wanted it to have a rhythmic "dance" feel. They knew this was not their strongest forte, so for inspiration they took a listen to George McCrae's disco classic 'Rock Your Baby'. That's where they found the right groove. Then, after discussions between Michael Tretow and drummer Roger Palm, a touch of elastic New Orleans rhythm, courtesy of Dr. John's Gumbo album, was added to the mix.

Even when the basic backing track had been completed, Ulvaeus and Andersson had a recording that could evoke strong emotions in people. When the later brought home a tape to play for Frida Lyngstad, she thought it so beautiful she started to cry. And after Agnetha Fältskog and she had laid down their lead vocals, and further overdubs had been added, it was pretty clear they had a winner on their hands.

"We knew immediately it was going to be massive," Fältskog recalled.

However, in early 1976, there was another strong track besides 'Dancing Queen' that had just been completed – 'Fernando'. It was high time to release a new single, and both tracks had hit potential. Stig Anderson insisted that 'Fernando' was the right song to go with at this point – a ballad seemed like a fresh contrast against the previous single, the uptempo 'Mamma Mia' – and Ulvaeus and Andersson eventually agreed with him. 'Dancing Queen' would have to wait another five months before it reached record shops.

Meanwhile, the song was introduced in some parts of the world long before its release as a single. The most famous occasion was on June 18, 1976, the day before the wedding of King Carl XVI Gustaf of Sweden and Silvia Sommerlath, when a televised gala in their honour was held at The Royal Swedish Opera in Stockholm. Abba, as the only representative of pop music, were invited to appear, and chose to perform their upcoming, most appropriately-titled single. For this occasion they dressed up in baroque outfits as a suitably tongue-in-cheek attempt to go along with the atmosphere of the ceremonious gala.

Then, a couple of months later, 'Dancing Queen' was finally released as a single. It didn't take long before the song occupied the number one spot in charts all over the world: it reached the top in at least a dozen countries – it was Abba's only US number one – and went Top five in plenty more. The group's biggest-ever hit, its jubilant sound, characterised by Andersson's trademark piano figures and Lyngstad and Fältskog's soaring vocals, made it an immediate classic, its inviting rhythms sending people on to the dance floor in an instant ever since.

Knowing Me, Knowing You

(Benny Andersson/Stig Anderson/Björn Ulvaeus)

An undisputed highlight of the entire Abba catalogue was this UK number one hit, an unexpectedly mature reflection on the break-up of a marriage, recorded at the very start of the

Arrival album sessions proper on March 23, 1976. For the first time, the group truly acknowledged in song that they were four adults. Couplets like, "In this old familiar room, children would play", indicate that 'Knowing Me, Knowing You' could never have been about any old teenage romance. Frida's chanteuse delivery, and the American West Coast-flavoured sound of the recording, paved the way for Abba's future role as a kind of European Fleetwood Mac.

Ulvaeus has pointed out that 'Knowing Me, Knowing You' was written well before either of the two couples had split up, thus ruling out the assumption that its lyrics reflected the state of the inter-Abba marriages at that point in time. "Even if the roots are somewhere deep inside, from something that has happened to you, it's still 90 per cent fiction," he said many years later. "I was just working from images. I saw a man walking through an empty house for the last time as a symbol of divorce. I just described what I saw. I hadn't been through that myself then."

In a sad irony, however, the lyrics of 'Knowing Me, Knowing You' were unusually prescient insofar as both of the Abba marriages would break up in the fullness of time.

Take A Chance On Me

For all the ambition and sometimes pretension that marked *ABBA – The Album*, Andersson and Ulvaeus had not forgotten their love of catchy, bouncy, straightforward pop, represented here by 'Take A Chance On Me'. Perhaps the way the title of the song came to Ulvaeus says it all. He was out on one of his usual jogging rounds in his neighbourhood, when the "t-k-ch" sound came into his head as a constantly repeated pattern, following his jogging rhythm. It was the perfect sound, and all he had to do now was to extend the consonant sounds into a complete phrase: "Take A Chance On Me". Never had their been a better illustration of Ulvaeus' philosophy that the mere sound of the words in a pop lyric are of equal importance to their meaning, a rule that he certainly believed very strongly in back then.

Recording began on August 15, 1977, after an attempt

earlier in the month had been ditched. This was Abba at their most energetic and forceful, with Fältskog and Lyngstad's razor-sharp, harmonised vocals slicing their way through the speaker membrane. 'Take A Chance On Me' was the second single from *ABBA – The Album*, and it was quite successful as well, reaching number one in several places – including the UK – and peaking at number three in the US, making it Abba's best-placed American single after 'Dancing Queen'. In many ways, 'Take A Chance On Me' was Abba's farewell to the more innocent, bubblegum-inflected pop that had marked their breakthrough years.

Mamma Mia
(Benny Andersson/Stig Anderson/Björn Ulvaeus)

'Mamma Mia', the cracking opening song on 1975's eponymous album, instantly signalled the arrival of a new Abba. This was not a group who were about to apologise for wanting to make brilliant pop music, although they were from "backward" Sweden. With its opening tick-tocking marimba and piano figure, it demanded attention, and when the spirited joint lead vocal by Fältskog and Lyngstad kicked in, surrender was the only possible option. The lyrics were throwaway, but no more so than any number of love-themed words penned by Brill Building-style songwriters over the years. Clearly, Stig Anderson's approach to lyric writing was still good and strong – 'Mamma Mia' was 'Waterloo' revisited: a concept that could be said and understood by everybody everywhere.

Abba's first UK number one since 'Waterloo' was also the very last song to be recorded for the *ABBA* album, with sessions beginning on March 12, 1975. It was the fourth and last worldwide single to be taken off the album, which had everything to do with Abba's breakthrough in Australia in 1975. The promo clips directed by Lasse Hallström – today a prominent Hollywood director – for a number of tracks off the album were shown on Australian television, and were instrumental in creating the Abbamania phenomenon down under. In particular, the clips for 'I Do, I Do, I Do, I Do, I Do' and 'Mamma Mia' caused a sensation. At the time, however, 'Mamma Mia' had not been released as a single and there were no plans to do so; the Swedes felt that the three singles released so far – 'So Long', 'I Do, I Do, I Do, I Do, I Do' and 'SOS' – were quite enough. But the pleading of the local record company, RCA, finally won through, and 'Mamma Mia' shot to number one in Australia and, subsequently, all over the world.

Lay All Your Love On Me

Often held up as a prototype for the electronic dance music of the Eighties, the Fältskog-led 'Lay All Your Love On Me' was certainly one of Abba's most compelling dance tracks. However, it wasn't necessarily going to be a dance floor filler from the beginning, since the hymn-like chorus suggested an altogether different arrangement. Finally, it was decided that the contrast between the half-tempo "congregation chanting" and the driving pulse of the full-tempo beat, would only make the song more effective. Indeed.

Unlike many other Abba albums, there were only two "official" singles released from *Super Trouper*: 'The Winner Takes It All' and the title track. However, a few territories, the UK included, released 'Lay All Your Love On Me' as a 12" single. In Great Britain, the single hit the Top 10, making it the highest-charting song to be released exclusively as a 12" disc up until that time.

Super Trouper

Recording for the second and last worldwide single from the album of the same name began on October 3, 1980; it was also the very last song to be started for the project. The new album was virtually completed by this point – indeed, on the evening following the day of the initial recording session, the ambitious shoot for the album sleeve and scenes for two promo clips had been scheduled. But Ulvaeus and Andersson felt that they needed something more, a song that would be strong enough to release as a single in conjunction with the album.

With the pressure of completing the album on them, the songwriting team afforded themselves the luxury of spending two days in the studio writing the song. The decision to name the album *Super Trouper*, in reference to the big spotlights used during stadium tours and such, had already been made. Most conveniently, the title happened to fit the hook part of this new tune as well, although the title posed some problems for lyricist Björn Ulvaeus: "Imagine trying to write about some damned spotlight!"

Those problems were overcome, however, and Ulvaeus hit upon the very logical solution of a story told from the perspective of a star on tour, longing to be in the arms of her lover. With a typically earnest Lyngstad lead vocal, and the usual accomplished arrangement with millions of counter-melodies and harmonies, 'Super Trouper' was a highlight on the album, as well as a successful single, giving Abba their ninth and final UK number one.

I Have A Dream

This ballad remains one of the more controversial Abba songs, largely due to the inclusion of a children's choir (this one came from the International School of Stockholm), pushing at the boundaries of what is generally accepted as credible pop music. Ulvaeus later acknowledged that many observers felt this was a bit over the top, but had no regrets himself. "It simply felt right to have them there," he said. Released as the fourth and last single from *Voulez-Vous* towards the end of 1979, 'I Have A Dream' reached number two in the UK, so it seemed that many agreed with his assessment.

The Winner Takes It All

'The Winner Takes It All' is the kind of masterpiece that almost defies description. Quite simply: anyone wanting confirmation of what brilliant pop music can aspire to need look no further than this recording. The song exemplifies Abba's ability to turn a simple tune – only two different melody lines are repeated throughout the song – into a wonder of versatility and variation. This is achieved through subtle changes in vocal interpretation, lyrical mood and arrangement devices throughout the song.

For all this minute attention to detail, the sound of Abba here is organic: it's the sound of urgency that comes when singers and musicians lift themselves by the hair in order to perform beyond their abilities. The third ingredient may simply be magic: the potency of four people coming together at a certain moment in time, just when they all happen to be on the same wavelength and most receptive to what each wants to achieve in their work. All of this can be heard in Abba's recording of 'The Winner Takes It All'.

It could all have gone very wrong, though, if they had used the backing track completed at the very first session, for that first attempt ended up way too stiff and metrical. Ulvaeus and Andersson realised their mistake when they listened to the recording in the car on the way home from work. A new backing track session was pencilled in for June 6, 1980, and in the meantime Andersson came up with the flowing, descending piano lines that occur throughout, loosening up its rhythms and giving it the right feel. The new backing track was exactly right. The composers even felt there was something French, chanson-like about the song, and Ulvaeus recorded demo vocals in French. At one point, there was even a suggestion that he should sing the lead vocals on the final track. "It's a good thing I didn't," he reflected later.

For the final, English lyrics, Ulvaeus drew inspiration from the collapse of his and Fältskog's marriage. Although he himself was now in a new and happy relationship – with his future wife, Lena – there was obviously still sadness over the failure of keeping it all together with Fältskog. Opening a bottle of whisky from which he drank freely, he sat down to write the lyrics. The words began pouring out of him – he later recalled 'The Winner Takes It All' as the quickest song he ever wrote. Then the group reconvened in the studio to overdub the vocals. The lead part was brilliantly handled by Fältskog; it was a masterful performance that tops everything she has done before or since.

Released as the first single from the album sessions, in

July 1980, 'The Winner Takes It All' returned Abba to the UK number one spot for the first time in more than two years. No song was more deserving of such a feat.

Money, Money, Money

This cabaret-tinged Lyngstad showcase is the song that is always dug up by television and radio producers whenever the subject of Abba's finances is to be dealt with. In the left-wing cultural climate of mid-Seventies Sweden, some observers felt that the song was an unashamed tribute to cold, crass commercialism. 'Money, Money, Money' was in fact meant to be a wry, tongue-in-cheek number, which is quite clear if the lyrics are analysed properly.

At the time, Andersson pointed to this track as his favourite on the *Arrival* album, viewing it as a song that stood on its own two feet and wasn't dependent on Abba's performance. "You could say that it's constructed like a stage number," he said. "I imagine someone else doing it, not necessarily us." Considering the musicals that he and Ulvaeus were imagining even back then, and which were to be their main occupation after the Abba years, this was a perceptive comment. The cabaret, "stage-performance" qualities of 'Money, Money, Money' were indeed emphasised when the group performed the song in concert.

SOS

(Benny Andersson/Stig Anderson/Björn Ulvaeus)

In terms of lead vocals, the *ABBA* album clearly belonged to Fältskog. Although she only had one more solo spot than Lyngstad, her vocal performance on 'SOS' was an undoubted highlight on the album, as was the song itself. It was among the first tracks to be recorded for ABBA – sessions began on August 22, 1974 – but despite its undoubted hit qualities it was only the third single to be lifted off the album.

Many consider 'SOS' to be Abba's first truly masterful pop single: Fältskog's first "heartbreak classic", wherein the tear-filled vocal delivery, her trademark, would blend an Anglo-

Saxon pop melody with a dash of Swedish melancholy, and an arrangement – characterised by Andersson's semi-classical keyboard flourishes – that was pure Abba. The synthesiser and guitar riffs that underpin the song, its defining characteristics, were added only at the last minute, late one night when Ulvaeus and Andersson stayed back to work on the track.

Again, Stig Anderson delivered a perfect "international" title, along with a set of lyrics that were quite heavily reworked by Ulvaeus, whose command of English was unquestionably superior to Anderson's. Although the words are hardly high poetry, there is something to be said for their simplicity, as Fältskog expresses these basic emotions like a primal scream of desolation.

All in all, the result was a brilliant recording that The Who's Pete Townshend once called "the best pop song ever written". Indeed, with the release of 'SOS' as a single in the autumn of 1975, Abba were finally back in the UK Top 10, and their credibility as purveyors of solid pop music was firmly restored. Incidentally, Fältskog also recorded a Swedish-language version of the song, included on her 1975 solo album, *Elva kvinnor i ett hus* (*Eleven Women In One House*).

Chiquitita

The first single released from Abba's *Voulez-Vous* album was this Latin American-flavoured, Fältskog-led ballad, a follow-up of sorts to Lyngstad's 'Fernando'. The song went through a couple of incarnations – the first entitled 'In The Arms Of Rosalita', recorded with a completely different backing track and featuring alternating lead lines from both women – before it finally became 'Chiquitita'.

Recording of the final version began on December 13, 1978. 'Chiquitita' was selected as the song for Abba to perform at a UNICEF benefit concert for The International Year Of The Child at the General Assembly Hall of the United Nations in New York. Moreover, they donated all future royalties of the song to UNICEF. It was very rewarding for the organisation, since 'Chiquitita' not only became a major hit at the time – reaching number two in the UK – but has endured as one of

Abba's most popular songs over the years, being included on most big-selling compilation albums.

Fernando
(Benny Andersson/Stig Anderson/Björn Ulvaeus)

The recording of 'Fernando', perhaps second only to 'Dancing Queen' in terms of single sales, actually began at the same time as that dance floor classic, on August 4 and 5, 1975. The song was not originally intended for Abba, but for Lyngstad's solo album *Frida ensam* (*Frida Alone*). Sessions for this album, which was produced by Andersson, had been going on intermittently since the spring of 1974, around the time of Abba's 'Waterloo' breakthrough. The LP consisted mainly of Swedish cover versions of foreign songs, but it was felt that Andersson, Ulvaeus and Anderson should contribute a brand new tune as well.

Soon enough it was clear that 'Fernando' had far too much hit potential to be confined to a Swedish Frida album. For the English lyrics, Ulvaeus spun his own theme around the 'Fernando' title: where Anderson had gone for an ordinary love story, Ulvaeus instead had a vision of "two old revolutionaries, sitting outdoors one night, reminiscing". Though the lyrics conjure up visions of the Spanish Civil War, he apparently never intended them to refer to any specific historical event.

Chosen as Abba's follow-up single to 'Mamma Mia' in March 1976 – in favour of 'Dancing Queen', no less – 'Fernando' ended up "between albums", and was never included on any proper studio album (except in Australia and New Zealand, where it was squeezed onto *Arrival*). However, in the UK it was featured on the blockbuster *Greatest Hits* LP, which, ironically, was to remain a bigger seller than any of Abba's regular albums in Great Britain.

Voulez-Vous

This song was a direct result of a songwriting trip Ulvaeus and Andersson undertook to the Bahamas in January 1979. Moreover, the excitement of finding themselves in the midst of a vibrant American pop music environment made them decide to record the backing track for the song right then and there. The Bahamas weren't too far away from Florida and the Criteria Recording Studios, at the time the super-hot location for many of The Bee Gees' disco-era recordings. On February 1, 1979, the backing for the new song was laid down in Miami, with the aid of members of the group Foxy (of 'Get Off' fame) and an array of producers and engineers, including Atlantic Records' legendary Tom Dowd. Even Michael Tretow flew over from Sweden to ensure that the recording would be technically compatible with the machines at Polar Music Studios.

Fältskog and Lyngstad share the lead vocals on the track that came closest to capturing the hedonistic spirit of disco: the lyrics were even set in a club environment, describing the intrigues and game-playing of a one night stand. 'Voulez-Vous' was chosen as the third single from the album, but was flipped-over in the UK, where the B-side, 'Angeleyes', was more heavily promoted.

The original 1992 issue of *ABBA Gold* featured an edit of the familiar 5.14 version of 'Voulez-Vous', down to 4.21, presumably to make it fit on what was considered maximum CD capacity in the early Nineties. By the end of the decade, there was sufficient space to include the original recording on all subsequent issues.

Gimme! Gimme! Gimme! (A Man After Midnight)

Abba's "disco" year of 1979 saw a fitting conclusion with this single, written and recorded just a few weeks before the group's tour of North America and Europe kicked off that September. Two earlier attempts at a new single to be released in conjunction with the tour – one a string-laden ballad, the other a straightforward pop song – had failed to come off. In keeping with their current mood, it was only when they found a song with a dance beat that Abba felt they had something that was good enough to release. Fältskog certainly helped out with her delivery of a typically yearning lead vocal against the relentlessly throbbing backing track. The group was rewarded with a hit single that, in global chart terms, was actually more successful than any of the singles off *Voulez-Vous*, with the exception of 'Chiquitita'.

It's no secret that Abba are much-loved among the world's gay communities, and this song is a particular favourite in gay clubs.

Does Your Mother Know

'Does Your Mother Know' marked the last time a song with Björn Ulvaeus lead vocals would be released as an Abba A-side. Recording began on February 6, 1979, shortly after he and Andersson had returned from the Bahamas. Originally the song featured a bit more rock-boogie-style backing, including a long, drum-based introduction, and this was how it was performed in the television special *ABBA In Switzerland*, taped in mid-February. However, on returning to Sweden and completing the *Voulez-Vous* album, the group decided to do some more work on the track, tightening-up the structure, and − surprise, surprise − emphasising its disco beat. Benny also came up with a completely new synth-bass introduction.

'Does Your Mother Know' was a fairly successful single, reaching the Top Five or Top 10 in most places. However, today Ulvaeus feels that if one of the girls had sung it instead of him they would have been rewarded with an even bigger hit. He's probably right.

One Of Us

'One Of Us' was one of the last tracks recorded for *The Visitors*, beginning on October 21. It was also the one major hit single from the album. The song opened with a lovely splash of melody, which led into a slightly reggae-inflected backing track with Italian mandolins and an immensely catchy chorus. It was easy to see why it became a favourite among fans: it offered many of the romantic, multi-layered Abba trademarks of yore, while Fältskog's delivery of yet another end-of-romance story contained all the heartbeat the public had come to expect of a group that now consisted of two divorced couples. 'One Of Us' was Abba's last UK Top Five hit, peaking at number three in 1981 – indeed, to date it is the last time they have featured inside the Top 15.

The Name Of The Game

(Benny Andersson/Stig Anderson/Björn Ulvaeus)

Just like 'One Man, One Woman', 'The Name Of The Game' was clearly inspired by American soft rock. There also seemed to be some influences from one of the group's biggest idols, Stevie Wonder; the bass-and-synthesiser riff that opens the song sounds very much like a slower variation on its counterpart in 'I Wish', a cut on Wonder's then-recently released *Songs In The Key Of Life* album. In an interesting illustration of the unpredictable routes music may travel for the unprejudiced, two decades later the riff travelled back across the Atlantic, where it was sampled from the Abba recording to form the basis of the hip-hop track 'Rumble In The Jungle' by The Fugees.

Indeed, 'The Name Of The Game' itself was a song that somehow defied genre definitions, being constructed in six separate parts that Andersson and Ulvaeus managed to fit together to make up one, cohesive whole. The song made outstanding use of Lyngstad and Fältskog's extraordinary vocal abilities: they each had their own parts, but they also drifted in and out of joint, harmonised sequences, at one stage blending into a short a cappella sequence of dreamlike, velvety smoothness. Over a slow-paced rhythm track, Andersson and Ulvaeus then piled their usual mix of keyboard pads, crisp acoustic guitar chords and electric guitar lines, topped off with a 'Penny Lane'-style synthesised piccolo trumpet. It was pure Abba.

'The Name Of The Game' was released as the first single off *ABBA - The Album* in October 1977, shooting to number one in the UK and reaching the Top Three or Top 10 almost everywhere else. Notably, it was also one of the last Abba songs with a Stig Anderson songwriting credit. By this time it seems his contribution was limited exclusively to titles. In this case, his genius mind turned the working title, 'A Bit Of Myself', into the decidedly more catchy and memorable 'The Name Of The Game'.

When *ABBA Gold* was first released in 1992, it featured a 4.01 edit of 'The Name Of The Game' – the original length of the track was 4.55 – which had first surfaced on a promo single in the United States in December 1977. This edit certainly constituted a drastic butchering of what was one of Abba's most accomplished recordings, ditching the entire second verse yet repeating the chorus twice in succession. This edit of 'The Name Of The Game' was given its first commercial release on the compilation double album *The Singles – The First Ten Years* in 1982, and then in 1992, presumably to save disc space, it was issued on *ABBA Gold*.

Unfortunately, a further consequence of its inclusion there was that the edit was used as the "official master" of the song for the next five years, appearing on the *Thank You For The Music* box set, and even the first pressings of the 1997 remastered version of *ABBA – The Album*. However, on the remastered version of *ABBA Gold*, issued in 1999, the original version of the song was reinstated. It also appears on all subsequent issues of the album, as well as on the currently available CD of *ABBA – The Album* issued in 2001.

Thank You For The Music

The first and most popular of the three songs from *The Girl With The Golden Hair*, Abba's mini-musical. Indeed, thanks to its title and its theme, this has become one of the most celebrated Abba songs of all time, although it was never a major single release. It was even included on the group's most successful "hits" collection, *ABBA Gold*, in favour of less well-known tracks that had actually been hits.

The version featured on the stage during *The Girl With The Golden Hair* was a much looser, cabaret-style interpretation, featuring slightly different lyrics. Then, in June, 1977, the first attempt at a studio recording was made, with rewritten lyrics. Finally, on July 21, the backing track for the version that ultimately ended up on *ABBA – The Album* was nailed. In a way, it could be said to be a cross between the live version and the first studio attempt, being less crisp and jaunty in rhythm than the June recording, but tighter and more focused than the live performance.

For many, 'Thank You For The Music' is something of a watershed recording in terms of how Abba are perceived. Some take its celebration of the power of music to heart and are won over by the usual Abba tunefulness, the attractive arrangement and Fältskog's earnest lead vocal; others, however, consider it a mum-and-dad toe-tapper, the ultimate in cabaret cheesiness, and a strong argument why Abba could never be taken seriously as a "happening" pop/rock band. Whatever your feelings about the track – and some opinions do fall in between – the expert craftsmanship can't be denied.

Waterloo

(Benny Andersson/Stig Anderson/Björn Ulvaeus)

A bit of classic girl-group pop, a dash of inspiration from contemporary Spector-influenced rock, such as Wizzard's 'See My Baby Jive', and a song title that could be understood and recognised by everyone – the perfect recipe for a hit that would conquer the international charts in 1974. Famously, 'Waterloo' was the song with which Abba won the Eurovision Song Contest in Brighton, England, on April 6, 1974.

Recording of the song began December 17, 1973, shortly after the songwriting trio of Andersson/Anderson/Ulvaeus had been invited to submit a new song in the Swedish selection for the contest, after the previous year's failure with 'Ring Ring'. Andersson and Ulvaeus wrote the tune in their cottage on an island in the Stockholm archipelago, where many of Abba's biggest hits were born.

Armed with a cassette demo of the tune, it took a while for Stig Anderson to come up with the right lyrics. He knew all too well the importance of coming up with a short and snappy title that would be easy to understand in all languages, like the name Abba itself. His first attempt was 'Honey-Pie', which has the same number of syllables, but he wasn't sufficiently inspired to write any lyrics based around that concept. Finally, he came up with 'Waterloo' – which referred to Napoleon Bonaparte's legendary defeat by British and German forces at the battle near the Belgian town on June 18, 1815 – and used that historical event as a metaphor for a girl surrendering to the courting of an insistent suitor. Not the greatest of lyrical concepts, but it worked.

After the Brighton victory, 'Waterloo' became a hit almost everywhere people were buying records, even in territories where Eurovision was virtually unheard of. The group recorded no other Abba song in as many languages: in addition to the familiar English recording, there were versions in Swedish, German and French. A planned Spanish recording seems never to have been completed.

R.E.M.

Automatic For The People

October 1992

By Peter Hogan

"NORMALLY PEOPLE WHO sell nine to ten million albums, you don't hear from them for four years," R.E.M. guitarist Peter Buck commented, explaining the fact that this was something the workaholic Georgia band wanted to avoid. In fact, Buck, bassist Mike Mills, and drummer Bill Berry were back in John Keane's Athens studio demoing new songs with producer Scott Litt mere months after the 1991 release of Out Of Time. This time, however, they were minus Peter Holsapple. The guitarist – supposedly unhappy about his status as a hired hand who earned a wage rather than a percentage, and who remained excluded from the songwriting process – quit to record an album, Mavericks, with his former dB's partner, Chris Stamey.

Peter Buck: "Things happen – you sell a lot of records and things get weird. It just isn't easy being the fifth member of our band. No one else is going to write songs with us. It's a closed shop and it's tough to deal with. I wouldn't want to be in a band where I didn't have input in the songwriting or arrangements and stuff. I wish money would have nothing to do with this. We played for free together for so long that it's a shame to have business things get in between us. But on the other hand, we write the songs, we're the band. It's fucked in a way, but we're not going to open it up. It's not a monetary thing; it's just the way that we are." Holsapple's lips remain sealed on the matter, probably for contractual reasons.

But Buck was enthusiastic about the new songs. Though the original intention had been to do a rock-guitar album (i.e. something they could play live more easily than the Out Of Time material), things weren't turning out that way, and he didn't seem to mind. "We'll have a folk-rock orchestra album," Buck told Spin magazine early on in the sessions. "The stuff is all turning out different. We've got a bunch of weird kind of Arabic folk songs."

If anything, the results would be even quieter than the previous album, the strings more lavish – in fact, "folk-rock orchestra" is a pretty good description. "We thought it was going to be a live-sounding rock album," Buck said after the album was completed. "But halfway through we realised it was going to be quiet and droney, so that's what we went with." Former Led Zeppelin bassist and keyboard player, John Paul Jones, provided string arrangements for four songs ('Drive', 'Everybody Hurts', 'The Sidewinder Sleeps Tonight' and 'Nightswimming'). "I was really impressed with how melodic and non-saccharine his arrangements were," said Buck. Thirteen orchestral musicians are credited on the sleeve, under the conductorship of George Hanson. Originally, half the songs were to contain no drums.

Once demos were completed, singer Michael Stipe joined the other members at Daniel Lanois' Kingsway studios in New Orleans. Recording continued at Bearsville in New York State, then Criteria in Miami and Bosstown in Atlanta. The album was finally mixed at Heart's Bad Animals Studio in Seattle. All of this studio-hopping probably had a lot more to do with seeing a bit of the country than with anything technical.

This time, the lyrics again seemed to concern personal matters, notably death and mourning. "I'm in the process of depoliticising myself," Stipe later told *Rolling Stone*. "I'm glad that people look at the band as politically active. I think that's healthy. But it's a lot to carry, and to quote myself, not everyone can carry the weight of the world. It's enough that people know that R.E.M. are thinking, compassionate people – human beings who support a number of causes, publicly and privately. I don't have to jump on top of a building and scream. I'm not a very good speaker – that's the end – all of it." But as he'd said around the release of *Out Of Time* : "I'm not saying that I will never write another political song – in fact, I think even though thematically this record is love songs, there's a great deal of politics involved and they're not just personal politics."

But Stipe's public solidarity with AIDS awareness – coupled with his gaunt appearance, his reluctance to appear in videos, the references to death on the record and the fact that the gay community wanted to believe he was gay, whatever he said (or didn't say) on the subject – fuelled rumours that Stipe himself was suffering from AIDS. It was one of rock's more bizarre rumours, which took a while to dissipate.

But as Buck pointed out: "Michael is one of the few writers I can think of who can actually write songs about friendship and stuff. You don't know who he's singing to or whether there's a sexual relationship involved." As to the media focus on Stipe's personal life, Buck said that the singer was (quite understandably) "just sick of it. The band are asked about guitar effects, but journalists want to talk to Michael about his childhood".

And anyway – though the media still find it hard to accept – R.E.M. have four voices, not one. In the songwriting process, Stipe doesn't necessarily write all the lyrics. As Buck told Q : "On every record there's one of us who has less of an involvement than maybe the next record, but nobody needs to know that. By the time we write the bridges and intros and rewrite stuff, it's all of ours anyway. Since we split the money equally, there's no real reason to get egotistical about it. Saying who wrote what is counterproductive, like family business. I like the idea of the four of us indivisible; you can't drive a wedge between us. That's how we stay together."

Automatic For The People took its title from a sign in a favourite diner, Weaver D's Fine Foods in Clarke County, Georgia, which read: "Delicious Fine Foods. Automatic For The People." The owner, Dexter Weaver, was approached for permission to use the slogan by Buck and Stipe, and he told them the saying meant: "Ready, Quick and Efficient". Stipe reportedly responded, "Woo, that's what we are". Within weeks of the album's release the sign was stolen by overzealous R.E.M. fans, who later returned it with $10 and a note of apology. Yup, sounds like R.E.M. fans.

Dexter Weaver: "Vice President Al Gore was here in Athens campaigning at the Tate Center over at the University of Georgia, and Michael introduced him at the rally. Gore said Bush and Quayle was 'Out Of Time', but him and Bill Clinton was going to be 'Automatic For The People'. I wasn't there, but everywhere I went that night in town, people were telling me that Al Gore used my slogan. That's great, because we need a President who is going to be 'For The People'."

The success of *Out Of Time* had evidently done wonders for R.E.M.'s self-confidence. *Automatic For The People* is an assured, mature work that combines polished production with polished performances and some of the band's best songs to date. It went straight in at number two in the US, number one in the UK and sold over 14 million copies worldwide.

All songs written by R.E.M.

Drive

"Smack, crack, bushwhacked" are the album's opening words, referring either to the increase of street drugs and resultant violence, or to the state of the nation under George Bush, or an optimistic prophecy of his defeat. Or all three. (Four years earlier, Stipe had placed a pro-Dukakis ad in an Athens student newspaper, urging people to vote Democrat with the phrase: "Don't get Bushwacked".). There are echoes of David Essex's UK hit 'Rock On' (though Essex was himself echoing Leon Russell). Broodingly atmospheric (and far from cheerful), with echoing vocals and booming bass set against delicate guitar and tasteful strings. Heck of a choice for a single, though.

Try Not To Breathe

Another of Stipe's "vomit songs", i.e. written quickly in one sitting. A message from an old man, tired of his life but still clinging to it. This doesn't sound like anybody else in pop, ancient or modern.

The Sidewinder Sleeps Tonight

The album's first vaguely happy track – bouncy pop, with Jones' gorgeously sweeping string arrangement. The title obviously references 'The Lion Sleeps Tonight', as does the opening yodel. The band actually recorded a cover of that song as well, so that may have been the jumping-off point for this.

Peter Buck: "Don't ask me what that's about. Part of it is trying to get into somebody's apartment to spend the night. The rest of it is just whatever Michael wanted to say. There are some things I just don't worry about. That's one of them."

A sidewinder is a small rattlesnake. The lyric includes the

kind of shopping list you'd imagine Stipe making in reality: can of beans, Dr. Seuss book, falling star ... Where do you buy falling stars, anyway?

Everybody Hurts

An anti-suicide song with lots of good advice – "hold on", "take comfort in your friends". The tastefulness of the arrangement mirrors the economy of the lyric; the song may have been aimed at teenagers, but it's proof of R.E.M.'s maturity. Peter Buck: 'Everybody Hurts' is like a soul ballad. If Otis Redding were alive I bet he'd have covered it."

Peter Buck: "If you ask Michael, he'll say that not one of the songs is about himself. I know that's bullshit. On 'Everybody Hurts' there was a line that went: 'When everything is wrong, everybody hurts, even the singer of the song'. But in the end he said, 'I'm not going to sing that'."

Mike Mills: "He came up with the lyrics in the time it took us to go through the song three or four times. None of us really thought it would see the light of day. It was kind of a joke song at first. But Michael, in my opinion, is the best lyricist alive, and that song's a great example of how he polished a turd."

Peter Buck: "I guess people think when Michael's being obscure it's because he can't express himself. In fact, he's trying to find another way to say things in a way that's real to him, that isn't a cliché. He wanted that particular song to reach teenagers and not be misunderstood. You don't want something that needs a maths degree to go through when you're trying to reach a 17-year-old and say, 'It's OK – things are tough, but they get better.' There's not a line out of place in there."

New Orleans Instrumental No. 1

So titled presumably because that's where it was recorded. Unlike most of the instrumentals from this period that turned up as single B-sides, this one has a tune: jazz-folk, with a bit of psychedelia round the edges.

Sweetness Follows

A song of grief and of coming of age. Losing a close relative is like joining a club: if you've been through it, you know what it's like; if you haven't, you don't. From the sound of it, R.E.M. do. Poignant folk-psychedelia featuring cello by Knox Chandler, making it sound reminiscent of The Beatles' 'Eleanor Rigby'.

Monty Got A Raw Deal

"Nonsense isn't new to me", sings Stipe (accurately), and many have no idea what this is about. Sounds almost like a traditional folk song, and again features cello by Knox Chandler.

Ignoreland

Overtly political rocker (there was a US election that year) that contains a litany of anti-Reagan/Bush bile ("I know this is vitriol, no solution, spleen-venting, but I feel better for having screamed, don't you?"). The following month Bill Clinton was elected to office. Both Mills and Stipe have gone on record as hating this one. (Mills: "I didn't like it the day we did it." Stipe: "We should have left it off the record.") Scott Litt plays clavinet and harmonica, and makes it sound like a brass section.

Star Me Kitten

R.E.M. turn their attention to sex (to which they would return for most of *Monster*). Peter Buck: "It's a real perverse love song, demented. It's an endearing term. It's not about cats." Just as well, since at one point Stipe gets audibly more direct, clearly singing, "Fuck me, kitten" (which was the song's original title, until Warners objected; the new title echoes The Rolling Stones having to change 'Starfucker' to 'Star Star').

Man On The Moon

Gentle but infectious, this one had "hit" written all over it. Buck called it "a goofy look at heaven". The song is addressed to the late Andy Kaufman, a radical stand-up comic best known outside of the USA for his role as Latka in the TV series *Taxi*. Kaufman often featured an Elvis impression in his act, hence Stipe's own (credible) Elvis impression here. Throughout the Third World, there are many who seriously believe the Apollo missions were all faked in Hollywood.

Robyn Hitchcock: "The first two verses of 'Man In The Moon' were written by Bill – you can tell by the weird way the guitar works against the voice that it's not what a conventional songwriter would have done – and Peter wrote the middle eight."

Michael: "That was kind of a 'vomit song'. But it took five months of working up to it. That song was written and recorded on the day that it was delivered to the record company. Although it was kind of a 40-hour day."

Nightswimming

Written before the *Green* album, apparently. A gentle ode to the joys of nude bathing, with wonderfully restrained orchestration, again courtesy of Jones.

Mike Mills: "It's something we used to do back in Athens. Twenty or 30 of us would go skinnydipping at two in the morning – you know, build a fire and get naked. There was a very real possibility of the sheriff coming up. We were drinking and doing who knows what, and we could have gone to jail. Whereas now, no one does it any more, except once in a while we take a friend up there to show them. And even if you do go to swim, it's still not like it used to be, because no one knows about it, and there's really no chance of anyone coming down and bothering you."

Peter Buck also remembered those days fondly: "We used to go swimming naked. It would be summertime, it would be 100 degrees, there'd be like 100 of us... We were all younger, it was pre-AIDS, so no one had this fear of sex. You'd assume what would happen and it did." But Buck's comment did seem to lend weight to those who saw in the line "fear of getting caught" a reference to AIDS, rather than just the thrill of illicit nudity. But it is possible to mourn the loss of innocence that comes simply through ageing without dragging AIDS into it.

Find The River

Another song seemingly about mourning, yet affirming life. The ocean is often used by Sufi mystics as a metaphor for God. Asked by Q's Adrian Deevoy whether his songs could make him cry, Stipe replied: "Sometimes. 'Find The River' to me has a lot of emotional baggage. It doesn't have that much to do with anything that would make sense to anyone else but me particularly. I know the place I wrote it. I know the connections I had with it when I wrote it. I know connections that came afterwards, people that died. So, yes, I can sing that song, but we've tried and tried to work it into some form which will translate live and for whatever reason we can't seem to play it. It's like a curse ... But I do love that song. Mike and I, when we wrote it, would drive around Miami in a convertible at three in the morning, and sing along to it. No words, just singing, both of us doing these climbing harmonics. It was so much fun to... cure yourself in that way."

RADIOHEAD

OK Computer
June 1997

By Mark Paytress

THE IDEA, RECKONED Thom Yorke, was to make a record that was both cool and yet easy to listen to while eating. "We could fall back on just doing another moribund, miserable, morbid and negative record," he added, shortly after *The Bends* was released, "but I really don't want to." It was some hope. The moment the singer began to note down any positive thoughts, his head was flooded with what he called "mental chatter". His struggle for serenity in a world where fatally flawed social structures were propped up by a seductive, drip-fed hyper-reality invariably supplied him with far more scope for Radiohead's next, eagerly anticipated album.

A rare instance of a contemporary record daring to take on the big issues of its time, *OK Computer* was instantly acclaimed as a key rock-music landmark, a *Sgt. Pepper* for the net generation, a richly textured slice of art-rock that both embodied its times and transcended them. Perched precariously, yet somehow perfectly, between art and commerce, between analogue and digital, between modern and postmodern, between crisis and comfort, between music and all else that lies beyond it, *OK Computer* showed what happens when worlds collide.

While accidents were by now integral to the Radiohead methodology, there appeared to be nothing unplanned about the record's scope and ambition, which had even the most jaded critics struggling to find new superlatives. Perhaps most remarkable of all was how the band took the mainstream indie rock audience with them, away from the trad-rock song structures that had dominated since the early Eighties towards a new, radical fusion of prog-rock and avant-punk.

While *The Bends* revealed that much progress had been made since the indie-rock orthodoxy of *Pablo Honey*, there was little to suggest that Radiohead would cross another major threshold for a second consecutive time. The secret of modern-day fame, after all, was to find a winning formula and – give or take a few superficial tweaks for the sake of novelty – stick to it. But Thom Yorke had been shuffling the cards in Brian Eno's pack of Oblique Strategies, taking particular note of the one that instructed, "Whatever worked last time, never do it again". And so, piqued by the progress they'd already made,

Radiohead set out, determined to put imagination before consolidation.

Self-sufficiency was crucial to their requirements, so they despatched engineer – and from this point on, co-producer – Nigel Godrich with instructions to build a studio. Several weeks – and £100,000 – later, Radiohead had their own state-of-the-art converted apple shed in the Oxfordshire countryside, which they duly dubbed Canned Applause.

The band spent much of January and February 1996 at the new studio with Godrich, who'd already been road-tested on the new, post-*Bends* song, 'Lucky', installed as their producer. The new, not-too-far-from-home surroundings proved conducive to work, too. For by the time Radiohead took off in March for yet another American tour, several new songs had all been worked up, almost all eagerly installed into the live set. Among these were 'Subterranean Homesick Alien', 'Let Down', 'Electioneering' and 'No Surprises', virtually the backbone for *OK Computer*.

As with *The Bends*, work on the album was fitted around the constant touring schedules – and Radiohead were back in the States in August supporting Alanis Morissette. But this time there was also their leap-in-the-dark attitude towards their work to contend with. For now, more than ever before, Radiohead were extending their collective palette. For Thom Yorke, it was the metronomic rhythms of early Seventies Krautrock. Jonny Greenwood bought himself a vintage, Theremin-like instrument called the Ondes Martenot. The others also searched for new perspectives on their instruments, bassist Colin Greenwood even squeezing in a round of private lessons between tours.

Having returned to Canned Applause during May and July, Radiohead broke out later that summer. Hiring St Catherine's Court, a stately residence near Bath owned by the famously fragrant actress Jane Seymour, they set up their equipment in the magnificent 15th-century ballroom. Alternating between mansion and converted apple shed, they emerged some time around Christmas 1996 with something approaching a finished album.

Various string parts were added at Abbey Road in the New

Year and, during the first few months of 1997, the finished material was mixed at several locations. (For old times' sake, Paul Q Kolderie and Sean Slade were asked to remix a couple of tracks, but their efforts went unused.) Sequencing the record proved no less difficult than any other stage in its making; Thom Yorke shuffling endlessly with the songs on his MiniDisc recorder until hitting on the perfect combination of pace and thematic consistency. (His MiniDisc also proved useful for grabbing various "slice of life" sounds heard on his travels, some of which were dropped into the album).

The blissful melancholia of 'Street Spirit', which closed *The Bends*, had dramatically signposted the future. And that was the mood maintained on Radiohead's first official post-*Bends* releases: 'Lucky', issued on *Help!*, a fundraising compilation, in September 1995, and 'Exit Music', recorded for the soundtrack to the 1996 film William Shakespeare's *Romeo + Juliet*. But it was when the band opted to release a six-minutes-plus epic as their first proper single in over a year, in May 1997, that the scale of Radiohead's latest achievement began to unfold.

The labyrinthine course of 'Paranoid Android' prompted the inevitable accusations of prog-rockery, forcing Yorke to counter that while he'd been listening to the music of the progressive rock dinosaurs, he thought it was "all awful". More pertinently, during the making of *OK Computer*, he said he'd been playing The Beatles' 'White Album' and Miles Davis's *Bitches Brew* ("A record for the end of the world," he declared). "You aim for these things," Yorke told band biographer Mac Randall, "and end up with your own version." There's little doubt, though, that the Fender Rhodes piano that was all over the album had been inspired by Davis' extraordinary late-Sixties work.

Further background influences, Yorke claimed, had been *The Tibetan Book Of The Dead* and assorted literature on the situationists and the student riots in Paris, May 1968. The singer was rather more vague when it came to possible meanings that might be drawn from the record. "It's not really about computers," he said, but the "noise that was going on in my head... mental chatter" aroused by travel, telephones, television and virtually everything else in the inescapable contemporary soundscape. That gave carte blanche for all manner of interpretations. Not since *Sgt. Pepper* or Pink Floyd's *The Dark Side Of The Moon* had a record been so thoroughly deconstructed, scrupulously scrutinised for secret "codes" to crack. Yet from its title in, *OK Computer* was always suggestive, rarely emphatic. However, one thing was certain: the album's kaleidoscopic character was a far cry from the transparently self-obsessed songs on *Pablo Honey*.

"Journalists like it, which is always ominous," Jonny Greenwood told Randall during the four-day media circus that descended on Barcelona for the launch of *OK Computer* in May 1997. No less worrying was the news that the band's American outlet, Capitol Records, had denounced the record as "commercial suicide", and had instantly cut its order from two million copies to a paltry half-million. Happily, they were proved wrong when, after topping the chart at home and debuting at an impressive 21 in the States, *OK Computer* proved that it was still possible to make a record that sounded like no other and yet still reap the commercial reward.

That summer, Radiohead made a triumphant return to Glastonbury, their Saturday-night show on the Pyramid Stage now regarded as one of the long-running festival's all-time highlights. Shortly afterwards, the readers of Q magazine voted *OK Computer* the best album of all time, a remarkable feat for a contemporary record. The jury might still be out on that one, but certainly the rock mainstream had not been blessed with an album this radical since... Patti Smith's *Horses*, perhaps? Compared to Radiohead's achievement, Nirvana's *Nevermind*, that other great overground/underground rock album from the Nineties, sounds one-dimensional and ordinary.

All songs written by Radiohead.

Airbag

While superficially similar to the rhythmically terse 'Planet Telex', which opened *The Bends*, 'Airbag' was a dizzying sonic sculpture. Motored by a looped three-second drum sample and augmented by dub-wise bass that evoked Jah Wobble's work on PiL's similarly spatial *Metal Box*, 'Airbag' instantly places OK Computer in an alternative musical sphere where all divisions between rock and dance music have fallen away. Thom Yorke's vocal, ruminating on car crashes and how to survive them, is disarmingly elegant; likewise, an intermittent guitar posing as a balalaika.

The total effect is heady and disorientating, hence the accusations of progressive rock. While it's true that 'Airbag' – originally performed acoustically and titled 'An Airbag Saved My Life' – has something in common with the dark, claustrophobic ultra-prog of Van Der Graaf Generator, its fragmented beats are closer to DJ Shadow or Aphex Twin. When, midway through the sessions, Colin Greenwood was asked what to expect from the new album, his "stoned Radiohead" quip wasn't too wide of the mark on this evidence.

Yorke, who takes great satisfaction in his work once the agony of creation is over, soon revealed his delight in the familiar manner, declaring 'Airbag' as his favourite track on the album. In fact, he'd recognised its worth right away, calling his girlfriend after completing one last, incredibly loud final mix of the song and exclaiming, "We've done something really great" down the phone.

Attempting to explain the meaning of the lyric to Q's Phil Sutcliffe, the singer returned to more familiar terrain. It was, he said, "more about the idea that whenever you go out on the road you could be killed... [and] about how the way I've been brought up and most of us are brought up, we are never given time to think about our own deaths."

Paranoid Android

The cardinal rule laid down by punk rock in the late Seventies and which, more or less, has been slavishly adhered to ever since, is that no pop song need ever extend its welcome longer than three minutes. 'Paranoid Android' brilliantly explodes that notion, and for that and several other reasons remains one of the cornerstones of the Radiohead catalogue. Clocking in at almost six-and-a-half minutes, the recorded version had been significantly abbreviated since the Alanis Morissette tour, when it featured a lengthy instrumental play-out based around Jonny Greenwood's Hammond organ. More shocking still is the song's constantly shifting structure, its quicksilver dynamics and intermittent eruptions of sound – fast becoming a Radiohead trademark – which again sounded distinctly more Van Der Graaf than Nirvana.

In fact, while The Beatles' 'Happiness Is A Warm Gun' (from the 'White Album') is widely acknowledged as the inspiration for the song's labyrinthine, three-part format, 'Paranoid Android' could just as easily be regarded as a younger, more compact cousin to VDGG's 20-minute epic, 'A Plague Of Lighthouse-Keepers'. Many other names have been dropped into the inspirational mix at various times, including Queen's similarly tangential 'Bohemian Rhapsody', Ennio Morricone, Can and the omnipresent Pixies and DJ Shadow. And yet, unlike so much deliberate, conspicious sourcing, 'Paranoid Android' – like so much of Radiohead's work – leaves virtually no obvious trace of its genesis behind.

Remarkably, the song, titled after Marvin The Paranoid Android, the boorish robot in Douglas Adams' *The Hitchhiker's Guide To The Galaxy*, gave the band a Top Three hit. Not since those heady hippy days had such a mind-blowing, convention-defying song – in the vein of The Beach Boys' 'Good Vibrations' and The Beatles' 'Strawberry Fields Forever' – been merrily embraced by a mainstream audience. The vibe, though, is significantly less love-filled.

"Basically it's just about chaos, chaos, utter fucking chaos," explained Yorke, playing down the barely concealed aggression and misanthropy in his lyric. The most cited evidence of that, the reference to the "kicking, squealing Gucci little piggy", came to Yorke in a bar in Los Angeles, as he wryly observed a bunch of coke-fuelled smart-asses going about their business. Acutely uncomfortable surrounded by all that well-heeled, self-satisfied "glamour", he retreated to his room, where he spent a sweat-filled night haunted by what he'd witnessed, worst of all the look in one woman's eye after someone had spilled a drink on her. The spectacle inspired some positively Robespierre-like fantasies ("When I am king you will be first against the wall", "Off with his head"), before his lone-wolf lyric veers off to invoke some natural catastrophe, closing with a deliciously ironic, "God loves his children, yeah!"

Subterranean Homesick Alien

Despite its blissful air, the sentiments of this song more neatly fit its original title, 'Uptight'. Continuing his assault on the spiritually bereft facts of contemporary life, Yorke has described the song as inspired by aliens "pissing themselves laughing at how humans go about their daily business". Clearly siding with the visitors, the character in the song hopes they'll "swoop down in a country lane", take him away and show him the world "as I'd love to see it".

Characteristically happy/sad, the song's despair is obscured by an enchanting arrangement and fantastic imagery, richly evocative of the wide-angled melancholy of Jeff Buckley's father, Tim. Another beautiful and shockingly gifted happy/sad troubadour, Tim Buckley had died tragically young, an event strangely mirrored when his son drowned in an accident in May 1997, just prior to the release of OK Computer.

Continuing with the song's folkish associations, the title was clearly drawn from Bob Dylan's 1965 stream-of-consciousness epic, 'Subterranean Homesick Blues'. In fact, when it was first performed in 1995, 'Subterranean Homesick Alien' featured just Thom Yorke and Jonny Greenwood on acoustic guitars. But when work on OK Computer had begun in earnest, Yorke's head was filled with Miles Davis's genre-busting Bitches Brew, "nauseating chaos" he reckoned on first listen, before admitting it had been "at the core of what we were trying to do".

That probably explains how 'Subterranean Homesick Alien', one of the first tracks to be completed for the album, was transformed from a song into an incantation. Yorke's Fender Rhodes is heavily reverbed in classic late-Sixties Davis fashion, while Greenwood – who wrote the intro and the chorus – follows suit with some mellifluous guitar lines.

Exit Music (For A Film)

If this song feels like a parting gesture, then that's because it was conceived that way – as the play-out music for Baz Luhrmann's 1996 film version of *William Shakespeare's Romeo + Juliet*. But it was more, much more than that. For while a second contribution, 'Talk Show Host', appears on the film's soundtrack CD, Radiohead declined to give permission for the producers to use 'Exit Music', claiming the song was "too personal". And unlike 'Talk Show Host', which had already appeared on the B-side of the 'Street Spirit' single, 'Exit Music' had yet to form part of the official Radiohead canon.

"The song is written for two people who should run away before all the bad stuff starts," Yorke later explained, hinting at past hurts. He'd also viewed a 30-minute rough cut of the film for inspiration, and drew on his memories of Franco Zeffirelli's hippy-era telling of the story, which he saw as a 13-year-old, and was struck by the obvious on-screen charms of Olivia Hussey as Juliet. The main ingredient, though, is Thom Yorke himself, whose resigned vocal brilliantly foreshadows the mood of impending tragedy. Biographer James Doheny describes the voice as having a "tomb-like ambience", taped, appropriately enough given her penchant for historical roles, in the courtyard of Jane Seymour's mansion.

It's odd, then, that 'Exit Music' begins in the manner of a late-Sixties Johnny Cash song, with Yorke accompanying himself on acoustic. And stranger still that the bleak, fateful mood is intensified by fuzzed-up bass (the ghost of Soft Machine's Hugh Hopper, perhaps) and some shrill, Ennio Morricone-inspired guitar lines. Suitably twisted by a range of disparate influences, the song passes over to the other side with a parting, "We hope that you choke", repeated with cracked conviction. Yorke was dead pleased. "Every note of it made my head spin," he later said.

Let Down

The short silence between 'Exit Music' and 'Let Down', up there alongside many other wonder-filled moments on *OK Computer*, was proof that Radiohead were close to mastering the fine art of sequencing. The mysterious spell of silence is touchingly broken with a perfectly poised guitar arpeggio, Jonny Greenwood's homage both to "the Spector Sound" and Lou Reed's spidery notes that dart in and out of The Velvet Underground's 'All Tomorrow's Parties'. Both the song's motor and its heart-rending motif, the deliciously delicate notes sweeten the disappointment inherent in Yorke's lyric, and neatly capture the oddly serene sense of helplessness that invariably accompanies a long journey, clearly the song's subtext. "'Let Down' is about what speed and movement do to someone's mind... when you're staring out of a window in a moving train for an hour. All those people, cars and houses passing by," Jonny Greenwood later confirmed.

The song's sparkly light-headedness, neatly undermined by some of Yorke's most arresting imagery ("People clinging on to bottles", "Crushed like a bug in the ground", "Wings twitch, legs are going"), was eventually committed to tape one night in St Catherine's Court at 3am, a suitably magical time to nail what's undoubtedly one of the band's most enchanting, and oddly underrated, songs. Things might have been different if the song had been issued as a single, as once planned but, after commissioning a costly video, the idea was shelved.

Midway through the song, Yorke pleads, "Don't get sentimental, it always ends up drivel". It's an observation that sounds wonderfully perverse given that 'Let Down' is probably the most elegant, heart-tugging performance Radiohead had yet recorded.

Karma Police

Having spent most of his life raging against all manner of machines, as well as bullies and undergraduates, ignoramuses and indie-kids, Thom Yorke was soon disappointed to discover that life at the centre of the culture industries was no less creep-free. Already infamous for shunning the coke, canapés and champagne circuit that keeps the music industry up all night, Radiohead didn't suffer fools gladly. Undesirables penetrating their privacy invariably prompted mock-desperate cries for the "karma police". It was Ed O'Brien who first suggested turning the catchphrase into a song, and Thom Yorke who seemed to find the whole idea funnier than everybody else.

The track's musical backbone came from a well-trod historical source, The Beatles' 'White Album', and one track in particular, 'Sexy Sadie'. There were fewer laughs here, for the song had once made such a profound impression on Charles Manson (of "The Manson Murders" infamy) that he renamed Susan Atkins, one of his murderous "lady lieutenants", 'Sadie'. The spectre of Manson, who often spoke of "levelling the karma" of the straight society he despised, seems to infect the song, from the otherwise amusing "arrest this man" hook, to the clearly sinister, "This is what you'll get if you mess with us", although there's no evidence that Yorke consciously drew on Manson for inspiration.

The second single lifted from the album, 'Karma Police' reached number eight in autumn 1997.

Fitter Happier

The thirst for list-making in rock journalism has now reached such proportions that we've even been distracted by guides such as "The Most Skipped Tracks On An Album". Invariably, 'Fitter Happier', the pivotal piece on OK Computer – and perhaps the ultimate, dehumanised source of its meaning – finds its way onto those lists every time. Given that the track itself is an imaginary two-minute "wish list" sketched out by the typical, mildly affluent Westerner, that's hardly inappropriate.

'Fitter Happier' was the only product of an otherwise barren three months when Thom Yorke found himself unable to write anything but lists. Basically a broadsheet supplement's survivors' kit to contemporary living, the lyric consists of 50 "wishes" covering a range of "issues" – from health and practical concerns to morality and spiritual matters. Idly running his check list of desires through SimpleText on his Apple Mac computer, Yorke inadvertently found a way to salvage something from his period of writer's block. Utilising the machine's "voice" to deliver the lyric also freed him from the prospect of him having to sing such goal-driven subject matter straight-faced.

The effect was so compelling/annoying that the subtle backdrop of meandering piano doodles and ominous patchwork of strings, loops and samples – including one from the 1975 film, *Three Days Of The Condor* – is virtually ignored. Yorke, nevertheless, was delighted by the outcome, describing 'Fitter Happier' as "the most upsetting thing I've ever written". Using technology commonly regarded as emotionally blank, he'd succeeded in bringing the lyric to life "in a fucking eerie way". And have "someone else" deliver a deliciously hideous sideswipe at the hidden cost of capitalism's "I want" culture, which was the purpose of the "pig in a cage on antibiotics" pay-off.

The 'Fitter Happier' monologue thrilled some, infuriated most. It also prompted many people to assume that *OK Computer* had been endorsed by high-profile philosopher/scientist Steven Hawking, who famously "speaks" utilising similar technology.

Electioneering

Leading neatly on from the automaton despair of 'Fitter Happier', this, Radiohead's first overtly political song, is vaguely reminiscent of late-Seventies agit-prop mavericks The Pop Group. As its title suggests, 'Electioneering' casts a cynical eye over how no one, least of all politicians, is able to stem the trickle-down greed peddled by the multinational corporations.

Yorke was moved to write this unsophisticated yet necessarily savage diatribe against "bullshit economies" and the politicians that prop them up after reading Will Hutton's *The State We're In*, and *The Age Of Extremes*, a Marxist's view of 20th century history written by Eric Hobsbawm. "I was completely fucking ignorant until I read those," he told *Time Out*'s Pete Paphides. Elsewhere, Yorke has admitted to a prior knowledge of the work of Noam Chomsky, and has also said that the song's fury was also inspired by memories of the Poll Tax riots of 1990.

Many rock musicians, especially over the past couple of decades, have worn their (invariably leftish) political colours in various shades of fashionable pastel. But not Yorke, whose conversion to political activism appears, like Lennon's, to have been motivated as much by an angry, disbelieving idealism as by private-club liberalism. And like the "revolutionary" ex-Beatle, he too tends towards a more apocalyptic vision of the new world order.

This early, unrefined intervention into politically charged rock channels that anger with what sounds like direct action. His cynicism plainly evident in slogan-like lyrics ("Say the right things when electioneering", "I trust I can rely on your vote"), Yorke's rant is neatly complemented by some of the most reductionist riffery Radiohead have ever set down on tape. 'Electioneering' is nothing less than the foul-mouthed gatecrasher at a sophisticated party, and not even the inventive, '68-era McCartney-style bassline played on a Novation Bass Station synth can dress up the song – a live favourite around this time – in any other way.

Climbing Up The Walls

From *10 Rillington Place* to *The Honeymoon Killers*, murder most foul – which most of us know only through films – moves slowly. And so it is with this pathologically inclined slice of doom rock, which begins with an institutionalised echo and climaxes in a string-induced cacophony of white noise. "Frightening music," admitted Jonny Greenwood.

Thom Yorke, who gives the song his most sinister performance yet, agreed. "This is about the unspeakable," he explained, meaning the seemingly irreversible increase in mass murderers at large. Declaring that he once worked in a mental hospital when the controversial Care In The Community initiative was introduced, he added that the decision to put mentally unstable patients back on the streets – and thus relieve the state of added financial burden – was hardly care at all. "It's one of the scariest things to happen in this country, because a lot of them weren't just harmless."

His heavily treated voice, which at times sounds so up close as to be inside the listener's own head, enhances the overriding mood of paranoia, which grows to head-beating, claustrophobic proportions by the song's end. "Some people can't sleep with the curtains open in case they see the eyes they imagine in their heads every night burning through the glass," Yorke further explained. "This song is about the cupboard monster."

No Surprises

From the terror-filled 'Climbing Up The Walls' to the childlike bliss of 'No Surprises' might seem a difficult journey to those who like their rock music confined to well-defined spaces, but Radiohead were by now becoming old hands in the ancient art of provocative juxtaposition. And besides, the lines between the two extremes are invariably more blurred than pop-vox assertions suggest.

Yorke was keen to dismiss claims that 'No Surprises' was in fact a suicide song. "We wanted it to sound like (Louis Armstrong's) 'What A Wonderful World' and Marvin Gaye," he said. "It's the sound of newly fitted double glazing – all hopeful, clean and secure." On the face of it, with Ed O'Brien's shimmering guitar line mimicking Jonny Greenwood's lullaby-like glockenspiel part, 'No Surprises' is innocence personified. But like a Douglas Sirk melodrama, it takes more than the shiny surfaces of modern domesticity ("Such a pretty house/And such a pretty garden") to keep darkness at bay, something confirmed by Yorke's opening words, "A heart that's full up like a landfill". A few lines later, he's reaching for "a handshake of carbon monoxide", forcing the child's music-box effect of the lead instruments to take on more sinister tones.

'No Surprises' was the first song to be recorded in the band's new Canned Applause studio, and the version used for the album was the first take, despite several attempts to improve on it. Originally written while touring with R.E.M. in August 1995 ("Colin goes nuts," wrote Yorke in his tour diary after unveiling the song backstage before the group's show in Oslo), 'No Surprises' was publicly premiered that December, a version that was considerably more downbeat than the one here. Apparently inspired by Sparklehorse's 'Sad

And Beautiful World', the studio take comes off sounding like the weirdly smiling offspring of The Beach Boys' 'Wouldn't It Be Nice' and The Velvet Underground's 'Sunday Morning'.

The third and final single from OK Computer, 'No Surprises' stalled at number three in the UK, a couple of places short of the Parlophone MD's expectations, but still impressive given that the album had been selling like mad for months.

Lucky

If 'Street Spirit' had suggested a sophisticated new musical future, then 'Lucky', the band's first high-profile post-Bends release, confirmed it. They had been toying with the song for weeks when, late in August 1995, Brian Eno's War Child charity, set up to send aid to the children of war-torn Bosnia, asked if the band had a song to contribute to a forthcoming fundraising album. Although their demands ran counter to the Radiohead way of working – all material had to be recorded on one day, Monday September 4, so that a finished album could hit the shops the following Saturday – the group accepted, passing the test in ways even they'd never imagined.

"'Lucky' is a song of complete release," Yorke later told NME, adding that it was the first in what he envisioned as a long line of "happy" material. But while the band managed to throw caution to the wind for the five-hour recording session, Yorke's opening salvo – "I'm on a roll this time/I feel my luck could change" – was hardly an emphatic declaration of levity. It was more like a moment's fanciful suggestion that life need not always be so problematic. Certainly, the procrastination they faced while making The Bends had been unblocked, albeit briefly. But Yorke's conversion into a smiley happy person was tentative, to say the least.

'Lucky' starts out like Neil Young's 'Heart Of Gold', before growing into a man-sized epic of early-Seventies symphonic rock proportions, complete with sampled choir. Yet it originated in some spontaneously strummed notes by Ed O'Brien while Radiohead were on tour in Japan. "I remember fiddling around [during] the soundcheck," he recalled, "putting together a different pedal order, and actually hitting the strings above the nut on the headstock. It was one of those moments." Not least because the sound reverberated via his delay pedal, thus lending the song its space-rock intro and its dreamy, Floyd-like ambience. Sophisticated and sonically spacious, 'Lucky' was, said Yorke, "the first mark on the wall" that would become *OK Computer*.

The Tourist

Had this been released in the Seventies, it would have been cited – alongside Nico's classic 'The End' – as a prime example of Mandrax-gripped musical torpor. And listlessness was indeed Jonny Greenwood's intention, having been inspired to write the music while watching a group of American tourists "do" the sights of a beautiful French town "in 10 minutes". 'The Tourist' is a song about speed," he confirmed, "about the amount of speed you live your life with." Like so many songs put forward for inclusion on albums, Greenwood imagined that his rare musical contribution would end up as a B-side at best. But, as the last song recorded at the *OK Computer* sessions, his weary hymn to drowsiness ("Idiot, slow down, slow down," choruses Yorke) virtually selected itself as the album's closer.

Once again, the spectre of Pink Floyd isn't far away, with Greenwood's Gilmour-like guitar trills sounding spectacularly pre-punk, especially when set against a sleepy waltz-beat that could have been plucked from any early-Seventies Grateful Dead album. The whole thing gives off the air of being recorded in an early morning mist, with Yorke barely able to remember adding his contribution, delivered for guide purposes only and with "no emotional involvement in it". And yet, in the tradition of the finest soul singers, something pure, spiritual even, seems to find an outlet from his exhausted body, a necessary catharsis at the end of an extraordinarily fertile period in the band's career. For, as *MOJO*'s Nick Kent later asserted, *OK Computer* was the record that made Radiohead "the most important rock band in the world".

LIST OF
CONTRIBUTORS

Geoff Brown

Geoff Brown is the Production Editor of *Mojo* magazine, a former editor of *Black Music*, and has written extensively on soul and R&B during a 35-year career in music journalism that began on *Melody Maker* during the early Seventies. He is the author of books on Otis Redding, Prince, Michael Jackson and Diana Ross. He lives in London.

David Buckley

Manchester-born David Buckley is a freelance writer now based in Munich. He has written an official biography of The Stranglers, *No Mercy*, and highly regarded books on David Bowie, R.E.M., Bryan Ferry & Roxy Music, and Elton John. David also contributes regularly to *Mojo* magazine, and has been commissioned by EMI Records to produce sleeve notes for the reissue of David Bowie albums.

Chris Charlesworth

Chris Charlesworth is the Editor-in-Chief of Omnibus Press, and a former News Editor and US Editor of *Melody Maker*. He has contributed to numerous magazines in the US and UK and written books on The Who, Pete Townshend, Deep Purple, Cat Stevens, Slade and David Bowie. In 1995, at Townshend's request, he compiled and co-produced The Who's 4-CD box set *30 Years Of Maximum R&B*, and was subsequently involved in the wholesale upgrade of The Who's back catalogue for remastered CDs. He lives in Surrey.

Andrew Doe

Andrew Doe is an acknowledged expert on Californian rock music who, together with John Tobler, has written books on The Beach Boys and The Doors. He is host of a Beach Boys reference website.

Peter Doggett

A former editor of *Record Collector*, Peter Doggett is an acknowledged expert on The Beatles who has written extensively about the group for numerous magazines. He has written several books, the most recent of which is *There's A Riot Going On: Revolutionaries, Rock Stars & The Rise of 60s Counterculture*. He is also the rock'n'roll memorabilia consultant to Christie's, the London auction house. He lives in Hampshire.

Tony Fletcher

Tony Fletcher is the author of biographies on Keith Moon, R.E.M. and Echo & The Bunnymen, and of the novel *Hedonism*. He hosts the website www.ijamming.net, and is presently at work on his latest book, a history of music in New York throughout the 20th century. He lives in upstate New York.

Bill Graham

The late Bill Graham was a regular contributor to Dublin's *Hot Press* magazine. He knew U2 from their earliest days as a schoolboy band and was instrumental in introducing them to their long-time manager, Paul McGuiness. Sadly, Graham died in 1996. A subsequent edition of *Complete Guide To The Music Of U2* has been updated by Caroline van Oosten de Boer.

Ed Hanel

Ed Hanel is among the world's foremost collectors of Who records, written material and miscellaneous memorabilia, and the author of the first reputable Who discography, published in 1981. He lives in Hawaii.

Peter Hogan

Peter Hogan is a veteran music journalist who has written for numerous British magazines including *Melody Maker*, *Vox* and *Uncut*. He is the author of books on The Doors, R.E.M. and The Velvet Underground. He lives in London.

Patrick Humphries

Patrick Humphries has been writing about popular music since 1976, when he began freelancing for *New Musical Express* as a "hip young gunslinger". Since then he has written numerous books, including definitive biographies of Nick Drake, Richard Thompson, Paul Simon and Tom Waits. He has also written for *The Times*, *Mojo* and *The Guardian*. He lives in London.

Dave Lewis

Acknowledged by the group and its fans as the UK's leading expert on Led Zeppelin, Dave Lewis is the editor and publisher of *Tight But Loose*, the acclaimed Led Zeppelin fanzine, and the author of several reference books on the band. In 1992, he was the co-organiser of the first Led Zeppelin fan convention held in London. He lives in Bedford.

Andy Mabbett

Andy Mabbett published and edited the Pink Floyd magazine *The Amazing Pudding* until it ceased publication in 1993. He has contributed to the books *Pink Floyd: The Visual Documentary* and *Crazy Diamond – Syd Barrett and The Dawn Of Pink Floyd*, and has written about the band for *Q* magazine. He lives in Birmingham.

Ian McCann

Ian McCann has written on reggae music for *New Musical Express*, *Q*, *Vox* and other magazines. He lives in London.

Carl Magnus Palm

Stockholm-based writer Carl Magnus Palm is recognised as the world's foremost Abba historian. He was involved in putting together the Abba CD box set *Thank You For The Music*, and has also contributed liner notes to several Abba-related CDs, most notably the remastered version of the compilation album *ABBA Gold* and the reissue of Abba's original albums. He is also the author of *Bright Lights Dark Shadows: The Real Story Of Abba*, which is now recognised as the definitive biography of the group.

Mark Paytress

Mark Paytress is the author of several music books, including *BowieStyle*, *The Rolling Stones Files* and *Rolling Stones - Off The Record*, and *Bolan: The Rise & Fall Of A 20th Century Superstar*. He has written extensively on popular music for a wide range of publications, including *Mojo*, *Select*, *Rolling Stone* and *Record Collector*, and is an acknowledged authority on the Stones. He lives in London.

Marc Roberty

Marc Roberty is the author of *Eric Clapton – A Visual Documentary* and *Eric Clapton In His Own Words*. He has written the text included in Eric Clapton concert programmes and edited *Slowhand*, the official magazine of the Eric Clapton fan club. He lives in London.

Rikky Rooksby

Rikky Rooksby's rock and pop writing has been published in numerous magazines. He is also a professional guitar teacher and author of the *Guitar Tutor* series of books. He lives in Oxford.

John Tobler

A key chronicler of American music for ZIGZAG, NME, and numerous other magazines, John Tobler has also supplied liner notes for countless reissues. He currently runs the Road Goes On Forever label in Tyneside, where he lives.